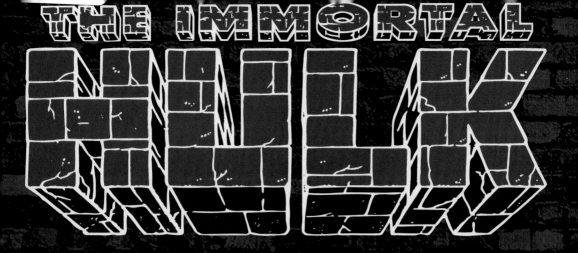

THE IMMORTAL HULK

BREAKER OF WORLDS

AL EWING
WRITER

JOE BENNETT [#22-25], **RYAN BODENHEIM** [#21] & **GERMÁN GARCÍA** [#25]
PENCILERS

RYAN BODENHEIM [#21], **RUY JOSÉ** [#22-25], **BELARDINO BRABO** [#21-24],
MARC DEERING [#24], **ROBERTO POGGI** [#24] & **GERMÁN GARCÍA** [#25]
INKERS

PAUL MOUNTS [#21-25] WITH
CHRIS O'HALLORAN [#25]
COLOR ARTISTS

VC's CORY PETIT
LETTERER

ALEX ROSS
COVER ARTIST

SARAH BRUNSTAD
ASSOCIATE EDITOR

WIL MOSS
EDITOR

TOM BREVOORT
EXECUTIVE EDITOR

COLLECTION EDITOR: **MARK D. BEAZLEY**
ASSISTANT EDITOR: **CAITLIN O'CONNELL**
ASSOCIATE MANAGING EDITOR: **KATERI WOODY**
SENIOR EDITOR, SPECIAL PROJECTS: **JENNIFER GRÜNWALD**
VP PRODUCTION & SPECIAL PROJECTS: **JEFF YOUNGQUIST**
BOOK DESIGNERS: **STACIE ZUCKER** with **ADAM DEL RE**

SVP PRINT, SALES & MA...
DIRECTOR, LICENSED PU...

...K
...BY

EDITOR IN CHIE...
CHIEF CREATIVE O...
PRESIDENT...
EXECUTIVE PR...

...LEE &
...KIRBY

IMMORTAL HULK VOL. 5: BREAKER OF WORLDS. Contains material originally published in magazine form as IMMORTAL HULK (2018) #21-25. First printing 2019. ISBN 978-1-302-91668-8. Published by MARVEL WORLDWIDE, INC., a subsidiary of MARVEL ENTERTAINMENT, LLC. OFFICE OF PUBLICATION: 135 West 50th Street, New York, NY 10020. © 2019 MARVEL No similarity between any of the names, characters, persons, and/or institutions in this magazine with those of any living or dead person or institution is intended, and any such similarity which may exist is purely coincidental. **Printed in Canada.** DAN BUCKLEY, President, Marvel Entertainment; JOHN NEE, Publisher; JOE QUESADA, Chief Creative Officer; TOM BREVOORT, SVP of Publishing; DAVID BOGART, Associate Publisher & SVP of Talent Affairs; DAVID GABRIEL, VP of Print & Digital Publishing; JEFF YOUNGQUIST, VP of Production & Special Projects; DAN CARR, Executive Director of Publishing Technology; ALEX MORALES, Director of Publishing Operations; DAN EDINGTON, Managing Editor; SUSAN CRESPI, Production Manager; STAN LEE, Chairman Emeritus. For information regarding advertising in Marvel Comics or on Marvel.com, please contact Vit DeBellis, Custom Solutions & Integrated Advertising Manager, at vdebellis@marvel.com. For Marvel subscription inquiries, please call 888-511-5480. **Manufactured between 9/27/2019 and 10/29/2019 by SOLISCO PRINTERS, SCOTT, QC, CANADA.**

10 9 8 7 6 5 4 3 2 1

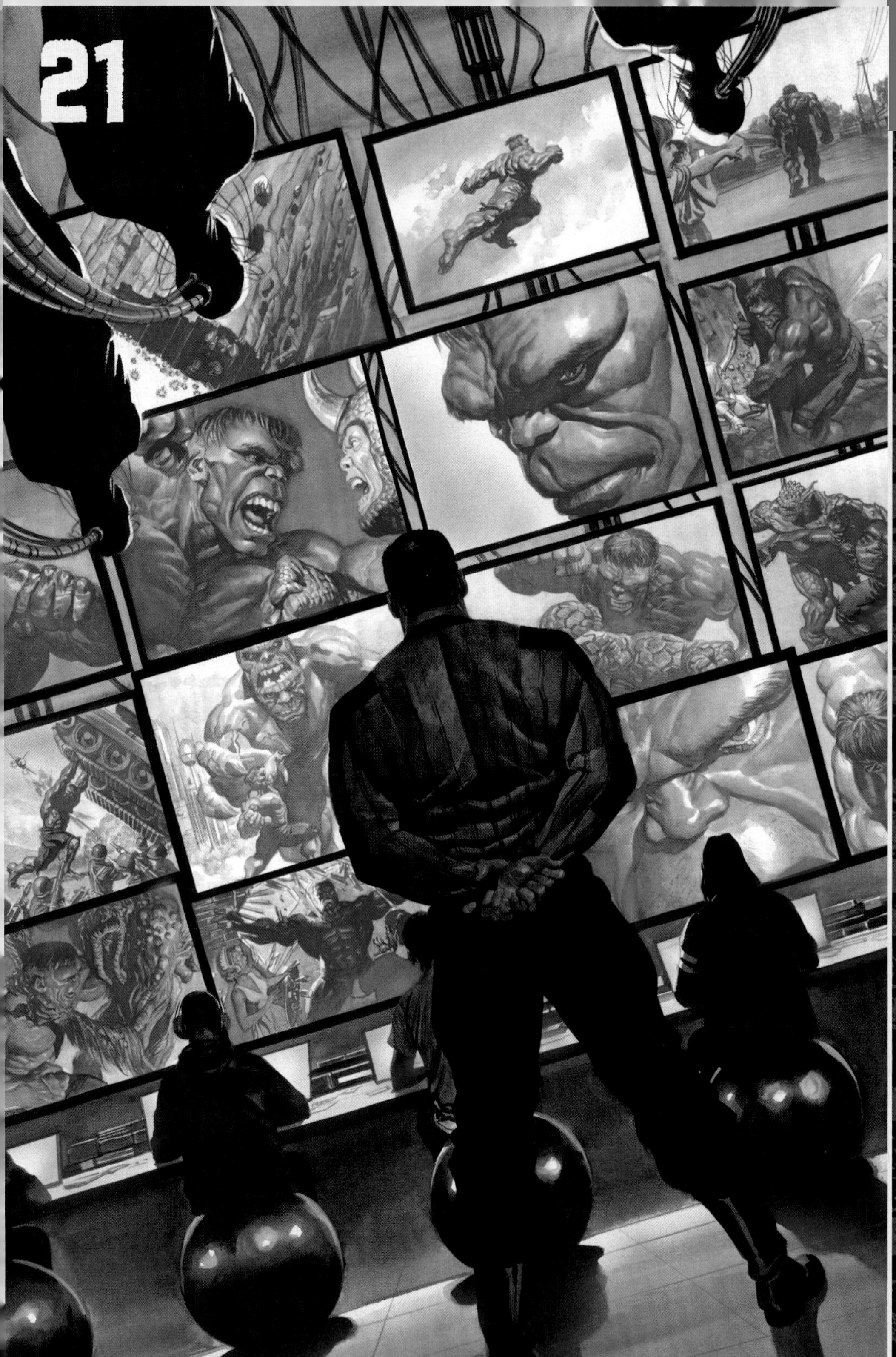
21

"...IN ALL CHAOS THERE IS A COSMOS, IN ALL DISORDER A SECRET ORDER..."

- CARL JUNG, *ARCHETYPES AND THE COLLECTIVE UNCONSCIOUS*

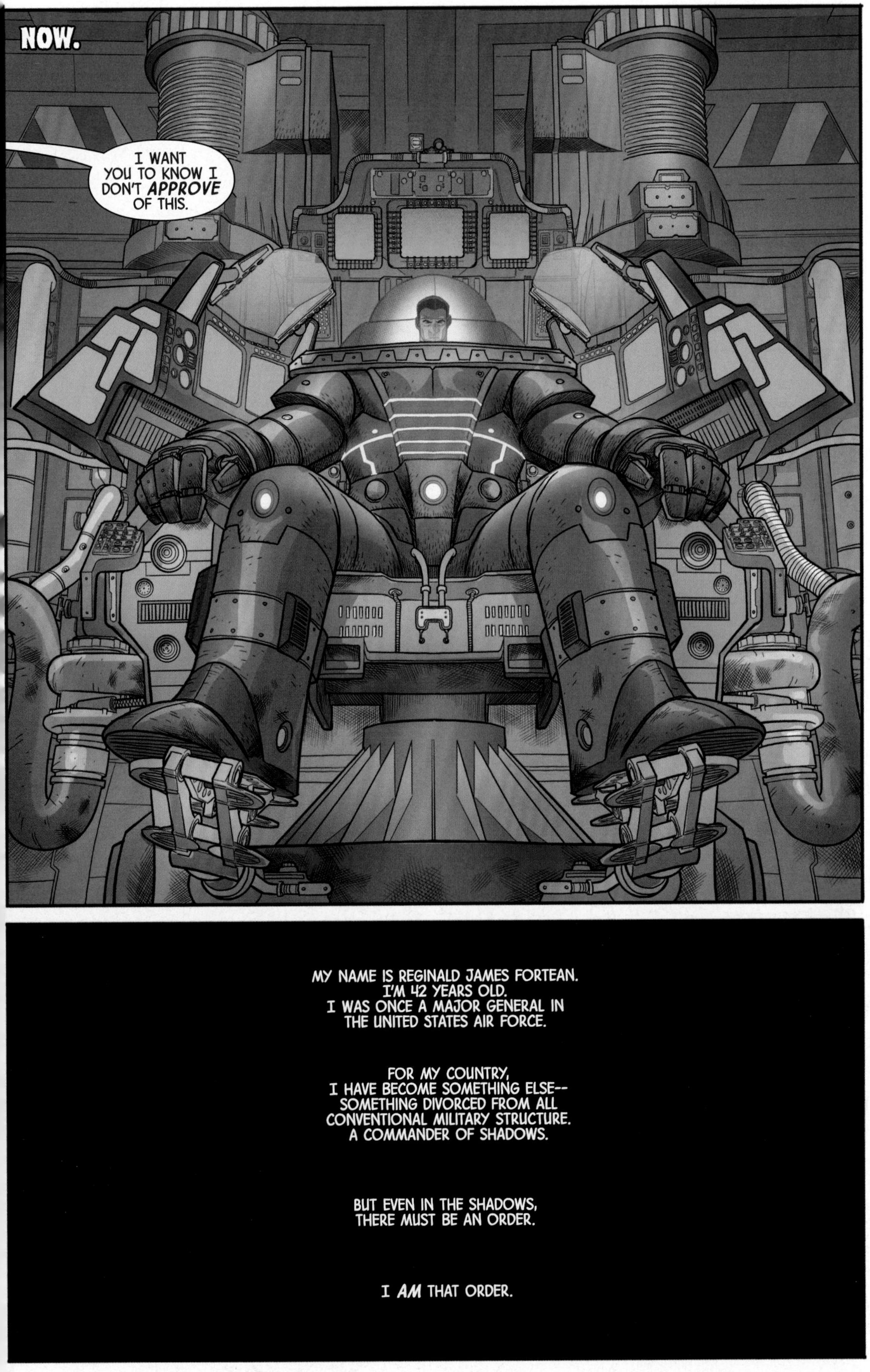
NOW.
I WANT YOU TO KNOW I DON'T *APPROVE* OF THIS.

MY NAME IS REGINALD JAMES FORTEAN.
I'M 42 YEARS OLD.
I WAS ONCE A MAJOR GENERAL IN
THE UNITED STATES AIR FORCE.

FOR MY COUNTRY,
I HAVE BECOME SOMETHING ELSE--
SOMETHING DIVORCED FROM ALL
CONVENTIONAL MILITARY STRUCTURE.
A COMMANDER OF SHADOWS.

BUT EVEN IN THE SHADOWS,
THERE MUST BE AN ORDER.

I *AM* THAT ORDER.

SO YOU'VE SAID.

YOU DON'T SEEM TO APPROVE OF *MUCH* LATELY, DR. McGOWAN.

IF YOU MEAN THE *MURDER OF CIVILIANS*--

COLLATERAL DAMAGE.

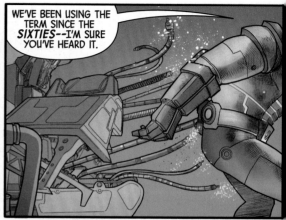

WE'VE BEEN USING THE TERM SINCE THE *SIXTIES*--I'M SURE YOU'VE HEARD IT.

WELL, I'VE REGISTERED MY COMPLAINTS ABOUT THAT. WHAT'S TROUBLING ME *NOW* IS YOU KILLING *YOURSELF.*

TRANSLOCATION IS EASILY THE MOST *DANGEROUS* METHOD OF INSTANT TRAVEL-- UNLESS YOU'RE A *REED RICHARDS* AND YOU CAN CALCULATE THE VARIABLES IN YOUR *HEAD.*

AND *YOU'RE* ABOUT TO TRANSLOCATE ALL THE WAY TO *EARTH ORBIT*--

HENCE THE *REDEEMER ARMOR.*

IT'S SEALED AND OXYGENATED FOR VACUUM. IF I MISS THE *TARGET,* I CAN *SURVIVE* IN OPEN SPACE.

UH-HUH. WHAT ABOUT ARRIVING HALFWAY THROUGH A *BULKHEAD?*

IT WON'T COME TO THAT.

WILL IT, DR. McGOWAN?

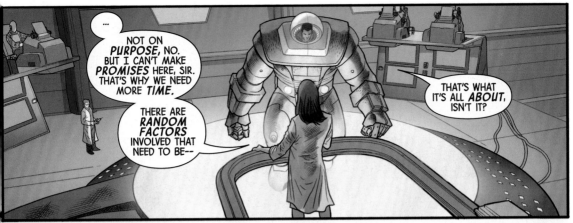

... NOT ON *PURPOSE*, NO. BUT I CAN'T MAKE *PROMISES* HERE, SIR. THAT'S WHY WE NEED MORE *TIME*.

THERE ARE *RANDOM FACTORS* INVOLVED THAT NEED TO BE--

THAT'S WHAT IT'S ALL *ABOUT*, ISN'T IT?

THE RANDOM FACTORS. THE *HUMAN ERRORS*. THE *SHADOWS*.

CHAOS. DO WE RULE CHAOS, OR DOES CHAOS RULE *US*?

I KNOW WHAT *MY* ANSWER WOULD BE.

IF I *DON'T* COME BACK, PROTOCOL PLACES *YOU* IN COMMAND, DOCTOR. UNTIL THEN...THE FINAL DECISION IS *MINE*.

SIR-- *DON'T*--

BEGINNING TRANSLOCATION... *NOW*.

NO! SHUT IT *DOWN*, GENERAL!

WE NEED TO DOUBLE-CHECK-- *TRIPLE*-CHECK! IF THERE'S BEEN *ANY* ERROR AT *ALL*--

THAT'S THE DIFFERENCE BETWEEN US, DOCTOR. I CHOOSE NOT TO BE *COWED* BY THE RANDOM FACTORS.

WE *CAN* RULE OVER CHAOS.

HAVE *FAITH*.

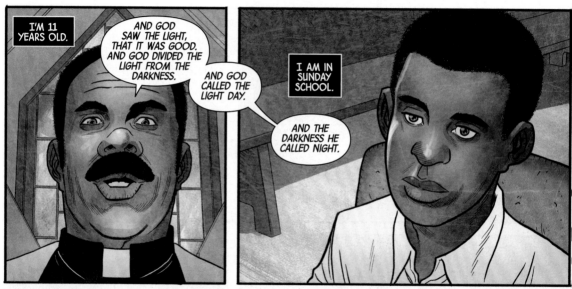

I'M 11 YEARS OLD.

AND GOD SAW THE LIGHT, THAT IT WAS GOOD. AND GOD DIVIDED THE LIGHT FROM THE DARKNESS.

AND GOD CALLED THE LIGHT DAY.

I AM IN SUNDAY SCHOOL.

AND THE DARKNESS HE CALLED NIGHT.

I AM LISTENING INTENTLY.

AND THE EVENING AND THE MORNING WAS THE FIRST DAY.

I WANT TO *PAUSE* THERE FOR A MOMENT.

WE'RE AT THE END OF THE FIRST DAY. THERE'S NO *PEOPLE* YET. NO *ANIMALS*--NOT EVEN *PLANTS*.

AND YET WHAT HAS GOD *ALREADY* DONE FOR US?

...

MADE THE *LIGHT?*

OF *COURSE.* BUT I'M THINKING OF SOMETHING EVEN MORE PROFOUND THAN *THAT.*

LET'S RETURN TO THE *SECOND* VERSE. *THE EARTH WAS WITHOUT FORM, AND VOID.*

WITHOUT *FORM.*

THINK ABOUT THAT.

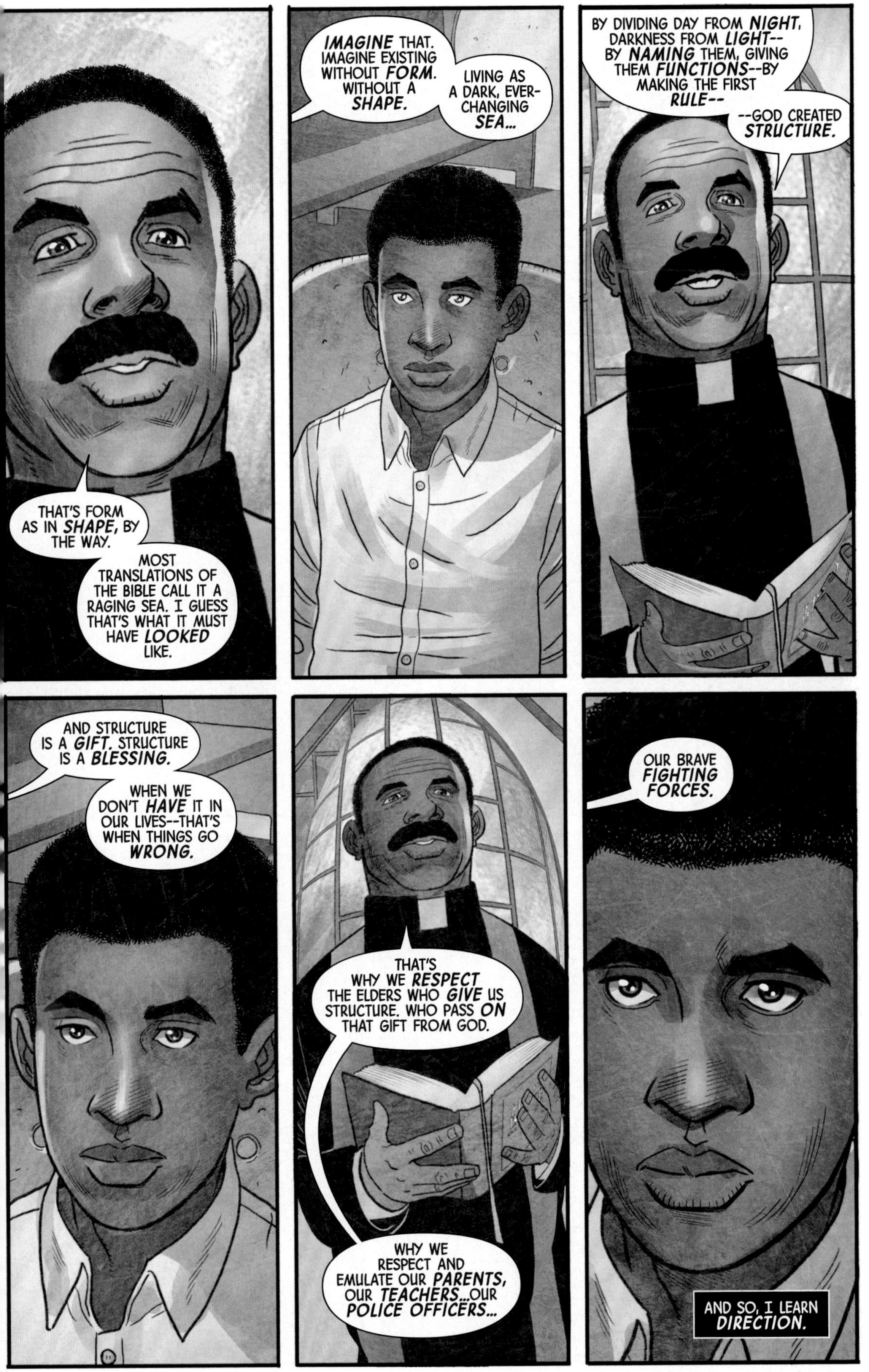
THAT'S FORM AS IN SHAPE, BY THE WAY.
MOST TRANSLATIONS OF THE BIBLE CALL IT A RAGING SEA. I GUESS THAT'S WHAT IT MUST HAVE LOOKED LIKE.
IMAGINE THAT. IMAGINE EXISTING WITHOUT FORM. WITHOUT A SHAPE.
LIVING AS A DARK, EVER-CHANGING SEA...
BY DIVIDING DAY FROM NIGHT, DARKNESS FROM LIGHT-- BY NAMING THEM, GIVING THEM FUNCTIONS--BY MAKING THE FIRST RULE--
--GOD CREATED STRUCTURE.
AND STRUCTURE IS A GIFT. STRUCTURE IS A BLESSING.
WHEN WE DON'T HAVE IT IN OUR LIVES--THAT'S WHEN THINGS GO WRONG.
THAT'S WHY WE RESPECT THE ELDERS WHO GIVE US STRUCTURE. WHO PASS ON THAT GIFT FROM GOD.
WHY WE RESPECT AND EMULATE OUR PARENTS, OUR TEACHERS...OUR POLICE OFFICERS...
OUR BRAVE FIGHTING FORCES.
AND SO, I LEARN DIRECTION.

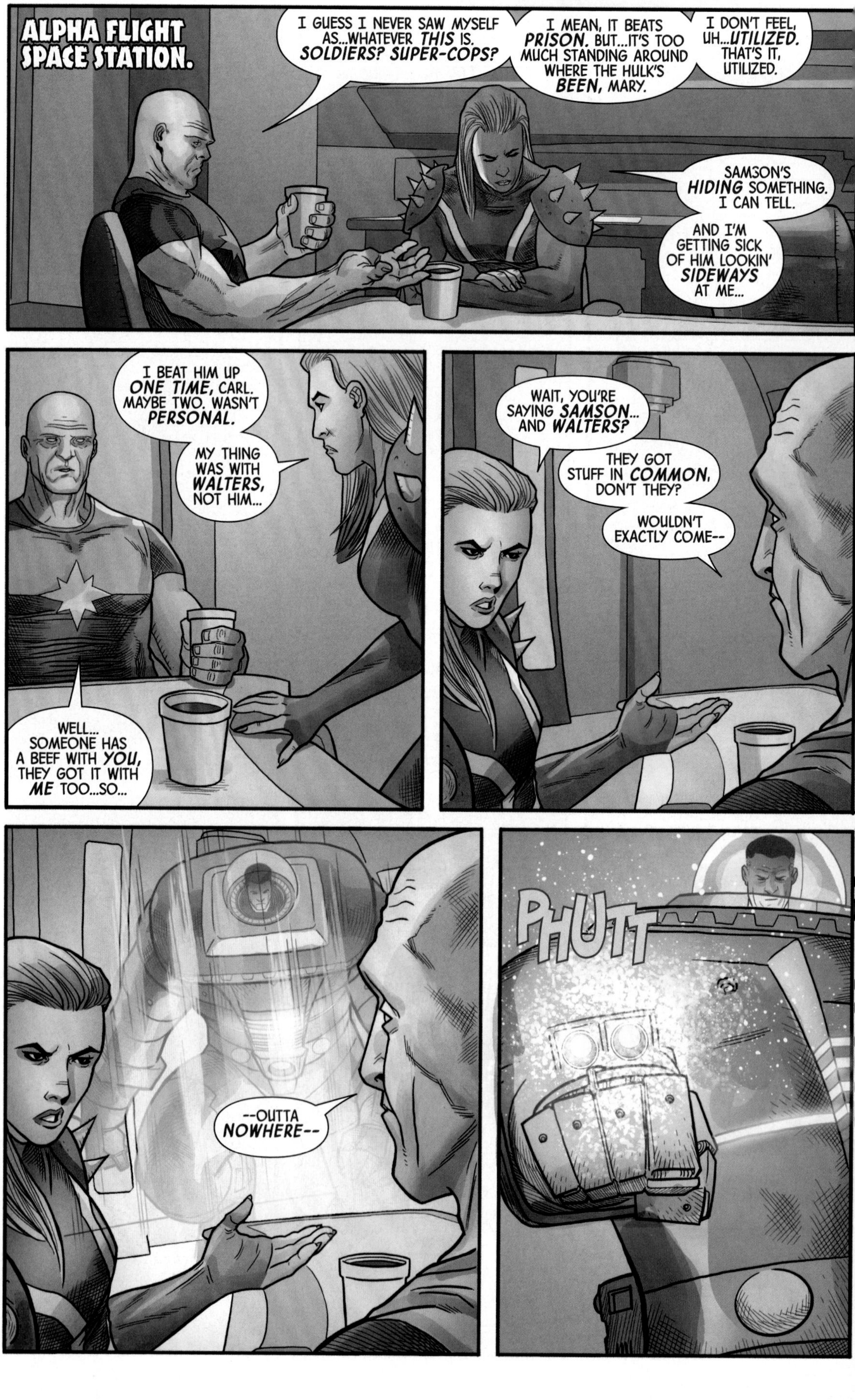
ALPHA FLIGHT SPACE STATION.
I GUESS I NEVER SAW MYSELF AS...WHATEVER THIS IS. SOLDIERS? SUPER-COPS?
I MEAN, IT BEATS PRISON. BUT...IT'S TOO MUCH STANDING AROUND WHERE THE HULK'S BEEN, MARY.
I DON'T FEEL, UH...UTILIZED. THAT'S IT, UTILIZED.
SAMSON'S HIDING SOMETHING. I CAN TELL.
AND I'M GETTING SICK OF HIM LOOKIN' SIDEWAYS AT ME...
I BEAT HIM UP ONE TIME, CARL. MAYBE TWO. WASN'T PERSONAL.
MY THING WAS WITH WALTERS, NOT HIM...
WELL... SOMEONE HAS A BEEF WITH YOU, THEY GOT IT WITH ME TOO...SO...
WAIT, YOU'RE SAYING SAMSON... AND WALTERS?
THEY GOT STUFF IN COMMON, DON'T THEY?
WOULDN'T EXACTLY COME--
--OUTTA NOWHERE--
PHUTT

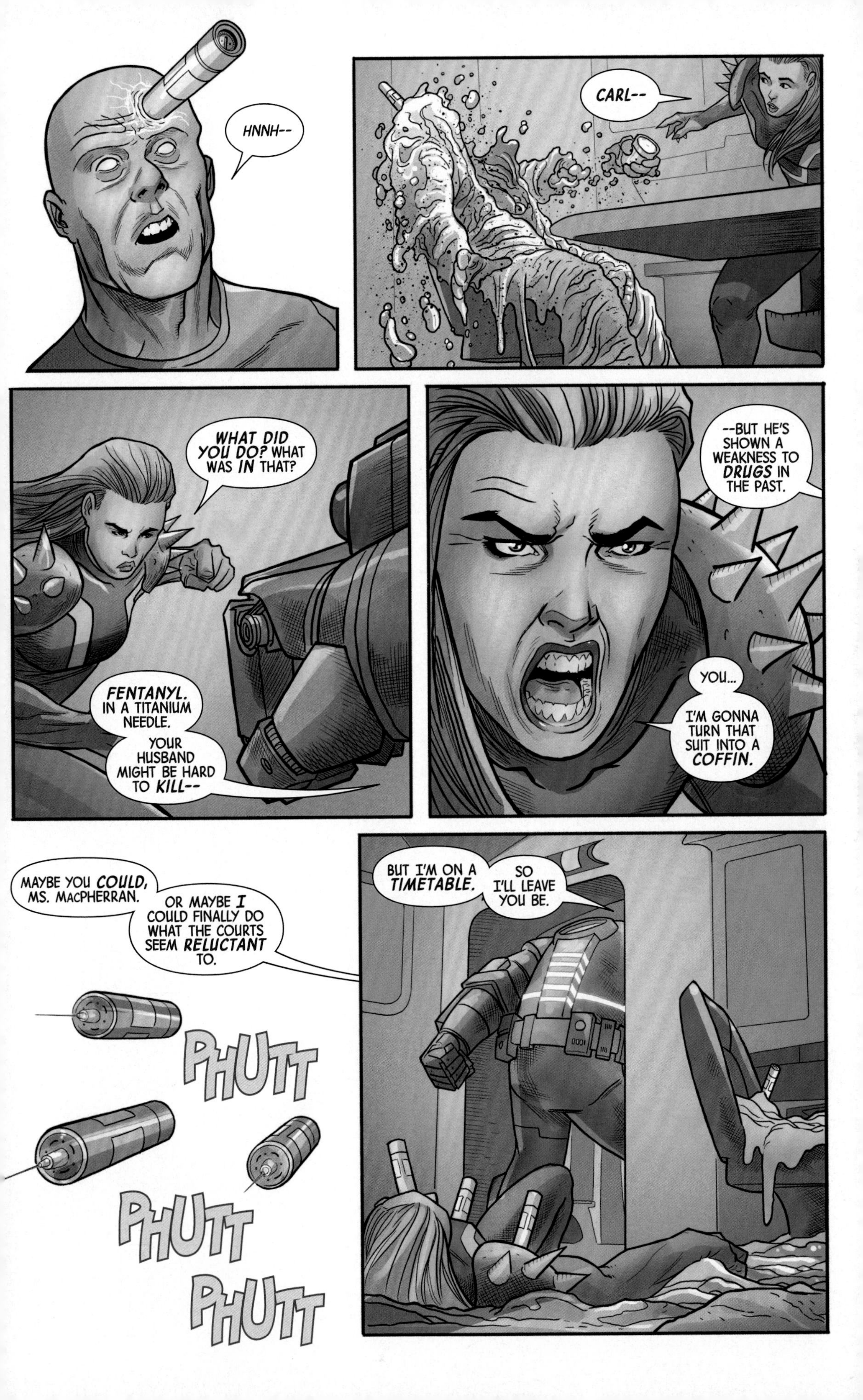

HNNH--
CARL--
WHAT DID YOU DO? WHAT WAS IN THAT?
FENTANYL. IN A TITANIUM NEEDLE.
YOUR HUSBAND MIGHT BE HARD TO KILL--
--BUT HE'S SHOWN A WEAKNESS TO DRUGS IN THE PAST.
YOU...
I'M GONNA TURN THAT SUIT INTO A COFFIN.
MAYBE YOU COULD, MS. MacPHERRAN.
OR MAYBE I COULD FINALLY DO WHAT THE COURTS SEEM RELUCTANT TO.
PHUTT
PHUTT
PHUTT
BUT I'M ON A TIMETABLE.
SO I'LL LEAVE YOU BE.

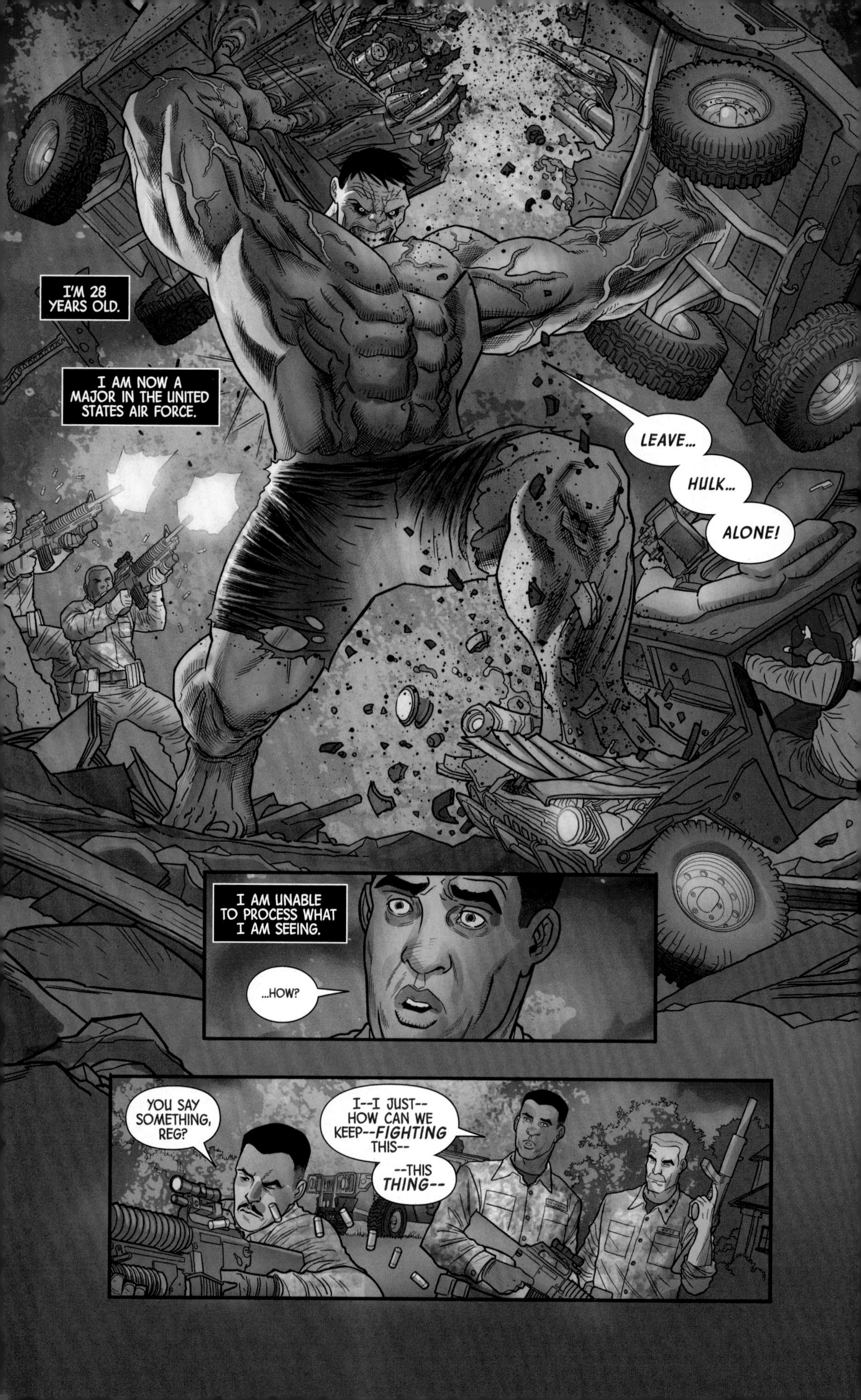
I'M 28 YEARS OLD.
I AM NOW A MAJOR IN THE UNITED STATES AIR FORCE.
LEAVE...
HULK...
ALONE!
I AM UNABLE TO PROCESS WHAT I AM SEEING.
...HOW?
YOU SAY SOMETHING, REG?
I--I JUST-- HOW CAN WE KEEP--FIGHTING THIS--
--THIS THING--

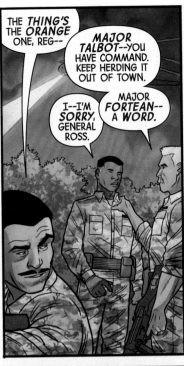

THE *THING'S* THE *ORANGE* ONE, REG--

MAJOR TALBOT--YOU HAVE COMMAND. KEEP HERDING IT OUT OF TOWN.

I--I'M *SORRY,* GENERAL ROSS.

MAJOR FORTEAN-- A *WORD.*

JUST--FOR A *MOMENT* THERE--

NEVER APOLOGIZE FOR BEING *HUMAN,* SON.

I'VE FELT IT *TOO*--WE *ALL* HAVE. THE *IMPOSSIBILITY* OF THIS... SITUATION.

BUT HERE'S HOW *I* HANDLE IT.

TAKE A LOOK OVER THERE. THAT *GIRL.*

SHE JUST LOST HER *HOME,* AND EVERYTHING *IN* IT. HER LIFE WILL *NEVER* BE THE SAME.

AND THERE ARE *HUNDREDS* LIKE HER. *HUNDREDS.* IN THIS ONE TOWN *ALONE.*

WHEN I HAVE MY MOMENTS OF...OF *DOUBT,* IN THE FACE OF THIS...I THINK ABOUT *THAT.* AND THEY *PASS.*

HOW ABOUT *YOU,* MAJOR?

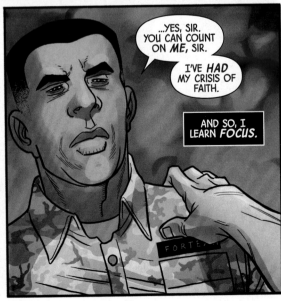

...YES, SIR. YOU CAN COUNT ON *ME,* SIR.

I'VE *HAD* MY CRISIS OF FAITH.

AND SO, I LEARN *FOCUS.*

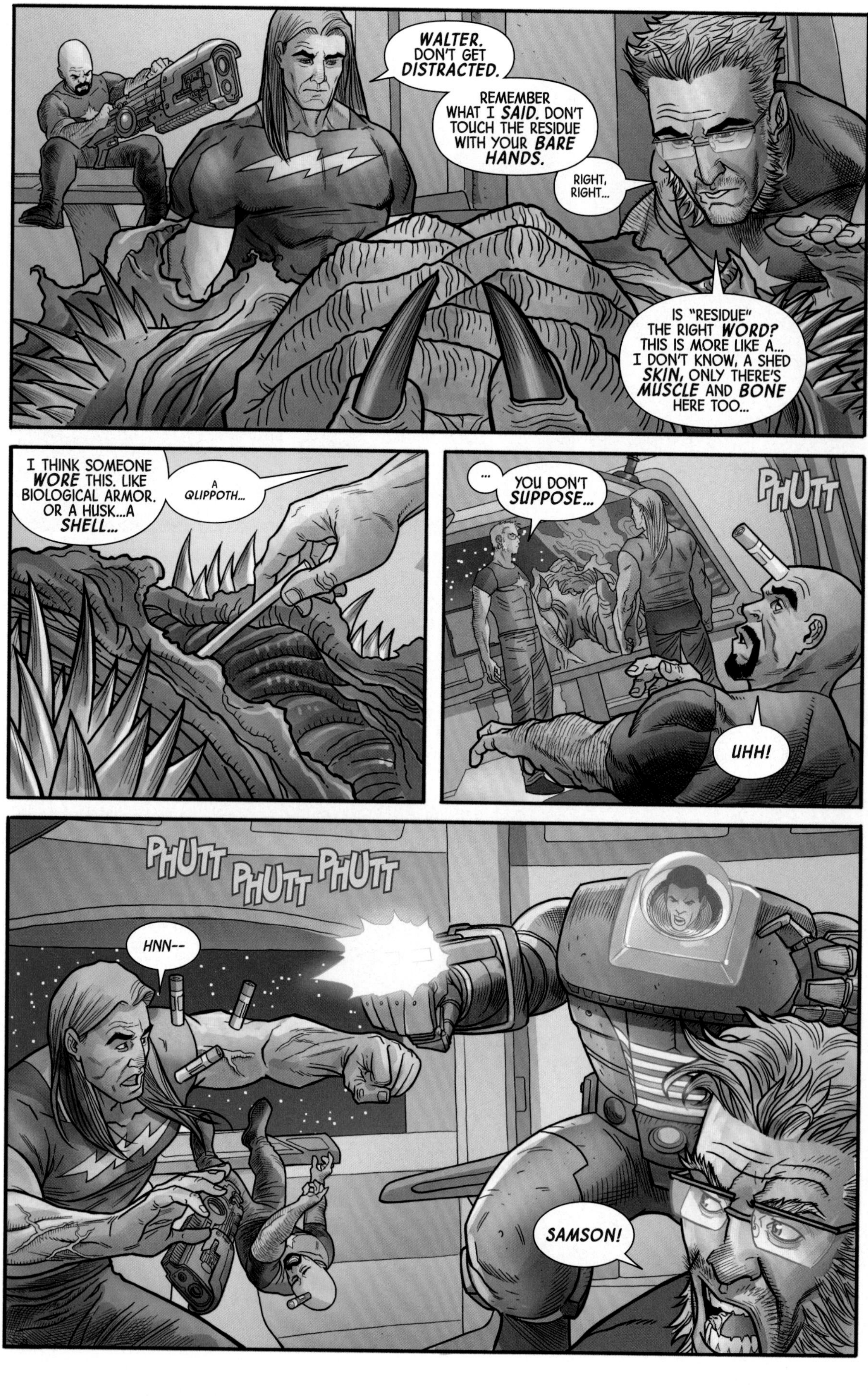
WALTER. DON'T GET DISTRACTED.
REMEMBER WHAT I SAID. DON'T TOUCH THE RESIDUE WITH YOUR BARE HANDS.
RIGHT, RIGHT...
IS "RESIDUE" THE RIGHT WORD? THIS IS MORE LIKE A... I DON'T KNOW, A SHED SKIN, ONLY THERE'S MUSCLE AND BONE HERE TOO...
I THINK SOMEONE WORE THIS. LIKE BIOLOGICAL ARMOR. OR A HUSK...A SHELL...
A QLIPPOTH...
...
YOU DON'T SUPPOSE...
PHUTT
UHH!
PHUTT PHUTT PHUTT
HNN--
SAMSON!

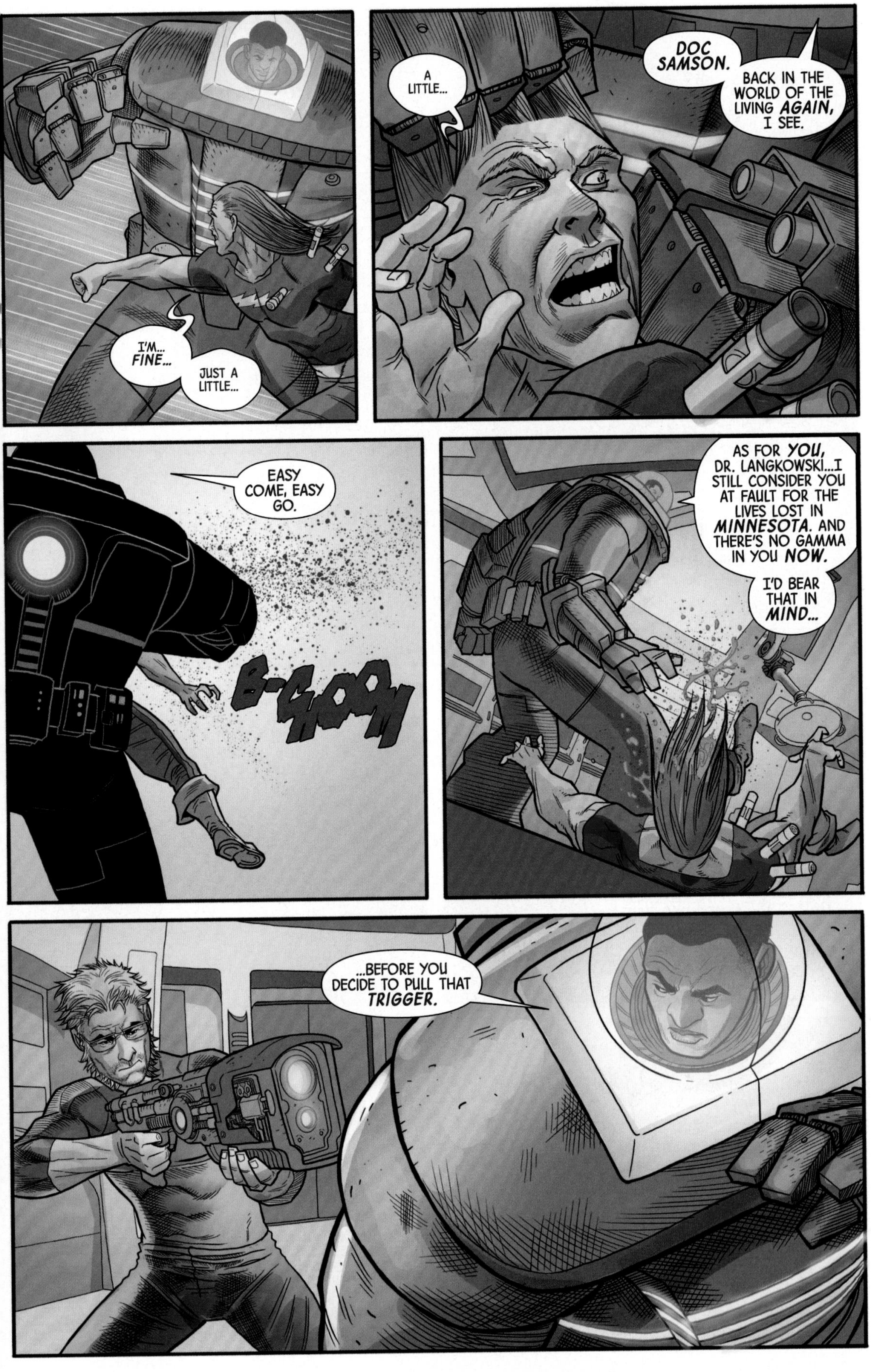
I'M... FINE...
JUST A LITTLE...
A LITTLE...
DOC SAMSON.
BACK IN THE WORLD OF THE LIVING AGAIN, I SEE.
EASY COME, EASY GO.
B-GOOM
AS FOR YOU, DR. LANGKOWSKI...I STILL CONSIDER YOU AT FAULT FOR THE LIVES LOST IN MINNESOTA. AND THERE'S NO GAMMA IN YOU NOW.
I'D BEAR THAT IN MIND...
...BEFORE YOU DECIDE TO PULL THAT TRIGGER.

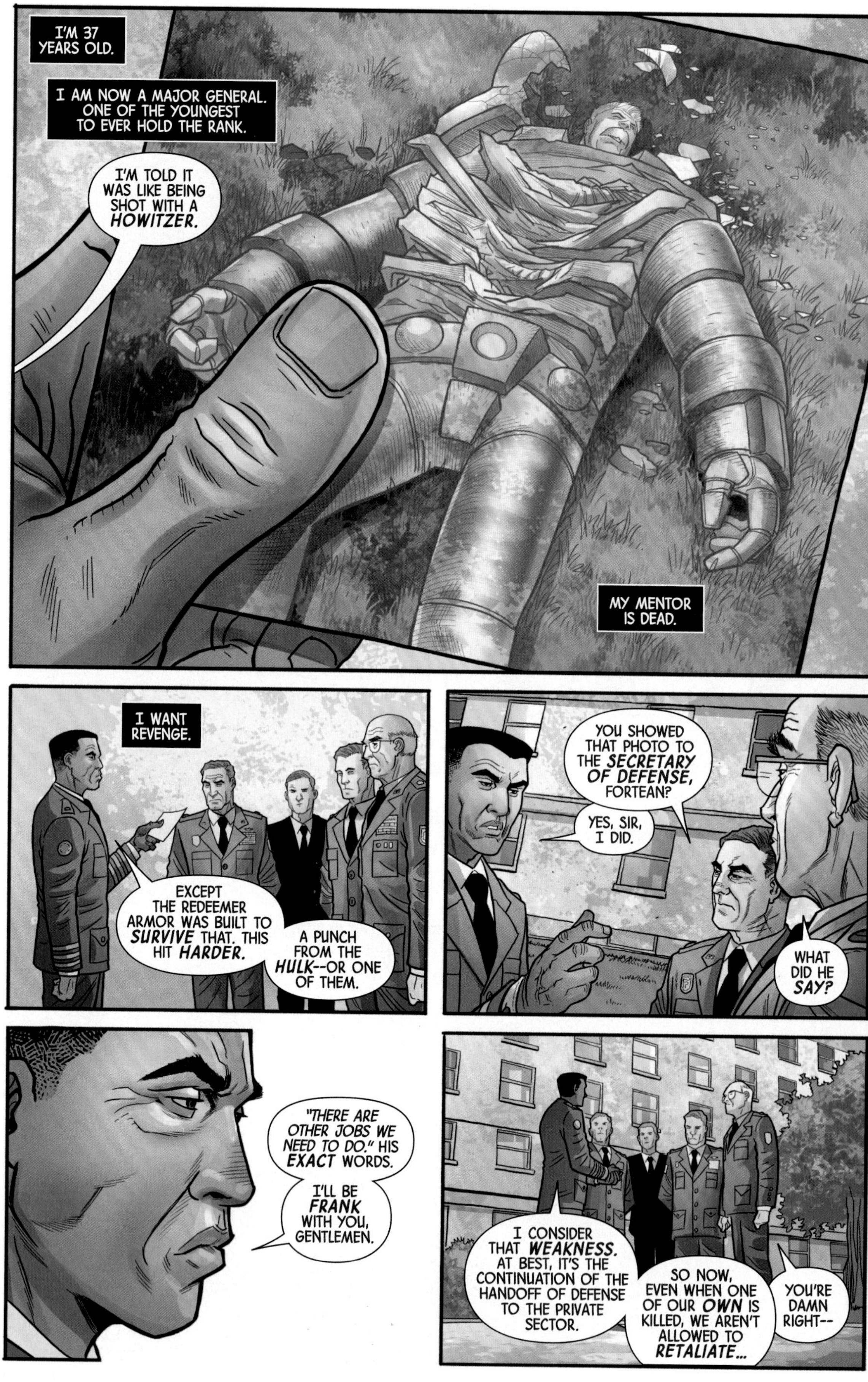
I'M 37 YEARS OLD.
I AM NOW A MAJOR GENERAL. ONE OF THE YOUNGEST TO EVER HOLD THE RANK.
I'M TOLD IT WAS LIKE BEING SHOT WITH A HOWITZER.
MY MENTOR IS DEAD.
I WANT REVENGE.
EXCEPT THE REDEEMER ARMOR WAS BUILT TO SURVIVE THAT. THIS HIT HARDER.
A PUNCH FROM THE HULK--OR ONE OF THEM.
YOU SHOWED THAT PHOTO TO THE SECRETARY OF DEFENSE, FORTEAN?
YES, SIR, I DID.
WHAT DID HE SAY?
"THERE ARE OTHER JOBS WE NEED TO DO." HIS EXACT WORDS.
I'LL BE FRANK WITH YOU, GENTLEMEN.
I CONSIDER THAT WEAKNESS. AT BEST, IT'S THE CONTINUATION OF THE HANDOFF OF DEFENSE TO THE PRIVATE SECTOR.
SO NOW, EVEN WHEN ONE OF OUR OWN IS KILLED, WE AREN'T ALLOWED TO RETALIATE...
YOU'RE DAMN RIGHT--

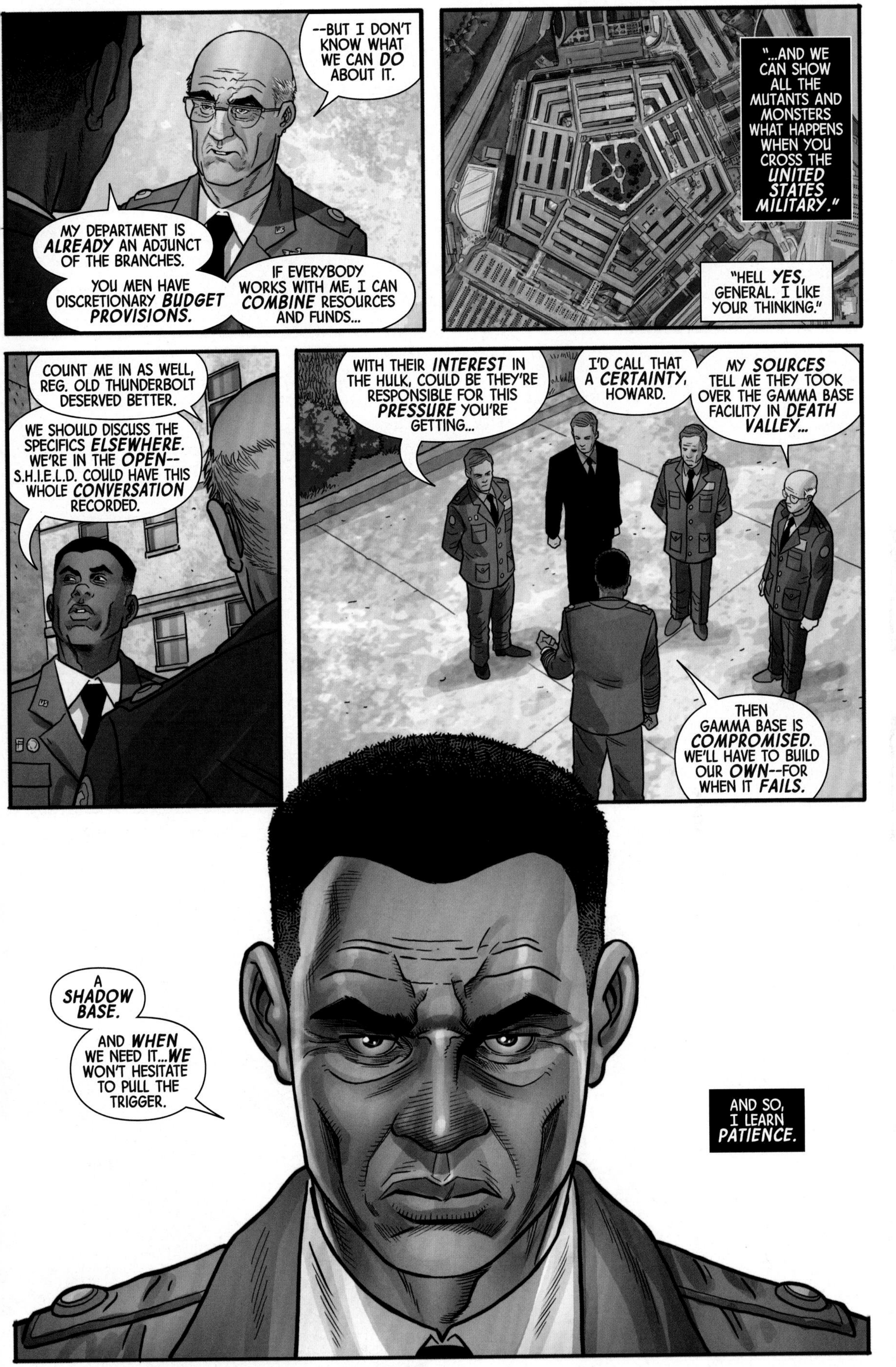
--BUT I DON'T KNOW WHAT WE CAN DO ABOUT IT.
MY DEPARTMENT IS ALREADY AN ADJUNCT OF THE BRANCHES.
YOU MEN HAVE DISCRETIONARY BUDGET PROVISIONS.
IF EVERYBODY WORKS WITH ME, I CAN COMBINE RESOURCES AND FUNDS...
"...AND WE CAN SHOW ALL THE MUTANTS AND MONSTERS WHAT HAPPENS WHEN YOU CROSS THE UNITED STATES MILITARY."
"HELL YES, GENERAL. I LIKE YOUR THINKING."
COUNT ME IN AS WELL, REG. OLD THUNDERBOLT DESERVED BETTER.
WE SHOULD DISCUSS THE SPECIFICS ELSEWHERE. WE'RE IN THE OPEN--S.H.I.E.L.D. COULD HAVE THIS WHOLE CONVERSATION RECORDED.
WITH THEIR INTEREST IN THE HULK, COULD BE THEY'RE RESPONSIBLE FOR THIS PRESSURE YOU'RE GETTING...
I'D CALL THAT A CERTAINTY, HOWARD.
MY SOURCES TELL ME THEY TOOK OVER THE GAMMA BASE FACILITY IN DEATH VALLEY...
THEN GAMMA BASE IS COMPROMISED. WE'LL HAVE TO BUILD OUR OWN--FOR WHEN IT FAILS.
A SHADOW BASE.
AND WHEN WE NEED IT...WE WON'T HESITATE TO PULL THE TRIGGER.
AND SO, I LEARN PATIENCE.

CLICK

EAT THIS--

OH NO--

MISFIRE. GUESS IT NEEDED *CLEANING.*

RANDOM FACTORS, DR. LANGKOWSKI.

CHAOS. DO WE RULE OVER *IT?*

OR DOES *IT* RULE OVER *US?*

WAIT-- JUST *WAIT* A SECOND--

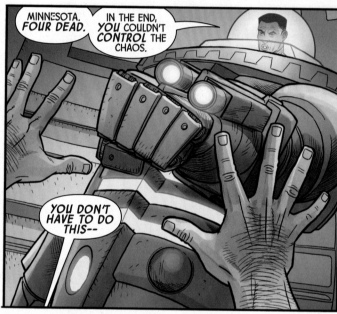

MINNESOTA. *FOUR DEAD.*

IN THE END, *YOU* COULDN'T *CONTROL* THE CHAOS.

YOU DON'T HAVE TO DO THIS--

B-GOOM B-GOOM B-GOOM

BUT I *CAN.* GOODBYE, WALTER.

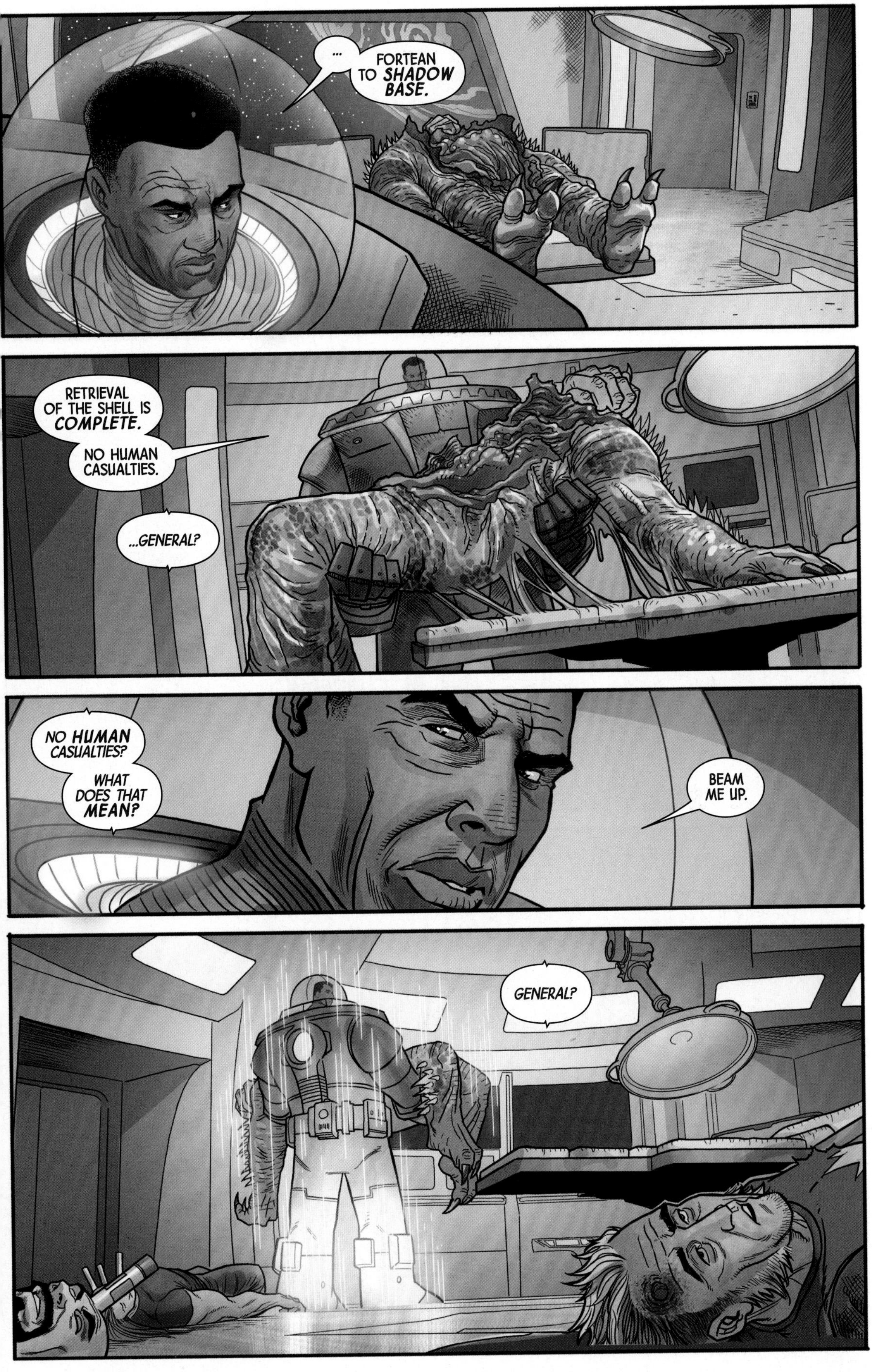

... FORTEAN TO SHADOW BASE.
RETRIEVAL OF THE SHELL IS COMPLETE.
NO HUMAN CASUALTIES.
...GENERAL?
NO HUMAN CASUALTIES?
WHAT DOES THAT MEAN?
BEAM ME UP.
GENERAL?

I'M 40 YEARS OLD.

I'M VISITING MY MENTOR IN HIS PRISON CELL.

...I HUNTED THE RED HULK FOR *MONTHS*, ROSS. TRYING TO AVENGE *YOUR DEATH.*

WHEN YOUR *DAUGHTER* BECAME A *GAMMA TERRORIST*-- I WENT *EASY* ON HER. IN *YOUR* MEMORY.

AND ALL THIS TIME, *YOU* WERE THE RED HULK. *YOU.* YOU BECAME THE VERY *MONSTER* YOU TRIED TO FIGHT.

WHAT WERE YOU *THINKING,* GENERAL?

I AM TRYING TO UNDERSTAND.

...DID YOU HEAR ABOUT THE *LAST* TIME I FOUGHT BANNER?

I DON'T SEE HOW THAT'S *RELEVANT*--

HE HAD *EXTREMIS* IN HIM. THAT NANO-JUNK *TONY STARK* MADE TO *PROGRAM* THE HUMAN BODY.

SAME STUFF BANNER USED TO TURN *ME* HUMAN FOR *KEEPS.*

HE'D USED IT ON *HIMSELF*-- TURNED THE HULK INTO A *GENIUS.* "DOC GREEN."

IT *WORE OFF* EVENTUALLY. BUT I TELL YOU, WHILE IT WAS *WORKING...*

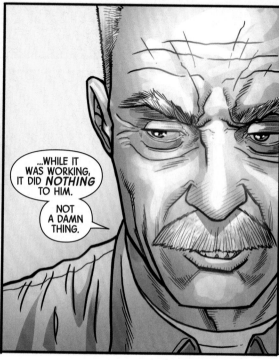

...WHILE IT WAS WORKING, IT DID *NOTHING* TO HIM.

NOT A DAMN THING.

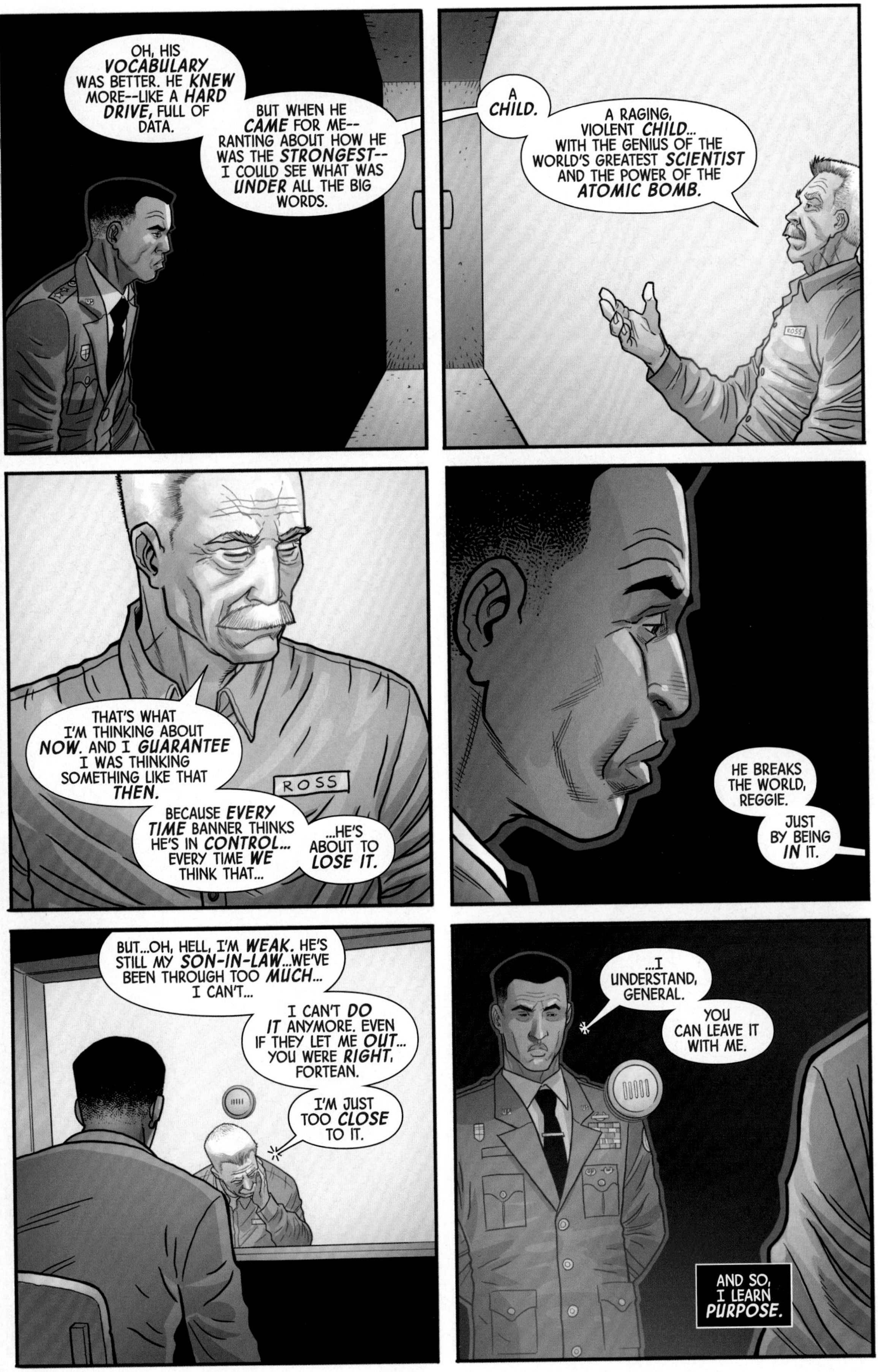
OH, HIS VOCABULARY WAS BETTER. HE KNEW MORE--LIKE A HARD DRIVE, FULL OF DATA.
BUT WHEN HE CAME FOR ME--RANTING ABOUT HOW HE WAS THE STRONGEST--I COULD SEE WHAT WAS UNDER ALL THE BIG WORDS.
A CHILD.
A RAGING, VIOLENT CHILD... WITH THE GENIUS OF THE WORLD'S GREATEST SCIENTIST AND THE POWER OF THE ATOMIC BOMB.
ROSS
THAT'S WHAT I'M THINKING ABOUT NOW. AND I GUARANTEE I WAS THINKING SOMETHING LIKE THAT THEN.
ROSS
BECAUSE EVERY TIME BANNER THINKS HE'S IN CONTROL... EVERY TIME WE THINK THAT...
...HE'S ABOUT TO LOSE IT.
HE BREAKS THE WORLD, REGGIE.
JUST BY BEING IN IT.
BUT...OH, HELL, I'M WEAK. HE'S STILL MY SON-IN-LAW...WE'VE BEEN THROUGH TOO MUCH... I CAN'T...
I CAN'T DO IT ANYMORE. EVEN IF THEY LET ME OUT... YOU WERE RIGHT, FORTEAN.
I'M JUST TOO CLOSE TO IT.
...I UNDERSTAND, GENERAL.
YOU CAN LEAVE IT WITH ME.
AND SO, I LEARN PURPOSE.

I'M 42 YEARS OLD.

I WAS ONCE A MAJOR GENERAL IN THE UNITED STATES AIR FORCE.

FOR MY COUNTRY... I HAVE BECOME SOMETHING ELSE.

SOMETHING DIVORCED FROM ALL CONVENTIONAL MILITARY STRUCTURE.

BRING IT HERE.

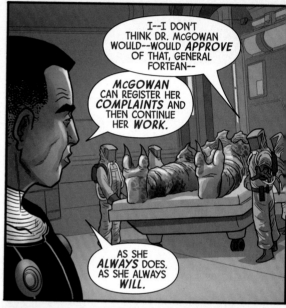

I--I DON'T THINK DR. McGOWAN WOULD--WOULD APPROVE OF THAT, GENERAL FORTEAN--

McGOWAN CAN REGISTER HER COMPLAINTS AND THEN CONTINUE HER WORK.

AS SHE ALWAYS DOES. AS SHE ALWAYS WILL.

NOW.

BRING IT HERE.

A COMMANDER OF SHADOWS.

BUT EVEN IN THE SHADOWS, THERE MUST BE AN ORDER.

SIR-- DON'T TOUCH IT--

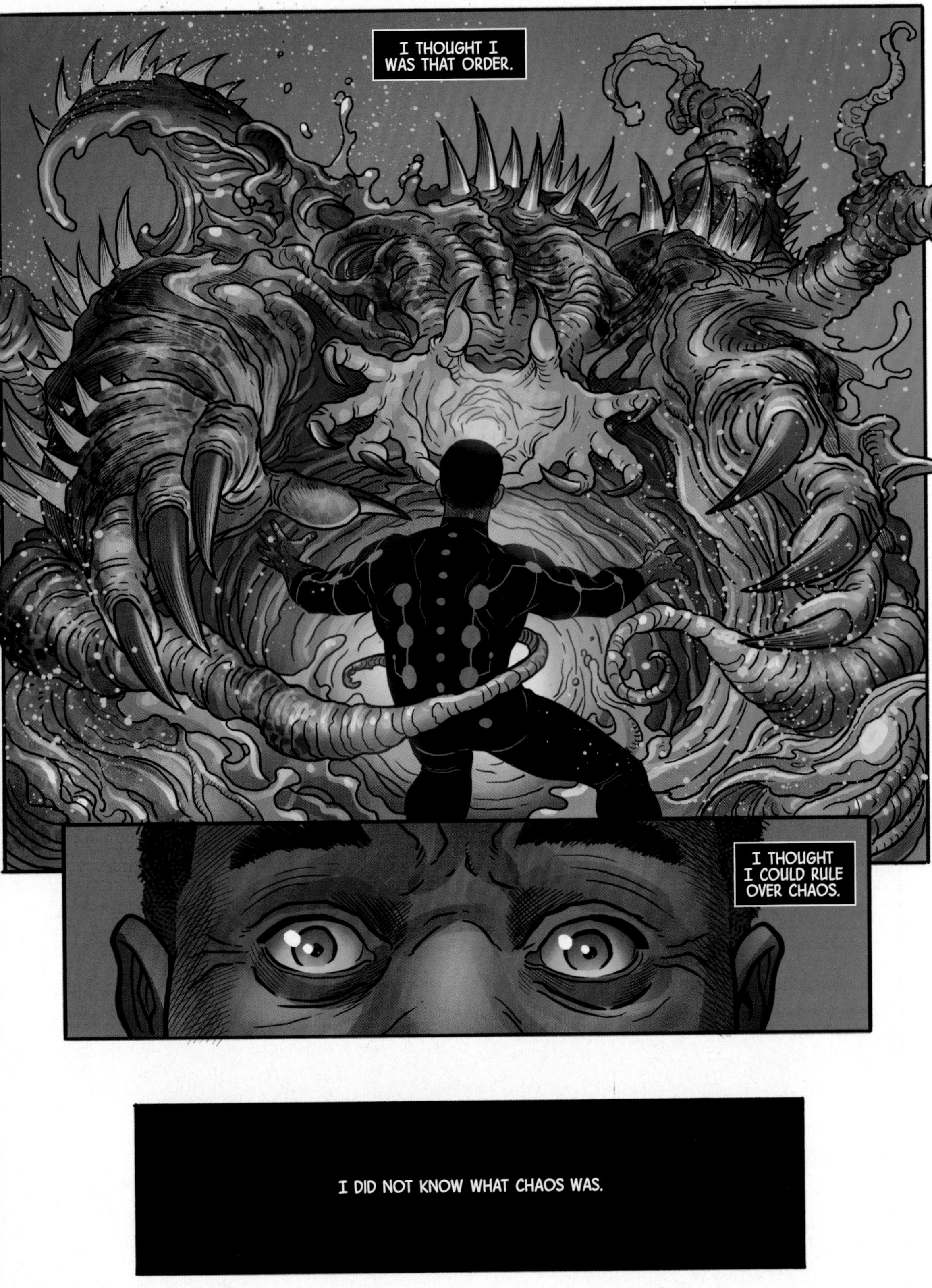
I THOUGHT I WAS THAT ORDER.
I THOUGHT I COULD RULE OVER CHAOS.

I DID NOT KNOW WHAT CHAOS WAS.

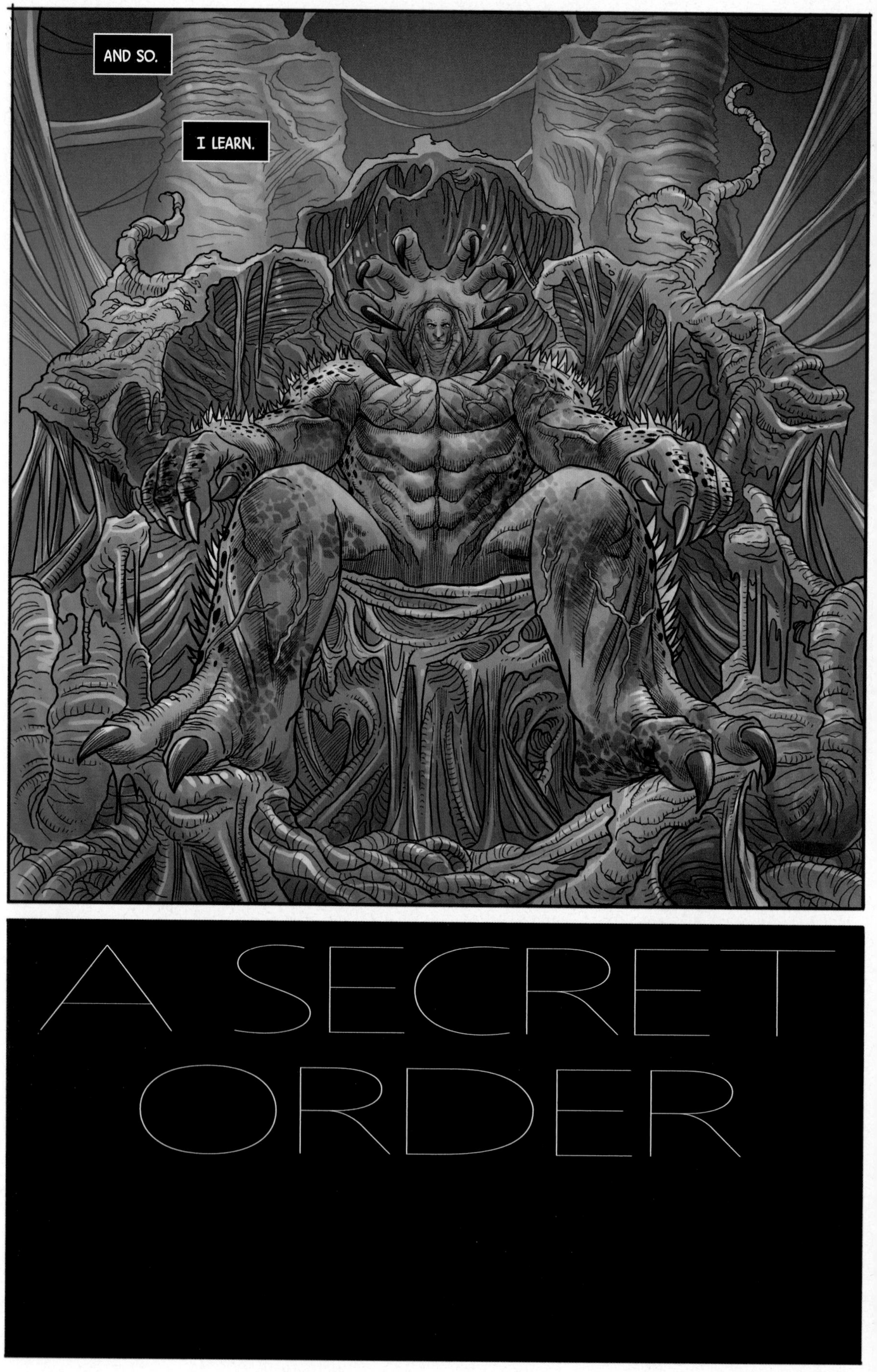
AND SO.
I LEARN.

A SECRET ORDER

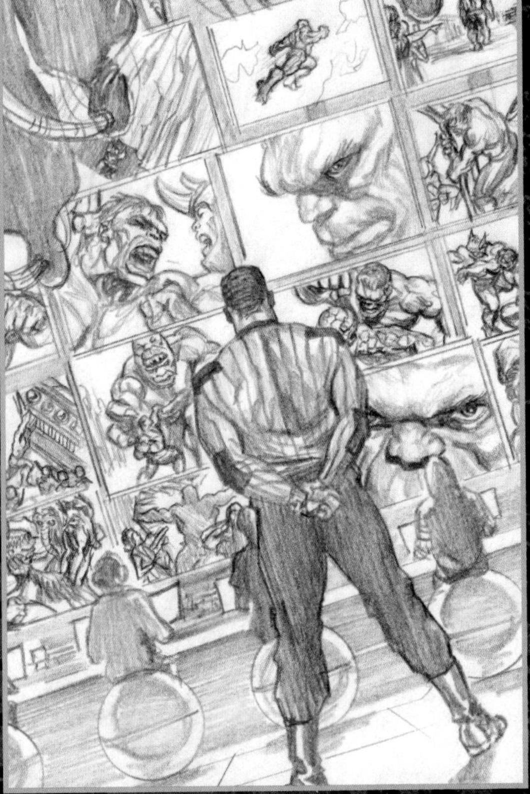

ALEX ROSS
#21 COVER PENCILS

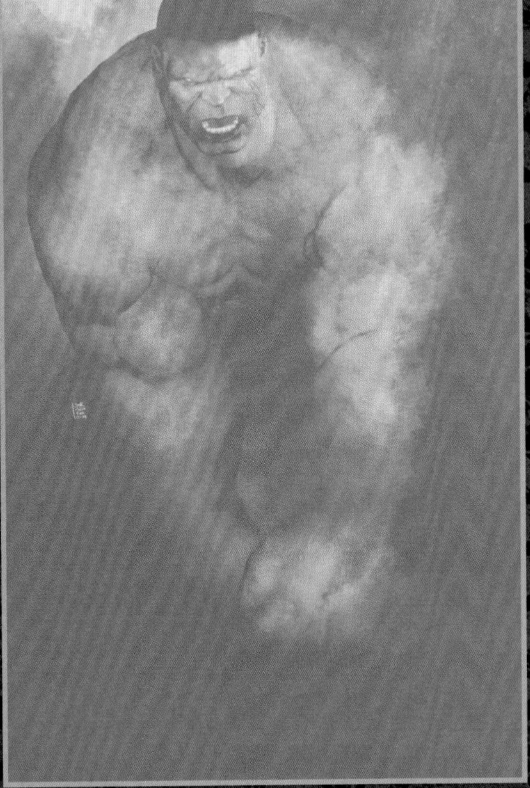

ANDREA SORRENTINO
#21 2ND PRINTING COVER

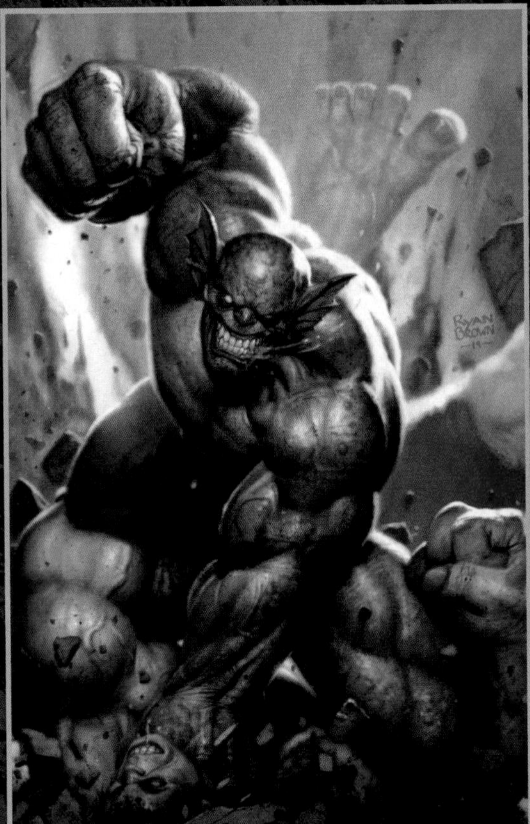

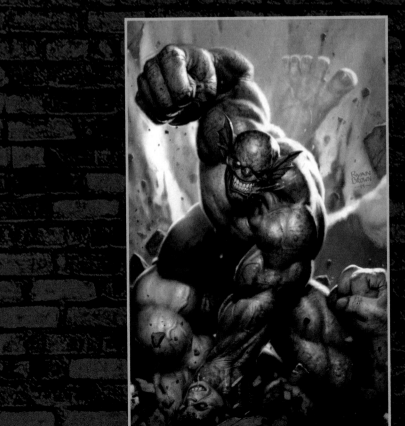

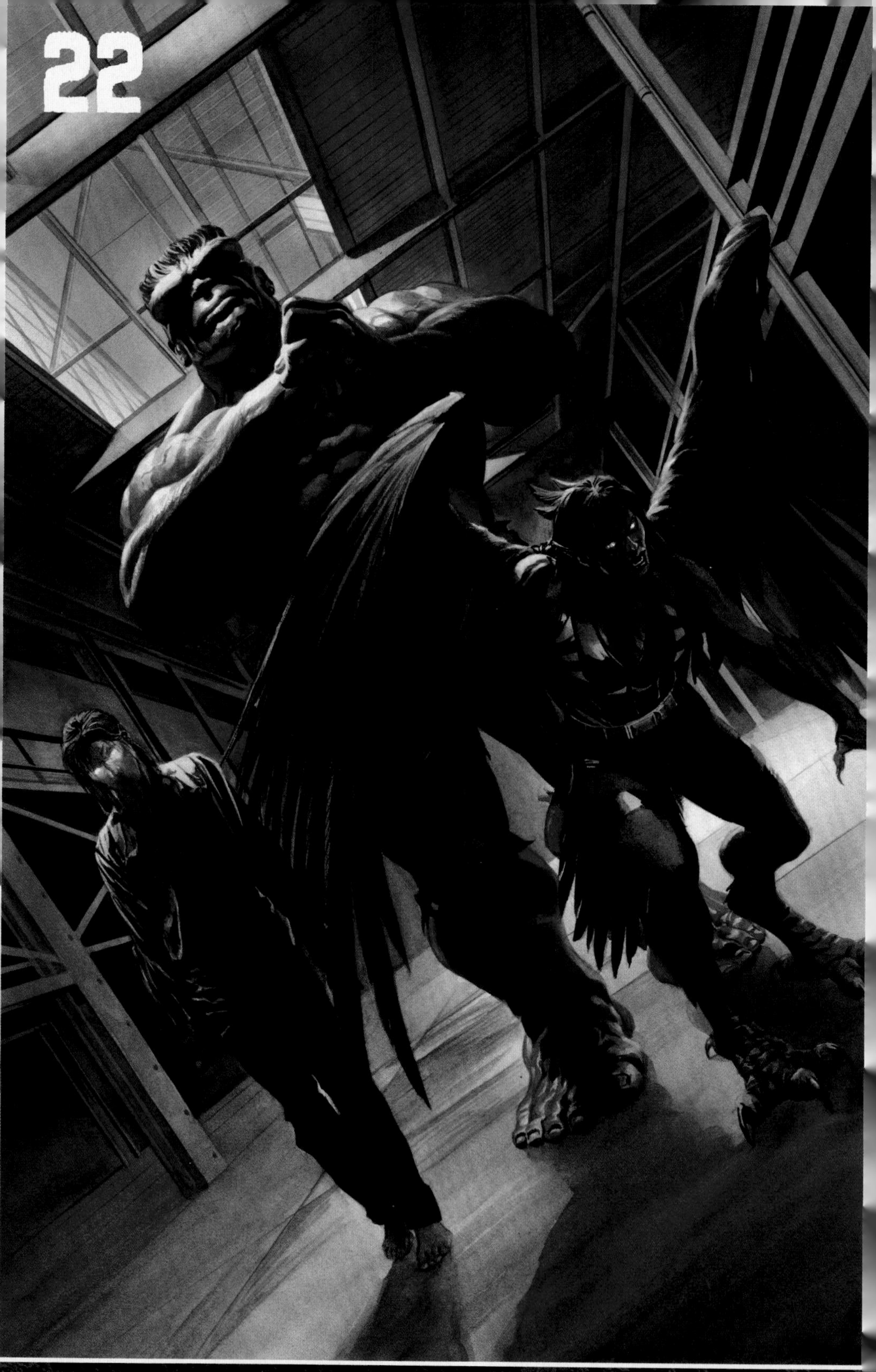
22

"HERE'S A KNOCKING INDEED! IF A MAN WERE PORTER OF HELL-GATE,

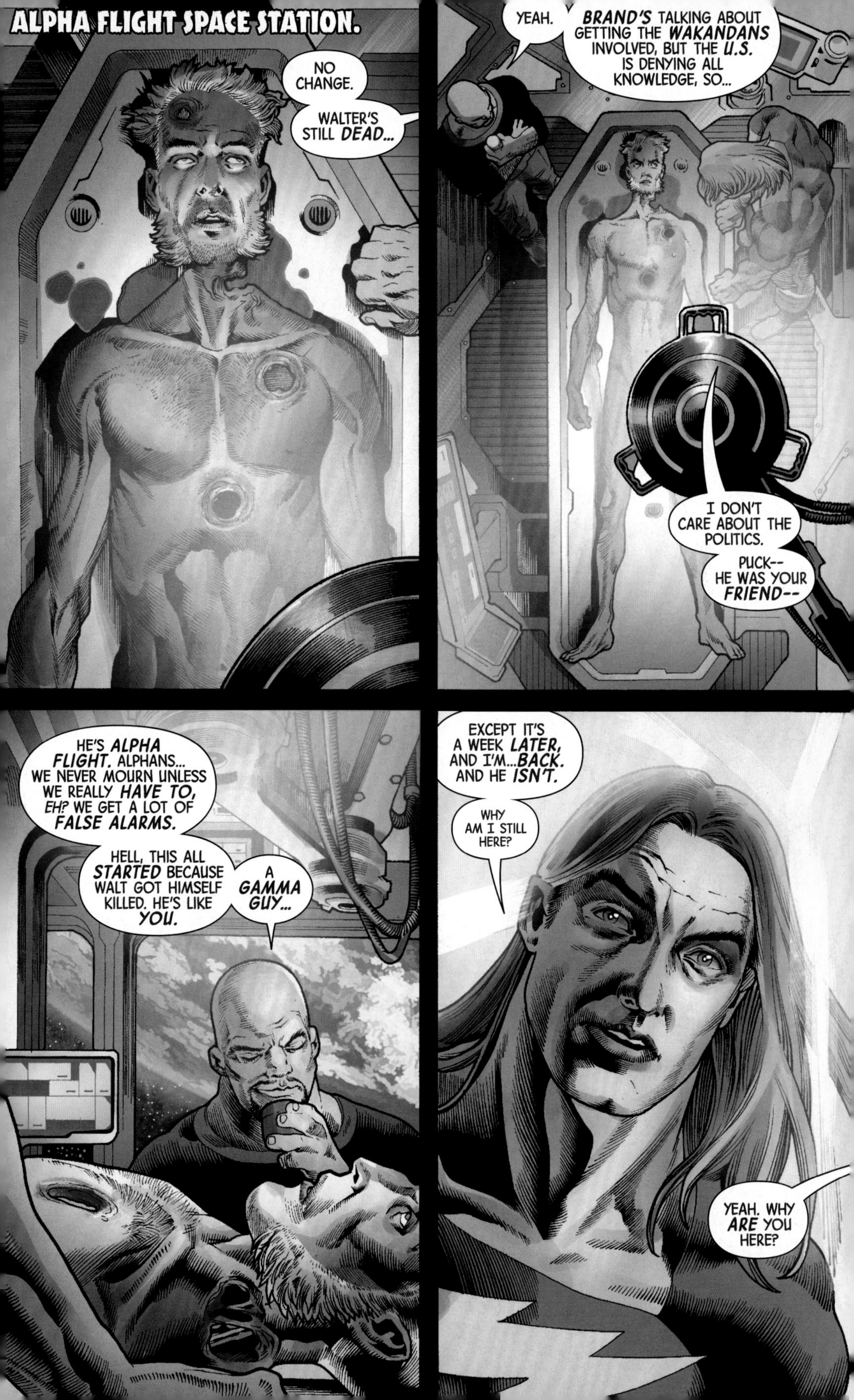
ALPHA FLIGHT SPACE STATION.
NO CHANGE.
WALTER'S STILL DEAD...
YEAH.
BRAND'S TALKING ABOUT GETTING THE WAKANDANS INVOLVED, BUT THE U.S. IS DENYING ALL KNOWLEDGE, SO...
I DON'T CARE ABOUT THE POLITICS.
PUCK-- HE WAS YOUR FRIEND--
HE'S ALPHA FLIGHT. ALPHANS... WE NEVER MOURN UNLESS WE REALLY HAVE TO, EH? WE GET A LOT OF FALSE ALARMS.
HELL, THIS ALL STARTED BECAUSE WALT GOT HIMSELF KILLED. HE'S LIKE YOU.
A GAMMA GUY...
EXCEPT IT'S A WEEK LATER, AND I'M...BACK. AND HE ISN'T.
WHY AM I STILL HERE?
YEAH. WHY ARE YOU HERE?

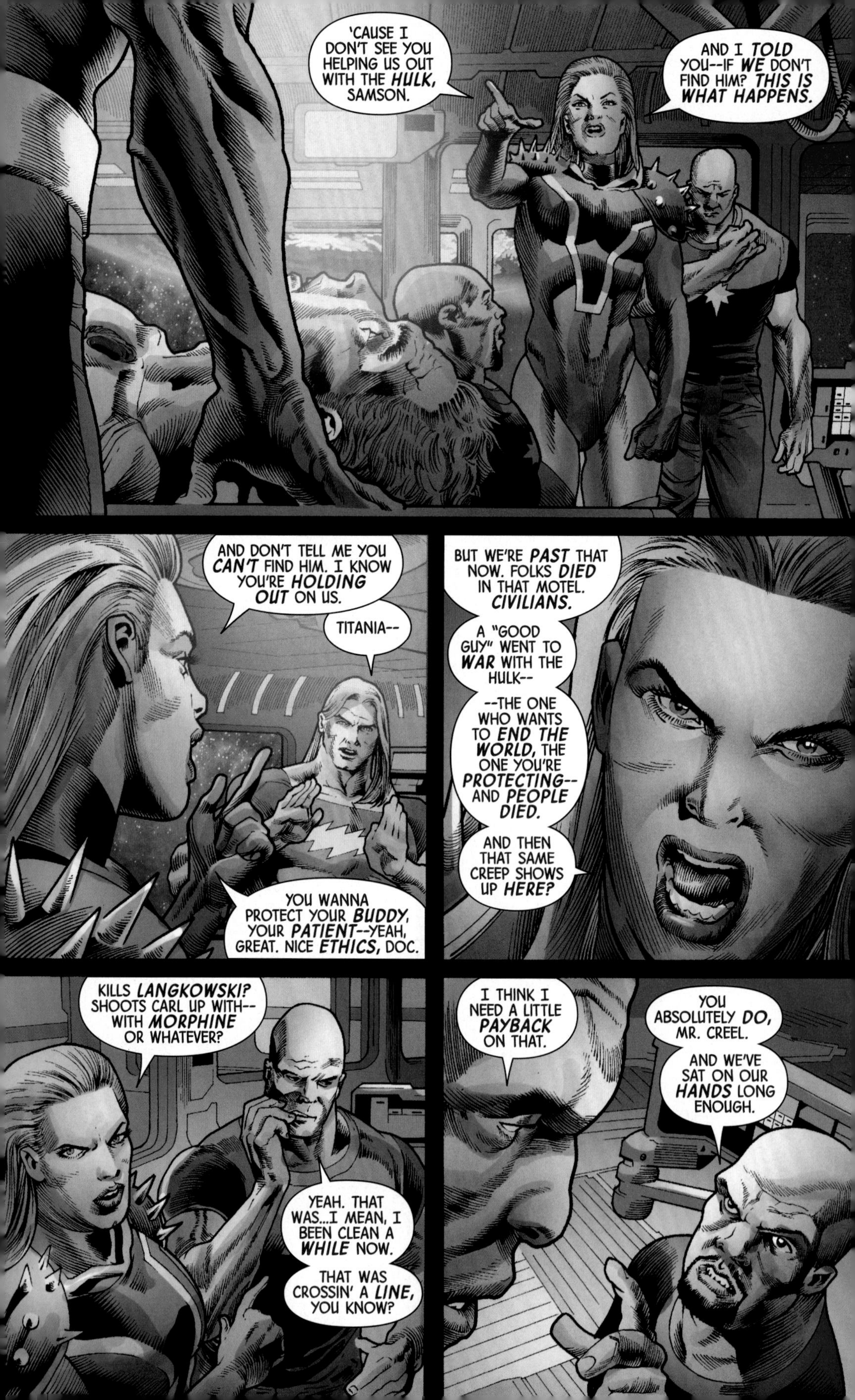

'CAUSE I DON'T SEE YOU HELPING US OUT WITH THE HULK, SAMSON.
AND I TOLD YOU--IF WE DON'T FIND HIM? THIS IS WHAT HAPPENS.
AND DON'T TELL ME YOU CAN'T FIND HIM. I KNOW YOU'RE HOLDING OUT ON US.
TITANIA--
YOU WANNA PROTECT YOUR BUDDY, YOUR PATIENT--YEAH, GREAT. NICE ETHICS, DOC.
BUT WE'RE PAST THAT NOW. FOLKS DIED IN THAT MOTEL. CIVILIANS.
A "GOOD GUY" WENT TO WAR WITH THE HULK--
--THE ONE WHO WANTS TO END THE WORLD, THE ONE YOU'RE PROTECTING--AND PEOPLE DIED.
AND THEN THAT SAME CREEP SHOWS UP HERE?
KILLS LANGKOWSKI? SHOOTS CARL UP WITH--WITH MORPHINE OR WHATEVER?
YEAH. THAT WAS...I MEAN, I BEEN CLEAN A WHILE NOW.
THAT WAS CROSSIN' A LINE, YOU KNOW?
I THINK I NEED A LITTLE PAYBACK ON THAT.
YOU ABSOLUTELY DO, MR. CREEL.
AND WE'VE SAT ON OUR HANDS LONG ENOUGH.

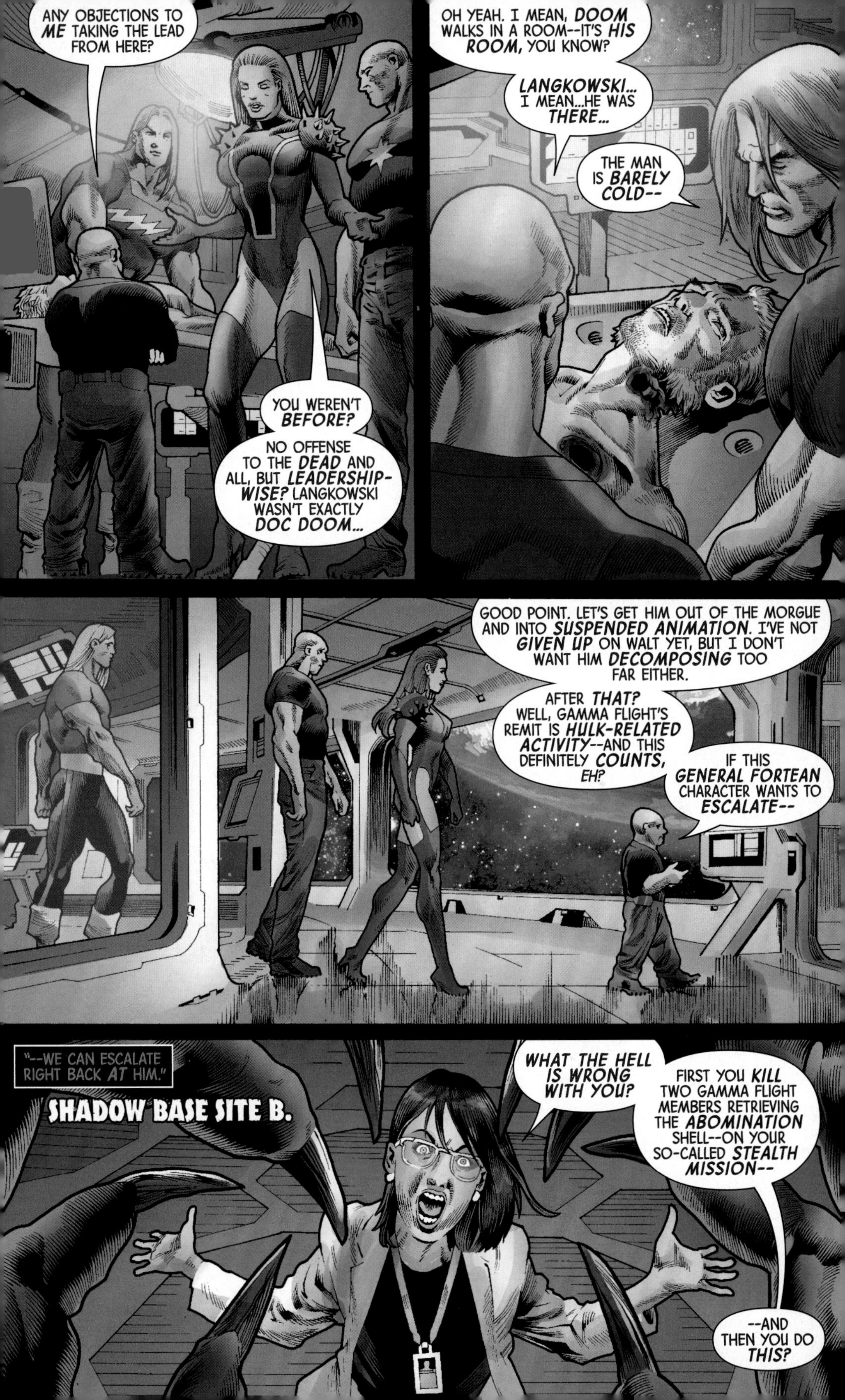
ANY OBJECTIONS TO ME TAKING THE LEAD FROM HERE?
YOU WEREN'T BEFORE?
NO OFFENSE TO THE DEAD AND ALL, BUT LEADERSHIP-WISE? LANGKOWSKI WASN'T EXACTLY DOC DOOM...
OH YEAH. I MEAN, DOOM WALKS IN A ROOM--IT'S HIS ROOM, YOU KNOW?
LANGKOWSKI... I MEAN...HE WAS THERE...
THE MAN IS BARELY COLD--
GOOD POINT. LET'S GET HIM OUT OF THE MORGUE AND INTO SUSPENDED ANIMATION. I'VE NOT GIVEN UP ON WALT YET, BUT I DON'T WANT HIM DECOMPOSING TOO FAR EITHER.
AFTER THAT? WELL, GAMMA FLIGHT'S REMIT IS HULK-RELATED ACTIVITY--AND THIS DEFINITELY COUNTS, EH?
IF THIS GENERAL FORTEAN CHARACTER WANTS TO ESCALATE--
"--WE CAN ESCALATE RIGHT BACK AT HIM."
SHADOW BASE SITE B.
WHAT THE HELL IS WRONG WITH YOU?
FIRST YOU KILL TWO GAMMA FLIGHT MEMBERS RETRIEVING THE ABOMINATION SHELL--ON YOUR SO-CALLED STEALTH MISSION--
--AND THEN YOU DO THIS?

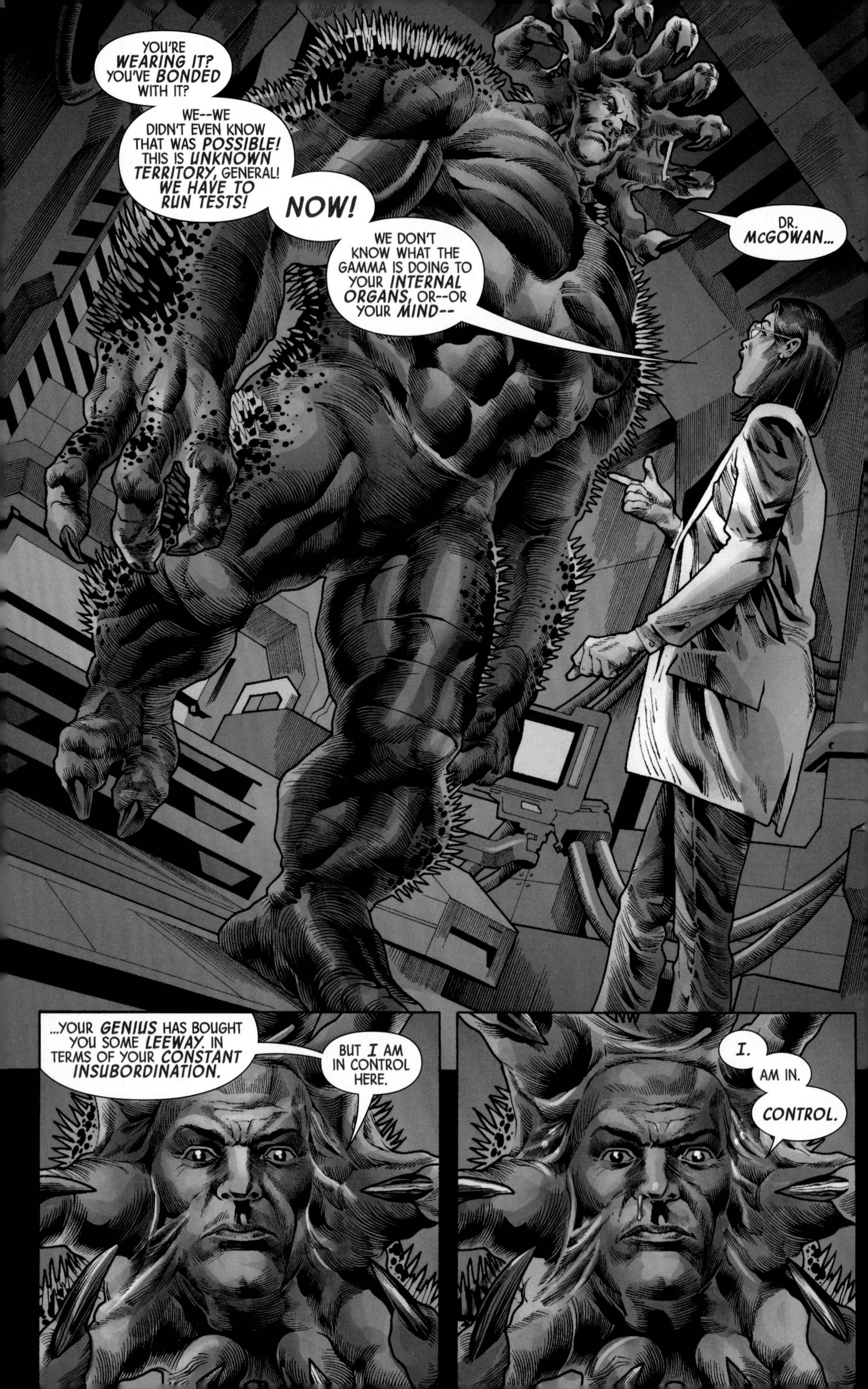
YOU'RE WEARING IT? YOU'VE BONDED WITH IT?
WE--WE DIDN'T EVEN KNOW THAT WAS POSSIBLE! THIS IS UNKNOWN TERRITORY, GENERAL! WE HAVE TO RUN TESTS!
NOW!
WE DON'T KNOW WHAT THE GAMMA IS DOING TO YOUR INTERNAL ORGANS, OR--OR YOUR MIND--
DR. McGOWAN...
...YOUR GENIUS HAS BOUGHT YOU SOME LEEWAY, IN TERMS OF YOUR CONSTANT INSUBORDINATION.
BUT I AM IN CONTROL HERE.
I.
AM IN.
CONTROL.

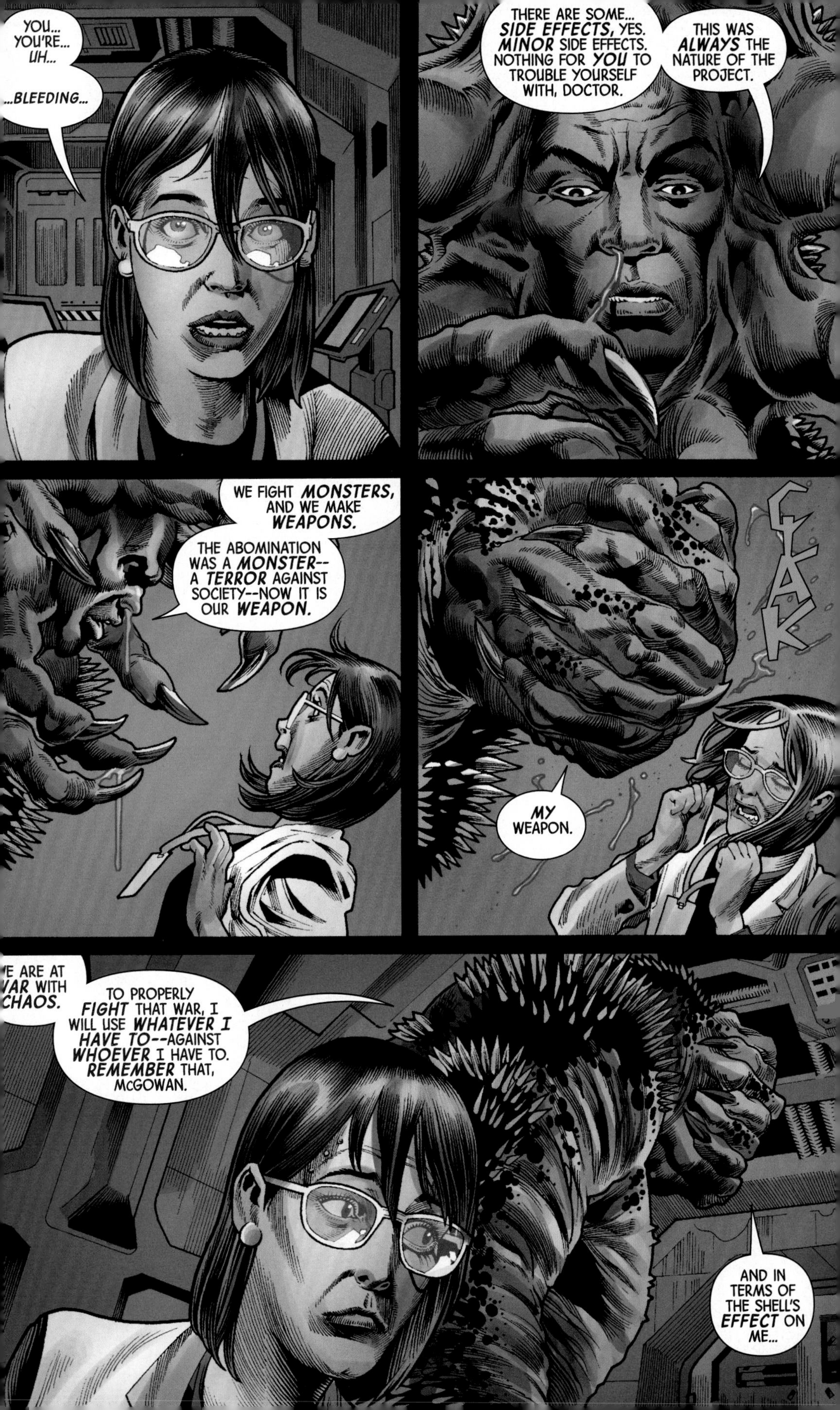

YOU... YOU'RE... UH...
...BLEEDING...
THERE ARE SOME... SIDE EFFECTS, YES. MINOR SIDE EFFECTS. NOTHING FOR YOU TO TROUBLE YOURSELF WITH, DOCTOR.
THIS WAS ALWAYS THE NATURE OF THE PROJECT.
WE FIGHT MONSTERS, AND WE MAKE WEAPONS.
THE ABOMINATION WAS A MONSTER-- A TERROR AGAINST SOCIETY--NOW IT IS OUR WEAPON.
CLAK
MY WEAPON.
E ARE AT VAR WITH CHAOS.
TO PROPERLY FIGHT THAT WAR, I WILL USE WHATEVER I HAVE TO--AGAINST WHOEVER I HAVE TO. REMEMBER THAT, McGOWAN.
AND IN TERMS OF THE SHELL'S EFFECT ON ME...

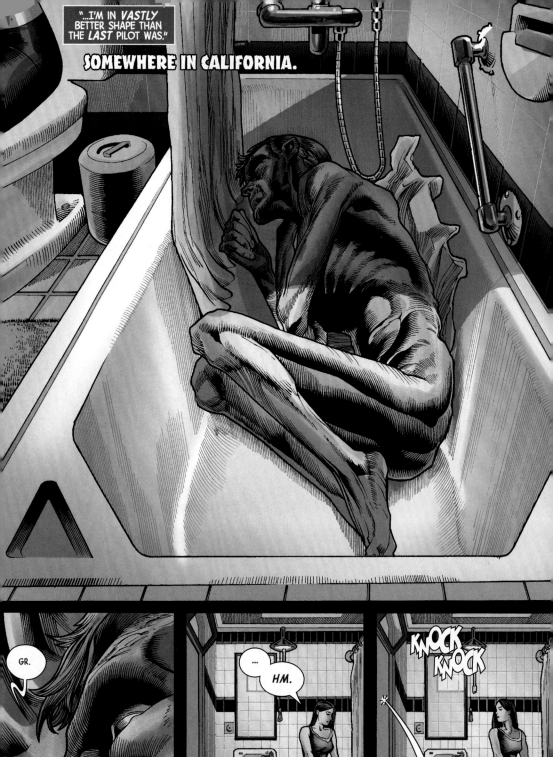

"...I'M IN *VASTLY* BETTER SHAPE THAN THE *LAST* PILOT WAS."

SOMEWHERE IN CALIFORNIA.

GR.

... HM.

KNOCK KNOCK

BETTY? ARE YOU *OKAY*?

YOU'VE-- YOU'VE BEEN IN THERE SINCE *DAWN*--

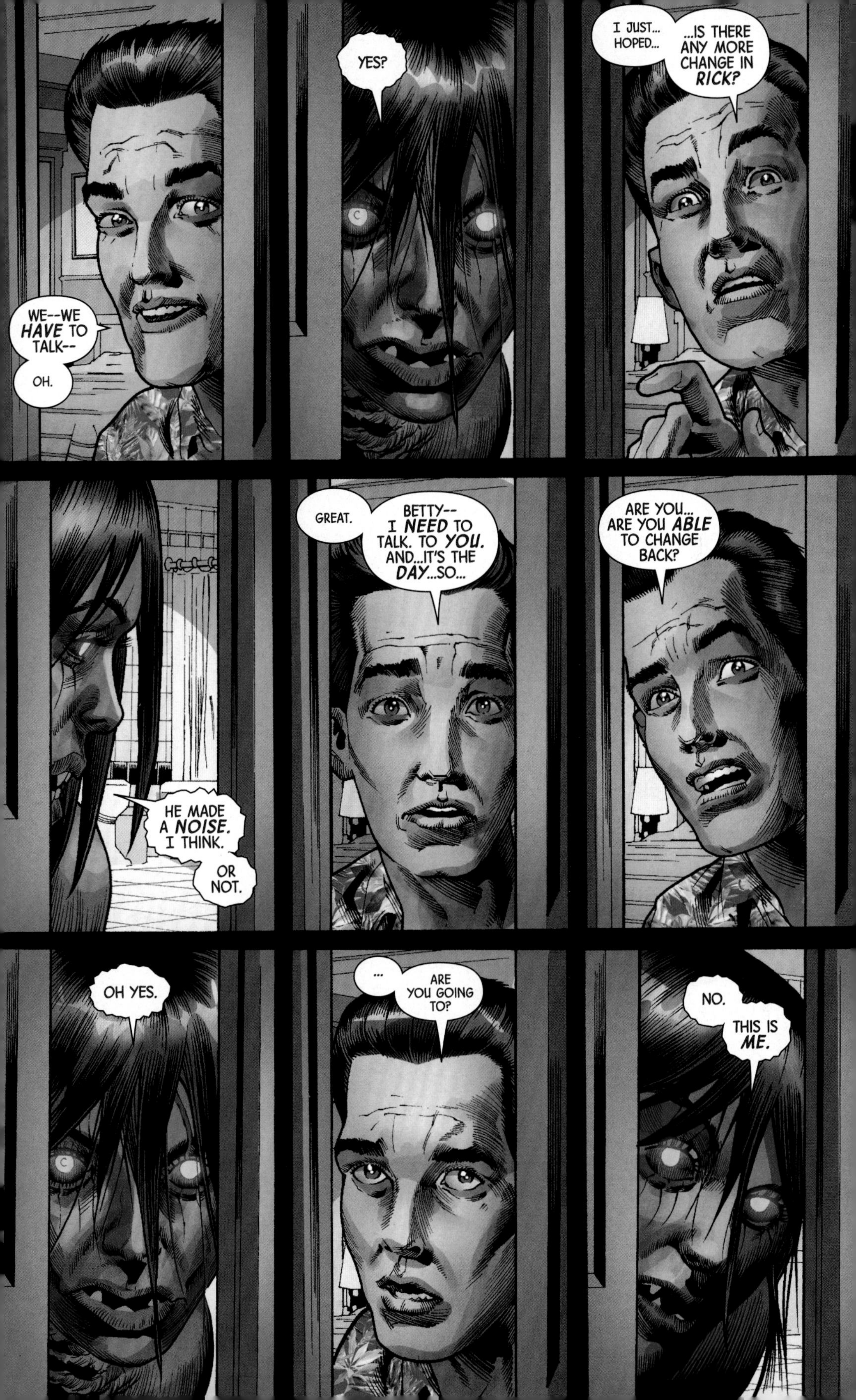
WE--WE HAVE TO TALK--
OH.
YES?
I JUST... HOPED...
...IS THERE ANY MORE CHANGE IN RICK?
HE MADE A NOISE. I THINK.
OR NOT.
GREAT.
BETTY-- I NEED TO TALK. TO YOU. AND...IT'S THE DAY...SO...
ARE YOU... ARE YOU ABLE TO CHANGE BACK?
OH YES.
...
ARE YOU GOING TO?
NO.
THIS IS ME.

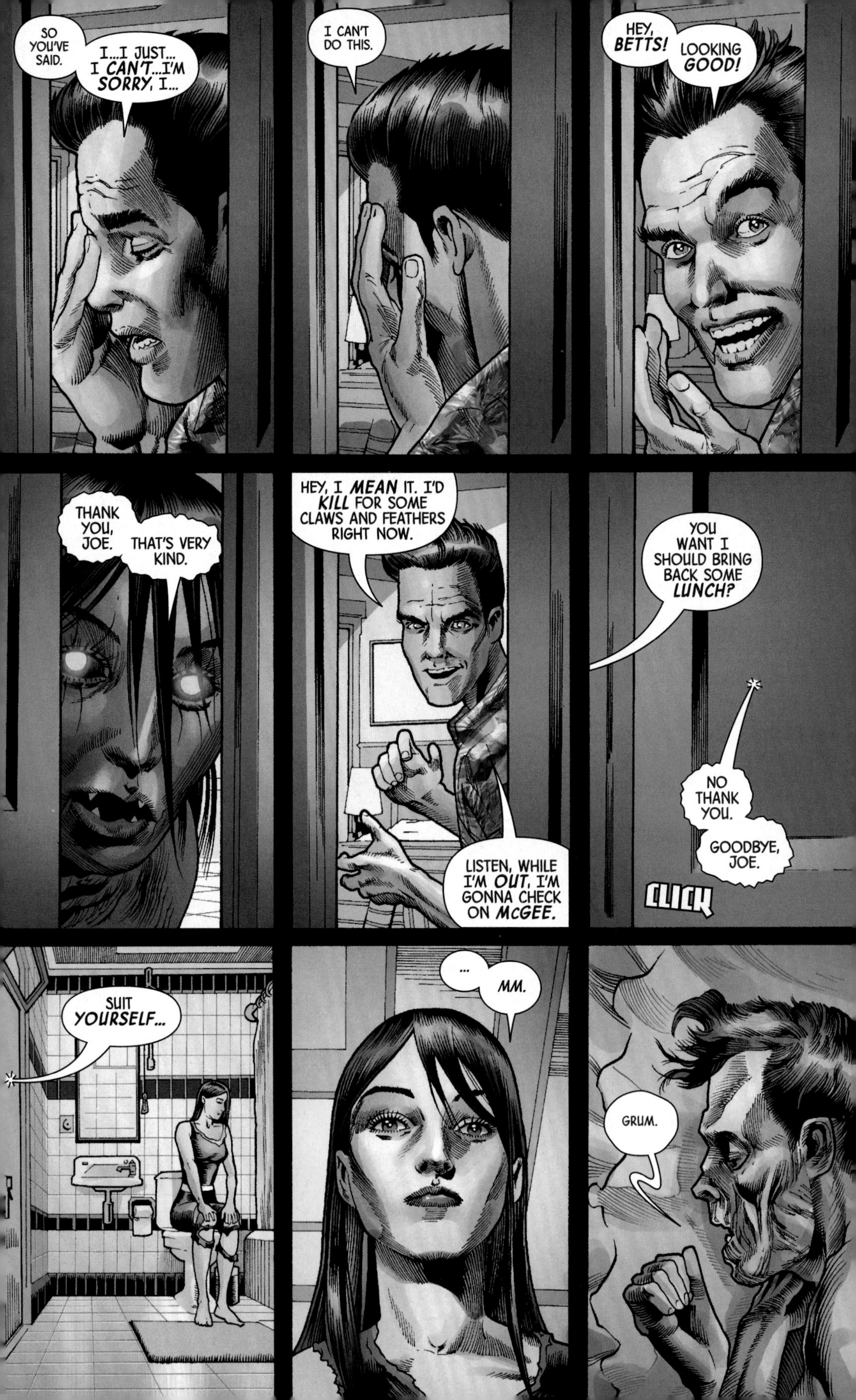
SO YOU'VE SAID.
I...I JUST... I CAN'T...I'M SORRY, I...
I CAN'T DO THIS.
HEY, BETTS!
LOOKING GOOD!
THANK YOU, JOE.
THAT'S VERY KIND.
HEY, I MEAN IT. I'D KILL FOR SOME CLAWS AND FEATHERS RIGHT NOW.
LISTEN, WHILE I'M OUT, I'M GONNA CHECK ON McGEE.
YOU WANT I SHOULD BRING BACK SOME LUNCH?
NO THANK YOU.
GOODBYE, JOE.
CLICK
SUIT YOURSELF...
...
MM.
GRUM.

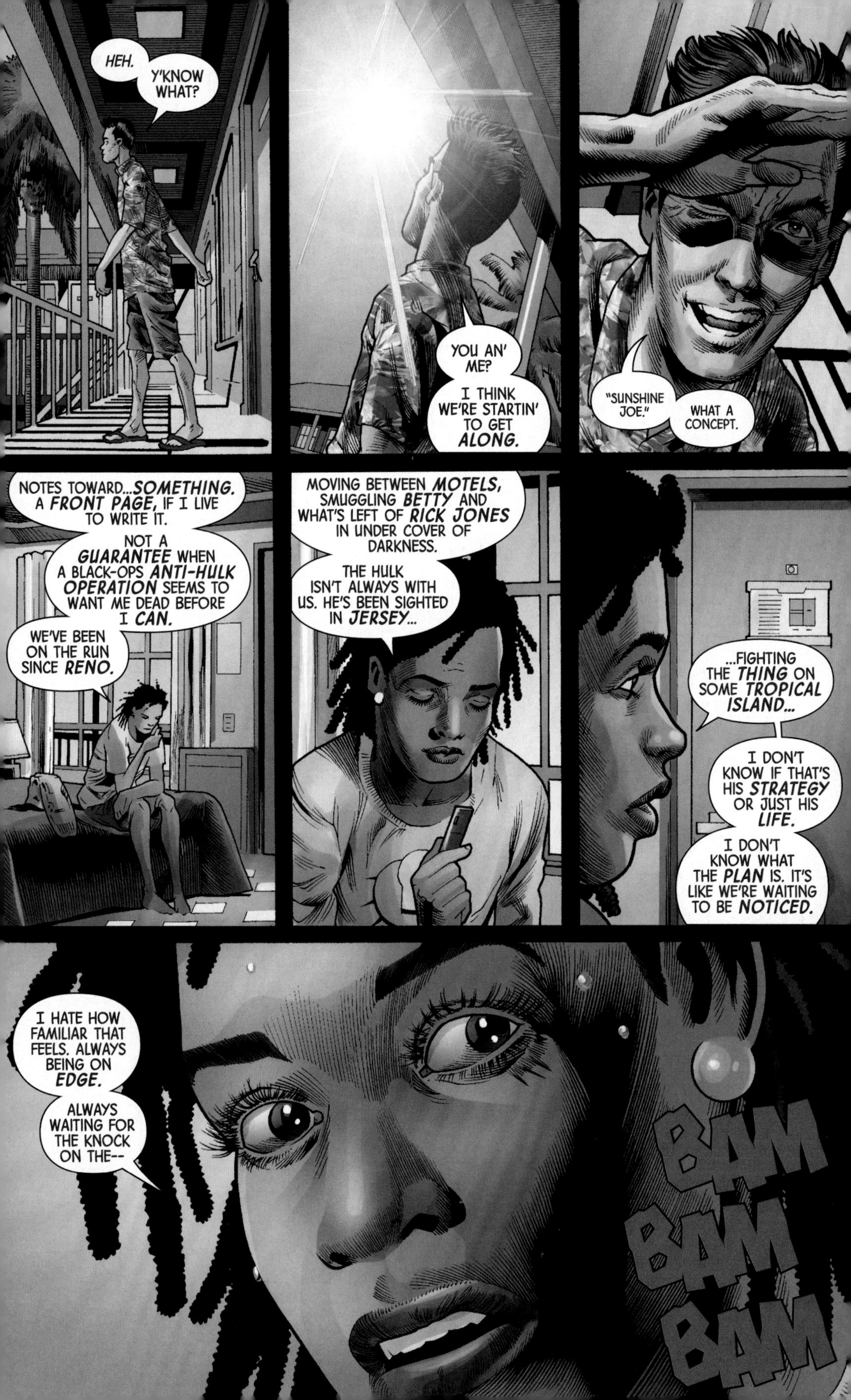
HEH.
Y'KNOW WHAT?
YOU AN' ME?
I THINK WE'RE STARTIN' TO GET ALONG.
"SUNSHINE JOE."
WHAT A CONCEPT.
NOTES TOWARD...SOMETHING. A FRONT PAGE, IF I LIVE TO WRITE IT.
NOT A GUARANTEE WHEN A BLACK-OPS ANTI-HULK OPERATION SEEMS TO WANT ME DEAD BEFORE I CAN.
WE'VE BEEN ON THE RUN SINCE RENO.
MOVING BETWEEN MOTELS, SMUGGLING BETTY AND WHAT'S LEFT OF RICK JONES IN UNDER COVER OF DARKNESS.
THE HULK ISN'T ALWAYS WITH US. HE'S BEEN SIGHTED IN JERSEY...
...FIGHTING THE THING ON SOME TROPICAL ISLAND...
I DON'T KNOW IF THAT'S HIS STRATEGY OR JUST HIS LIFE.
I DON'T KNOW WHAT THE PLAN IS. IT'S LIKE WE'RE WAITING TO BE NOTICED.
I HATE HOW FAMILIAR THAT FEELS. ALWAYS BEING ON EDGE.
ALWAYS WAITING FOR THE KNOCK ON THE--
BAM
BAM
BAM

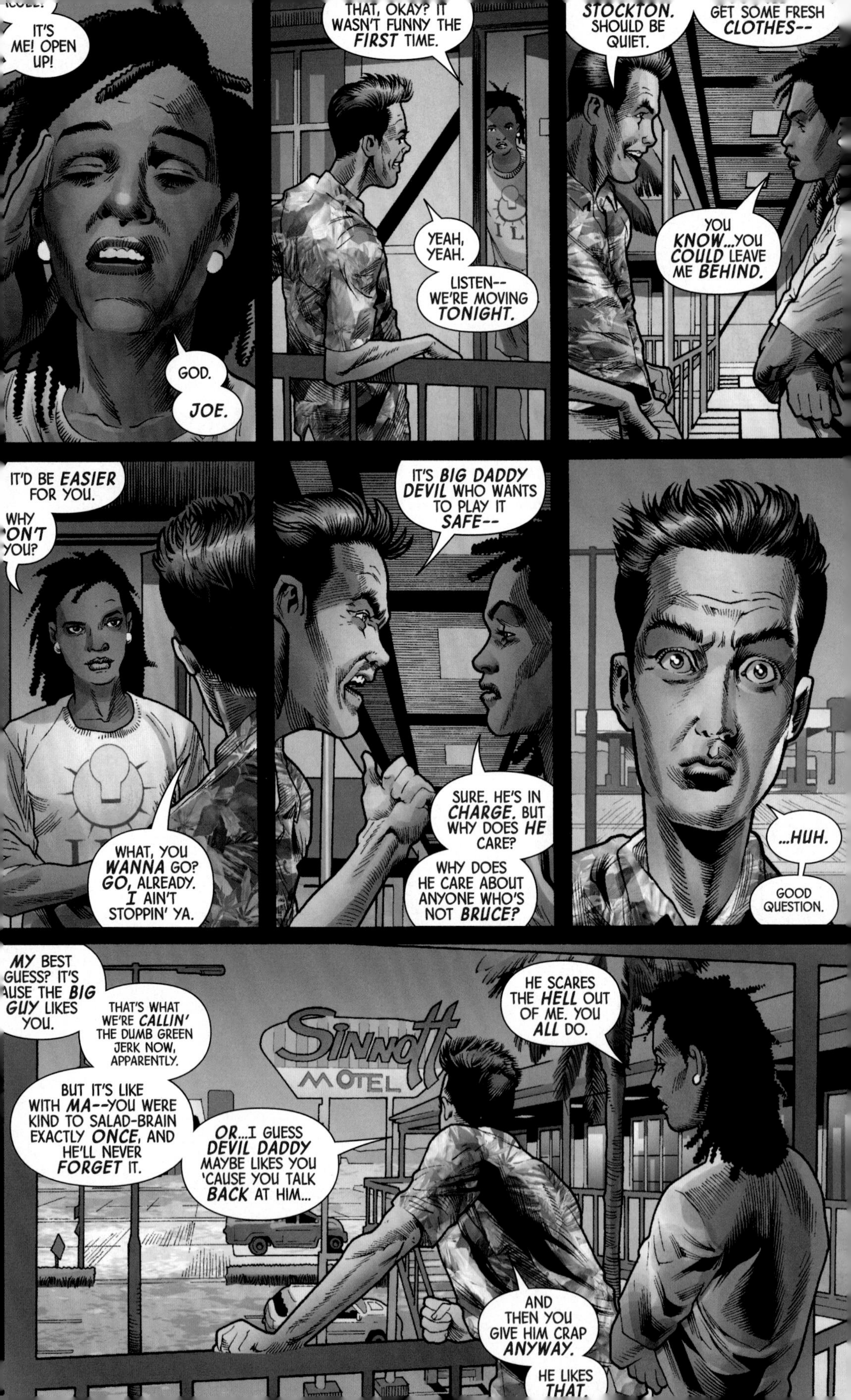
IT'S ME! OPEN UP!
GOD.
JOE.
THAT, OKAY? IT WASN'T FUNNY THE FIRST TIME.
YEAH, YEAH.
LISTEN-- WE'RE MOVING TONIGHT.
STOCKTON. SHOULD BE QUIET.
GET SOME FRESH CLOTHES--
YOU KNOW...YOU COULD LEAVE ME BEHIND.
IT'D BE EASIER FOR YOU.
WHY
ON'T YOU?
WHAT, YOU WANNA GO? GO, ALREADY. I AIN'T STOPPIN' YA.
IT'S BIG DADDY DEVIL WHO WANTS TO PLAY IT SAFE--
SURE. HE'S IN CHARGE. BUT WHY DOES HE CARE?
WHY DOES HE CARE ABOUT ANYONE WHO'S NOT BRUCE?
...HUH.
GOOD QUESTION.
MY BEST GUESS? IT'S
AUSE THE BIG GUY LIKES YOU.
THAT'S WHAT WE'RE CALLIN' THE DUMB GREEN JERK NOW, APPARENTLY.
BUT IT'S LIKE WITH MA--YOU WERE KIND TO SALAD-BRAIN EXACTLY ONCE, AND HE'LL NEVER FORGET IT.
OR...I GUESS DEVIL DADDY MAYBE LIKES YOU 'CAUSE YOU TALK BACK AT HIM...
SINNOTT MOTEL
HE SCARES THE HELL OUT OF ME. YOU ALL DO.
AND THEN YOU GIVE HIM CRAP ANYWAY.
HE LIKES THAT.

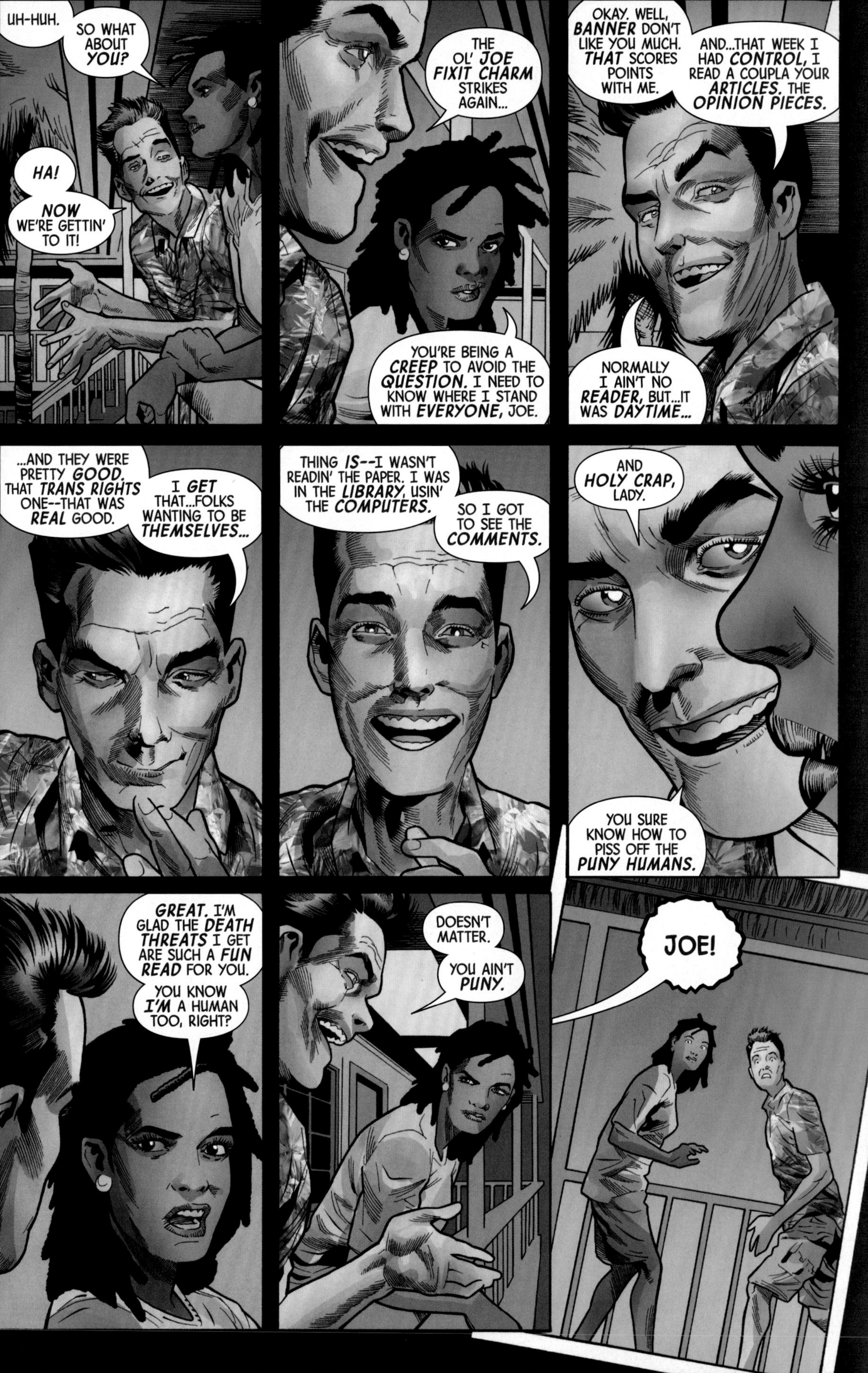
UH-HUH.
SO WHAT ABOUT YOU?
HA!
NOW WE'RE GETTIN' TO IT!
THE OL' JOE FIXIT CHARM STRIKES AGAIN...
YOU'RE BEING A CREEP TO AVOID THE QUESTION. I NEED TO KNOW WHERE I STAND WITH EVERYONE, JOE.
OKAY. WELL, BANNER DON'T LIKE YOU MUCH. THAT SCORES POINTS WITH ME.
AND...THAT WEEK I HAD CONTROL, I READ A COUPLA YOUR ARTICLES. THE OPINION PIECES.
NORMALLY I AIN'T NO READER, BUT...IT WAS DAYTIME...
...AND THEY WERE PRETTY GOOD. THAT TRANS RIGHTS ONE--THAT WAS REAL GOOD.
I GET THAT...FOLKS WANTING TO BE THEMSELVES...
THING IS--I WASN'T READIN' THE PAPER. I WAS IN THE LIBRARY, USIN' THE COMPUTERS.
SO I GOT TO SEE THE COMMENTS.
AND HOLY CRAP, LADY.
YOU SURE KNOW HOW TO PISS OFF THE PUNY HUMANS.
GREAT. I'M GLAD THE DEATH THREATS I GET ARE SUCH A FUN READ FOR YOU.
YOU KNOW I'M A HUMAN TOO, RIGHT?
DOESN'T MATTER.
YOU AIN'T PUNY.
JOE!

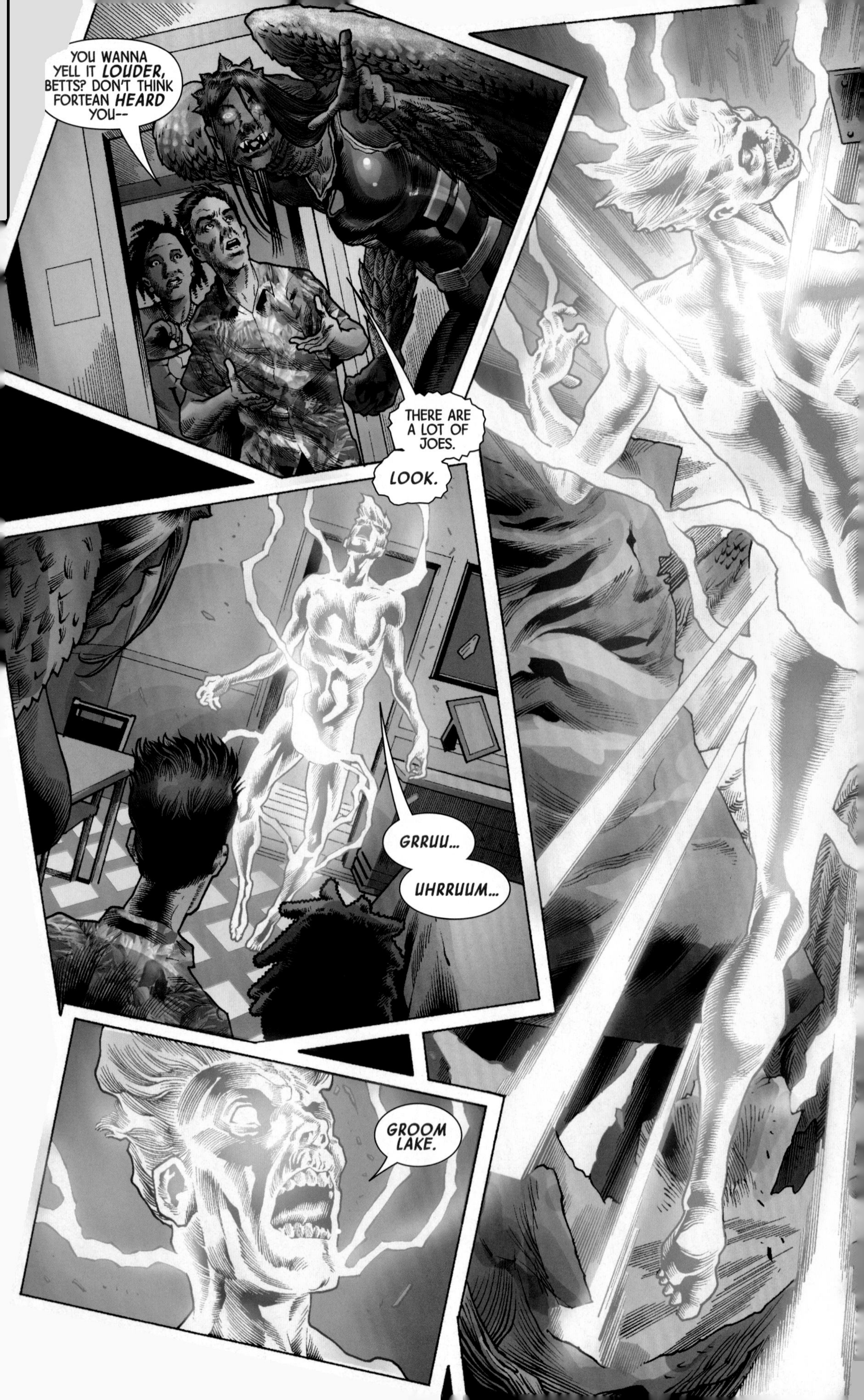
YOU WANNA YELL IT LOUDER, BETTS? DON'T THINK FORTEAN HEARD YOU--
THERE ARE A LOT OF JOES.
LOOK.
GRRUU...
UHRRUUM...
GROOM LAKE.

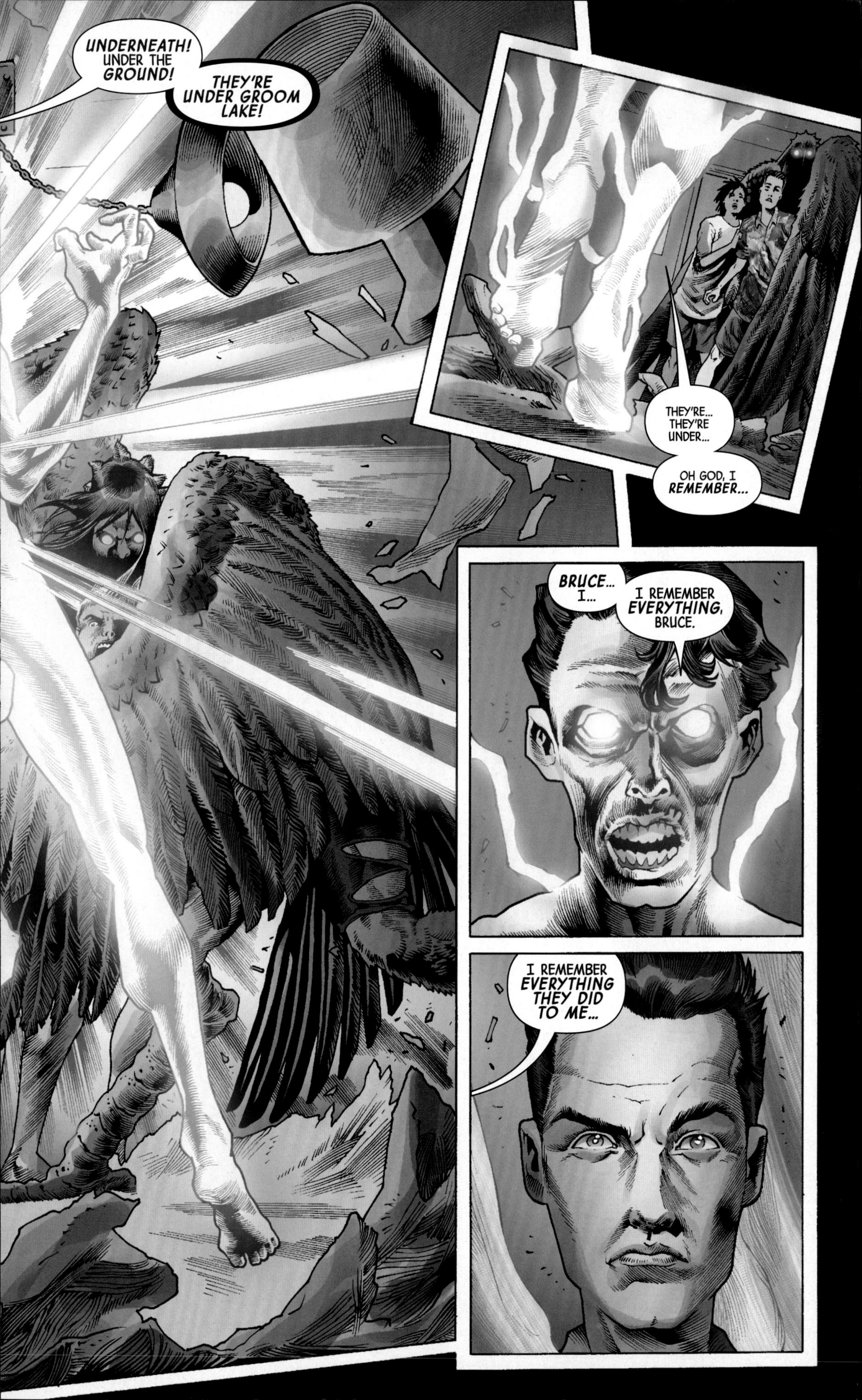
UNDERNEATH! UNDER THE GROUND!
THEY'RE UNDER GROOM LAKE!
THEY'RE... THEY'RE UNDER...
OH GOD, I REMEMBER...
BRUCE... I...
I REMEMBER EVERYTHING, BRUCE.
I REMEMBER EVERYTHING THEY DID TO ME...

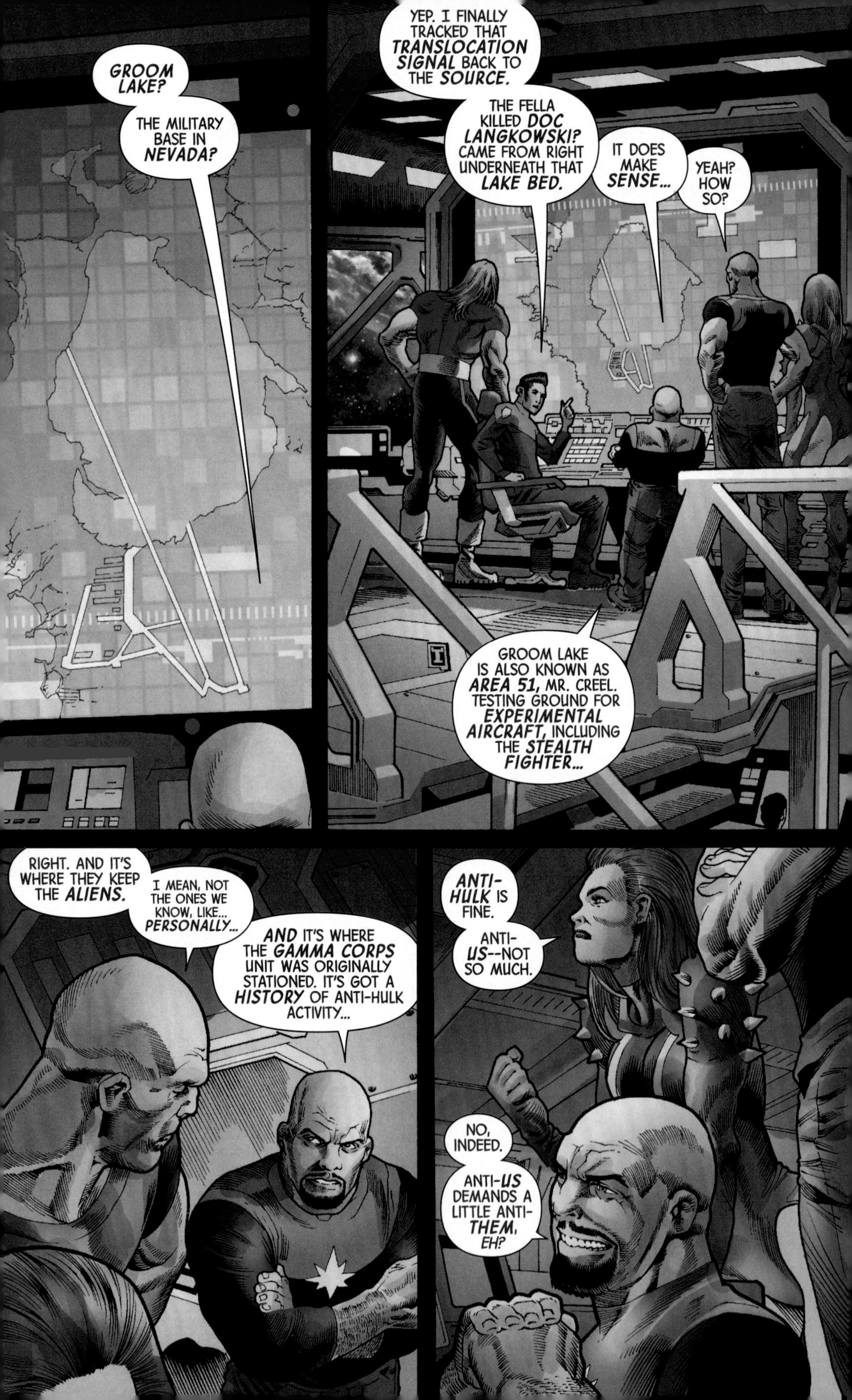
GROOM LAKE?
THE MILITARY BASE IN NEVADA?
YEP. I FINALLY TRACKED THAT TRANSLOCATION SIGNAL BACK TO THE SOURCE.
THE FELLA KILLED DOC LANGKOWSKI? CAME FROM RIGHT UNDERNEATH THAT LAKE BED.
IT DOES MAKE SENSE...
YEAH? HOW SO?
GROOM LAKE IS ALSO KNOWN AS AREA 51, MR. CREEL. TESTING GROUND FOR EXPERIMENTAL AIRCRAFT, INCLUDING THE STEALTH FIGHTER...
RIGHT. AND IT'S WHERE THEY KEEP THE ALIENS.
I MEAN, NOT THE ONES WE KNOW, LIKE... PERSONALLY...
AND IT'S WHERE THE GAMMA CORPS UNIT WAS ORIGINALLY STATIONED. IT'S GOT A HISTORY OF ANTI-HULK ACTIVITY...
ANTI-HULK IS FINE.
ANTI-US--NOT SO MUCH.
NO, INDEED.
ANTI-US DEMANDS A LITTLE ANTI-THEM, EH?

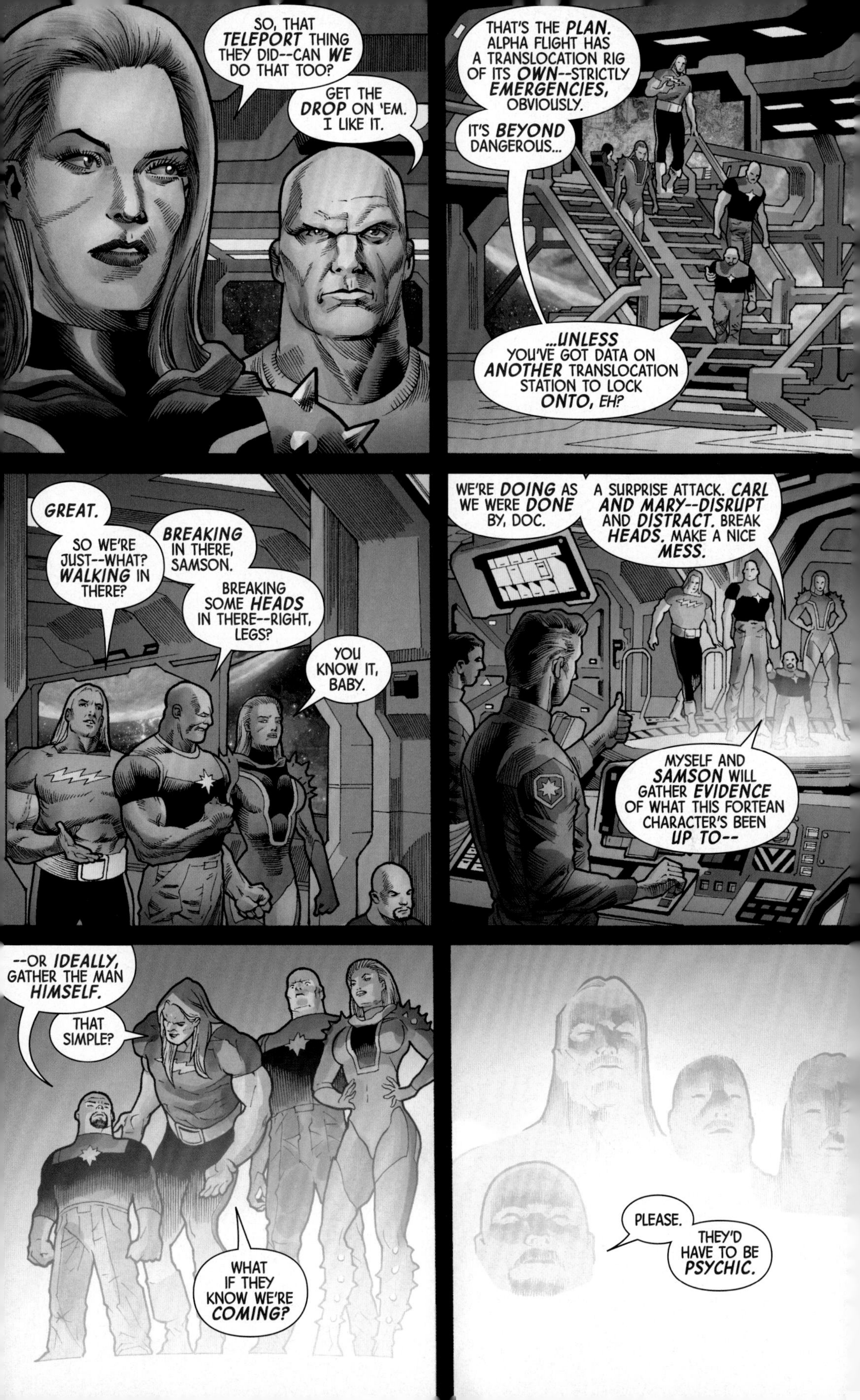
SO, THAT TELEPORT THING THEY DID--CAN WE DO THAT TOO?
GET THE DROP ON 'EM. I LIKE IT.
THAT'S THE PLAN. ALPHA FLIGHT HAS A TRANSLOCATION RIG OF ITS OWN--STRICTLY EMERGENCIES, OBVIOUSLY.
IT'S BEYOND DANGEROUS...
...UNLESS YOU'VE GOT DATA ON ANOTHER TRANSLOCATION STATION TO LOCK ONTO, EH?
GREAT.
SO WE'RE JUST--WHAT? WALKING IN THERE?
BREAKING IN THERE, SAMSON.
BREAKING SOME HEADS IN THERE--RIGHT, LEGS?
YOU KNOW IT, BABY.
WE'RE DOING AS WE WERE DONE BY, DOC.
A SURPRISE ATTACK. CARL AND MARY--DISRUPT AND DISTRACT. BREAK HEADS. MAKE A NICE MESS.
MYSELF AND SAMSON WILL GATHER EVIDENCE OF WHAT THIS FORTEAN CHARACTER'S BEEN UP TO--
--OR IDEALLY, GATHER THE MAN HIMSELF.
THAT SIMPLE?
WHAT IF THEY KNOW WE'RE COMING?
PLEASE.
THEY'D HAVE TO BE PSYCHIC.

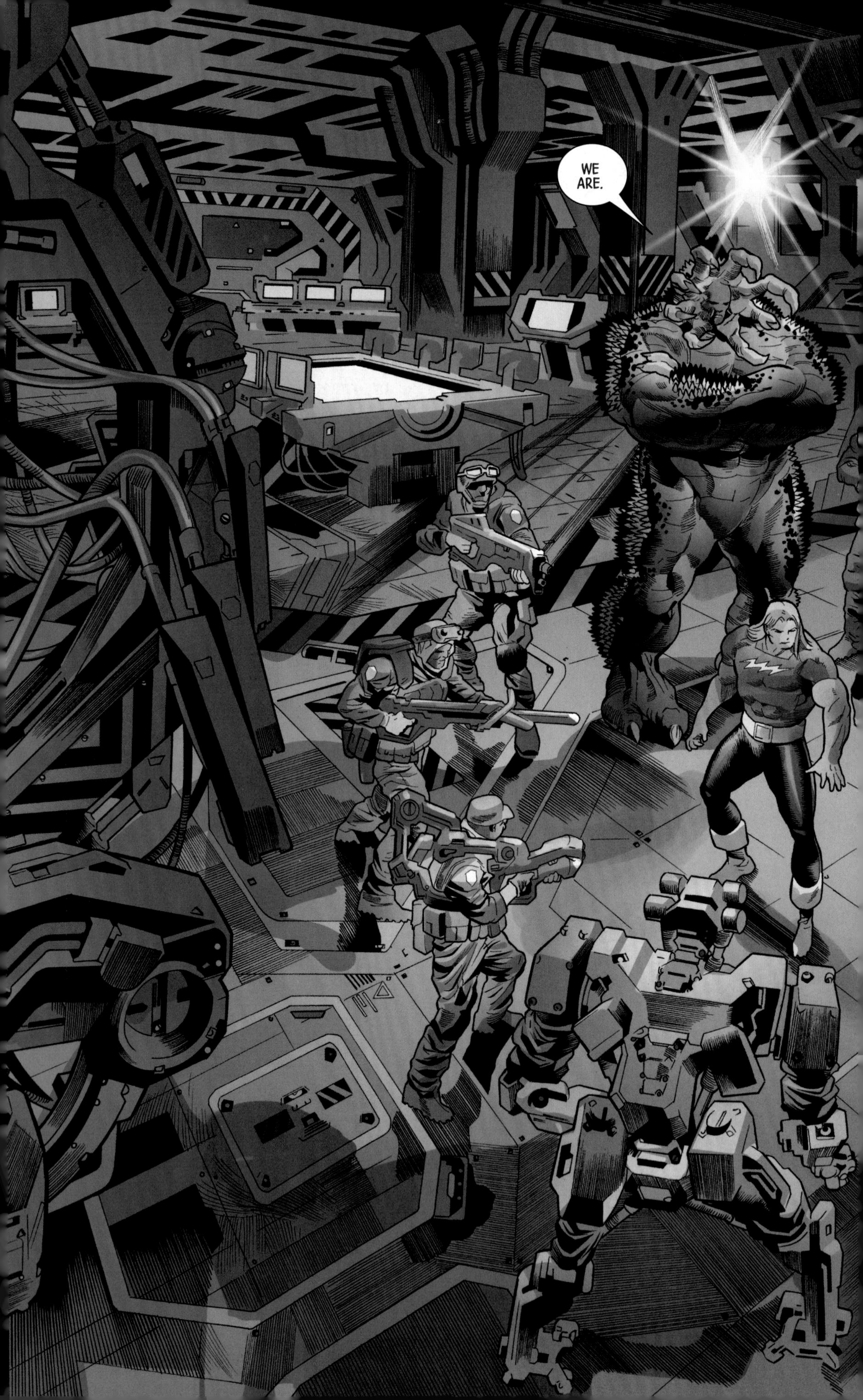
WE ARE.

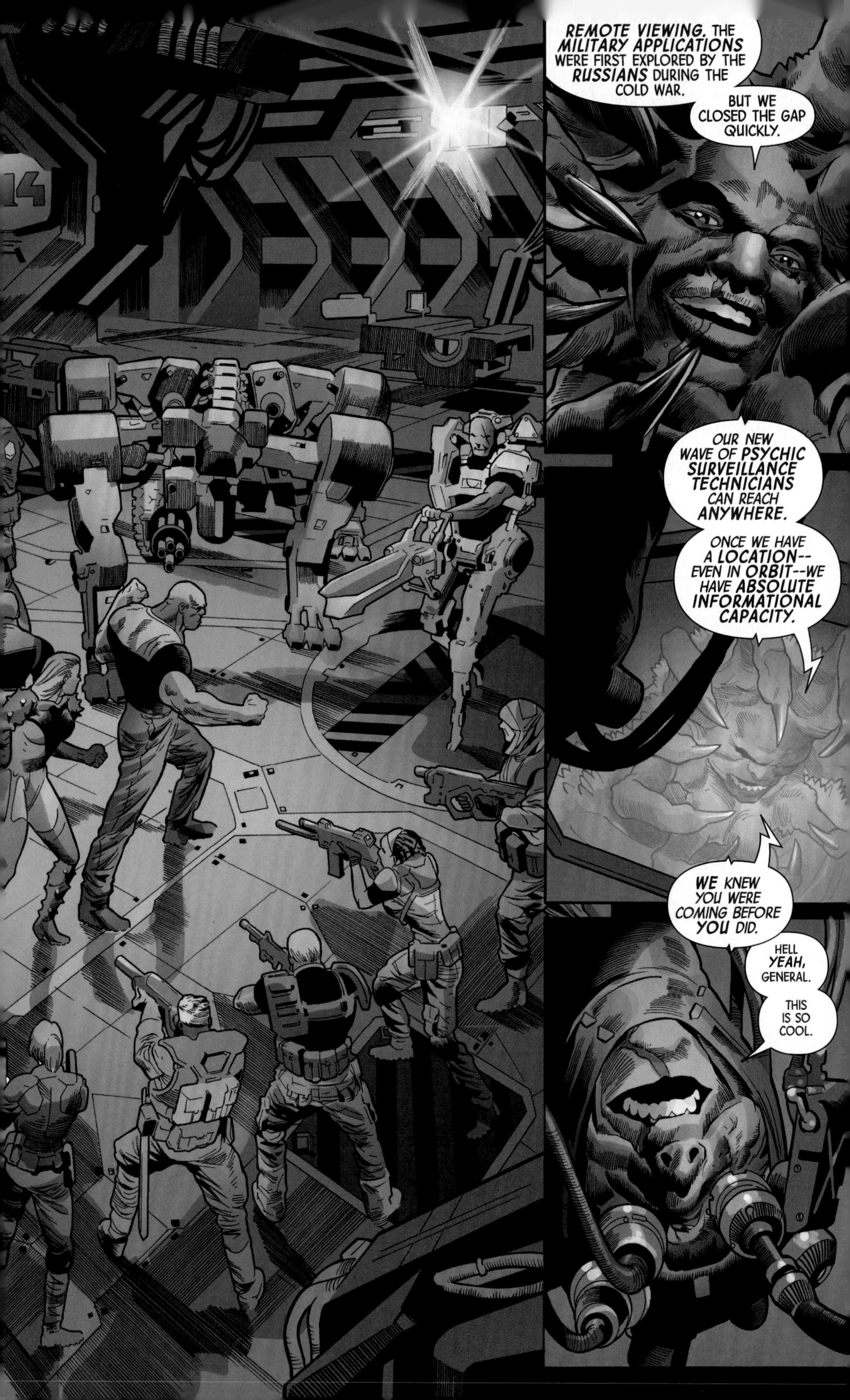
REMOTE VIEWING. THE MILITARY APPLICATIONS WERE FIRST EXPLORED BY THE RUSSIANS DURING THE COLD WAR.
BUT WE CLOSED THE GAP QUICKLY.
OUR NEW WAVE OF PSYCHIC SURVEILLANCE TECHNICIANS CAN REACH ANYWHERE.
ONCE WE HAVE A LOCATION--EVEN IN ORBIT--WE HAVE ABSOLUTE INFORMATIONAL CAPACITY.
WE KNEW YOU WERE COMING BEFORE YOU DID.
HELL YEAH, GENERAL.
THIS IS SO COOL.
14

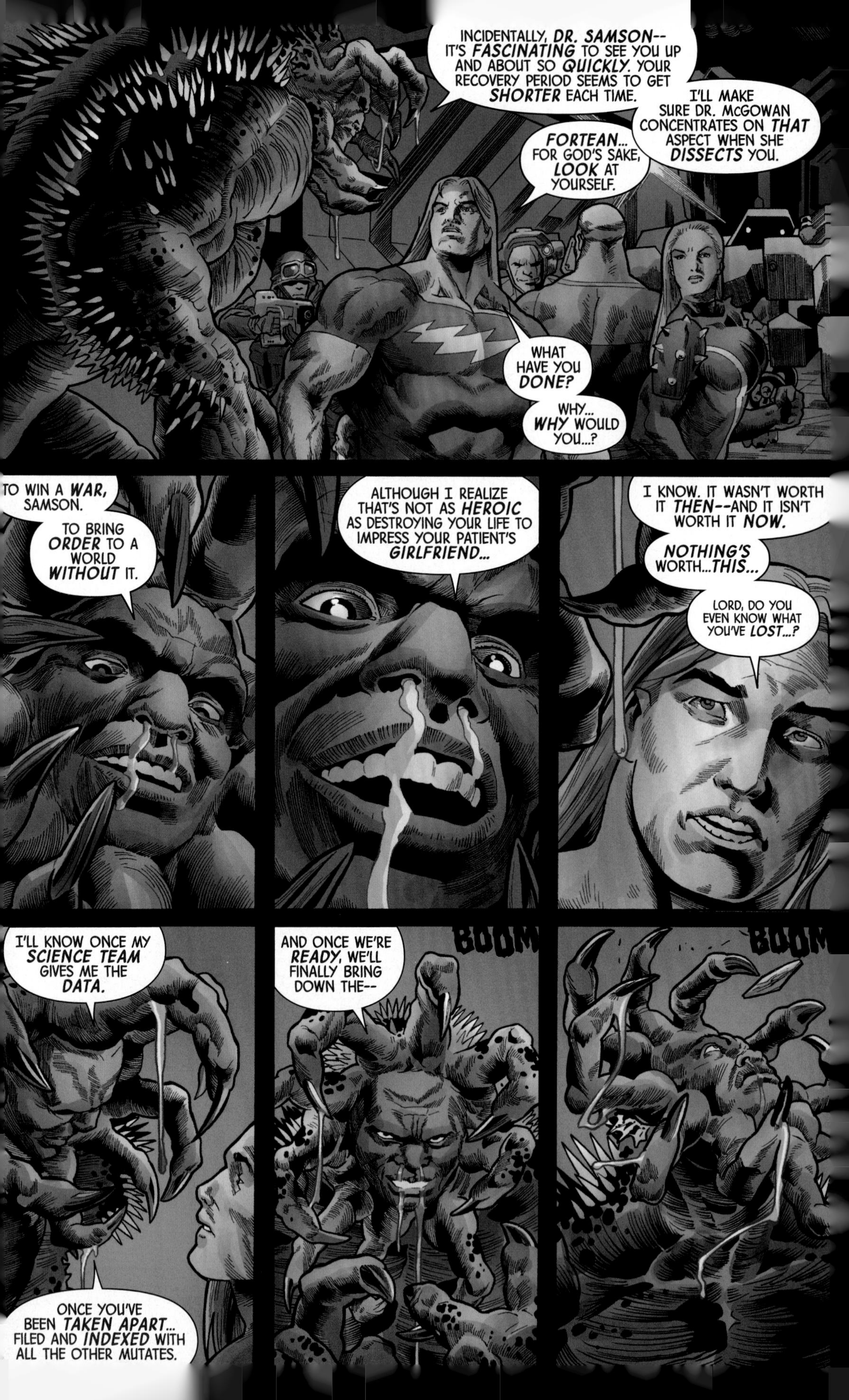

INCIDENTALLY, DR. SAMSON-- IT'S FASCINATING TO SEE YOU UP AND ABOUT SO QUICKLY. YOUR RECOVERY PERIOD SEEMS TO GET SHORTER EACH TIME.
I'LL MAKE SURE DR. McGOWAN CONCENTRATES ON THAT ASPECT WHEN SHE DISSECTS YOU.
FORTEAN... FOR GOD'S SAKE, LOOK AT YOURSELF.
WHAT HAVE YOU DONE?
WHY... WHY WOULD YOU...?
TO WIN A WAR, SAMSON.
TO BRING ORDER TO A WORLD WITHOUT IT.
ALTHOUGH I REALIZE THAT'S NOT AS HEROIC AS DESTROYING YOUR LIFE TO IMPRESS YOUR PATIENT'S GIRLFRIEND...
I KNOW. IT WASN'T WORTH IT THEN--AND IT ISN'T WORTH IT NOW.
NOTHING'S WORTH...THIS...
LORD, DO YOU EVEN KNOW WHAT YOU'VE LOST...?
I'LL KNOW ONCE MY SCIENCE TEAM GIVES ME THE DATA.
ONCE YOU'VE BEEN TAKEN APART... FILED AND INDEXED WITH ALL THE OTHER MUTATES.
AND ONCE WE'RE READY, WE'LL FINALLY BRING DOWN THE--
BOOM
BOOM

BOOM

BOOM BOOM

HEH.

...

YOU'RE SO HOT RIGHT NOW.

YOU AIN'T SEEN NOTHIN' YET.

BOOM

K KK-KRAKK

BOOM

HOW...

HOW DID HE...?

"ONCE WE'RE READY," YOU SAID.

NOBODY'S EVER READY.

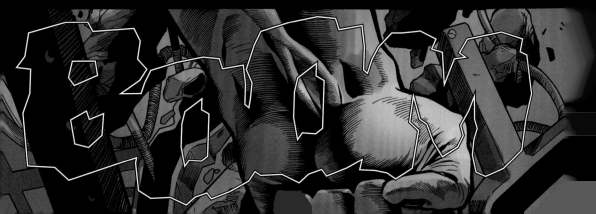

BOOM

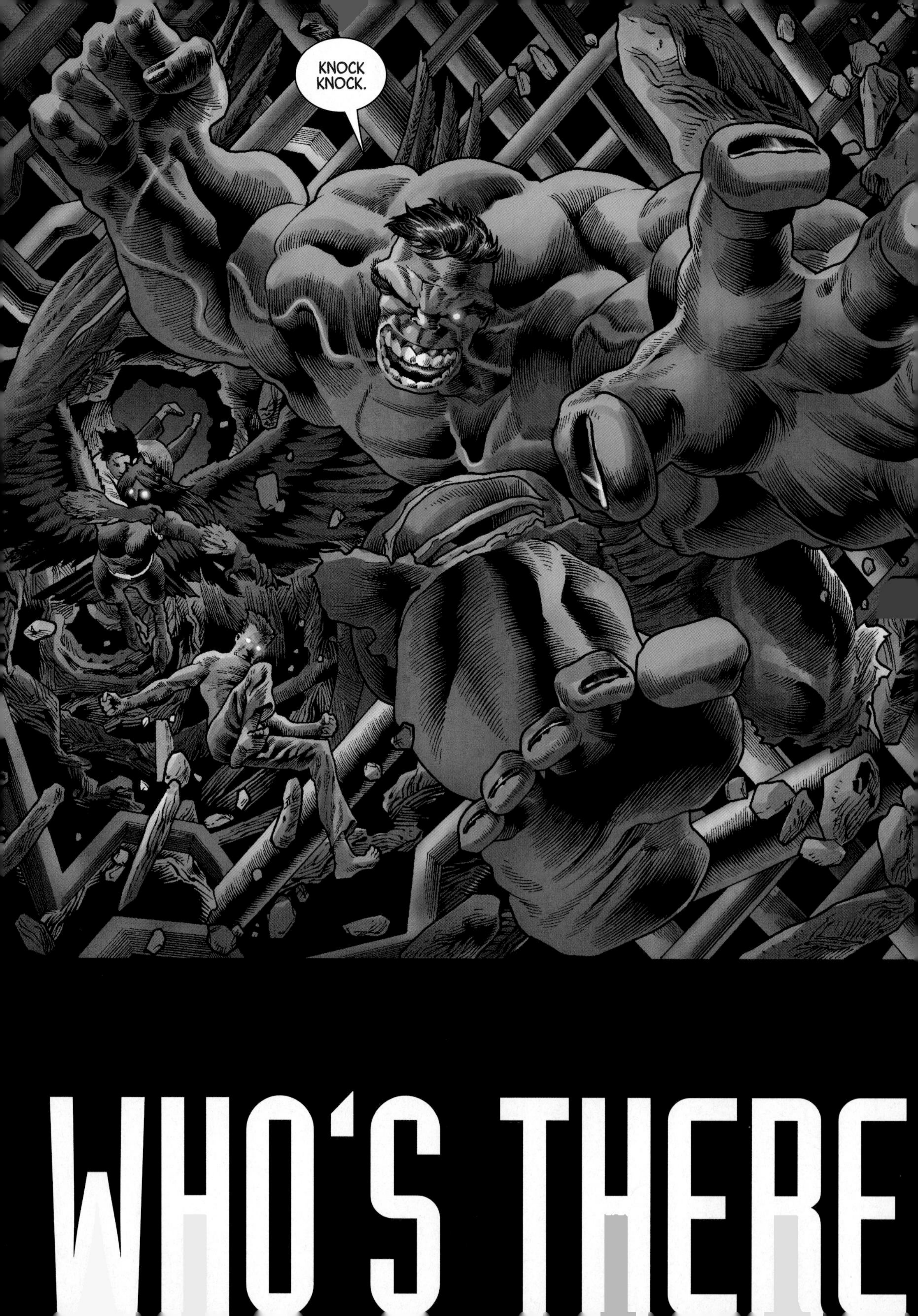
KNOCK KNOCK.
WHO'S THERE

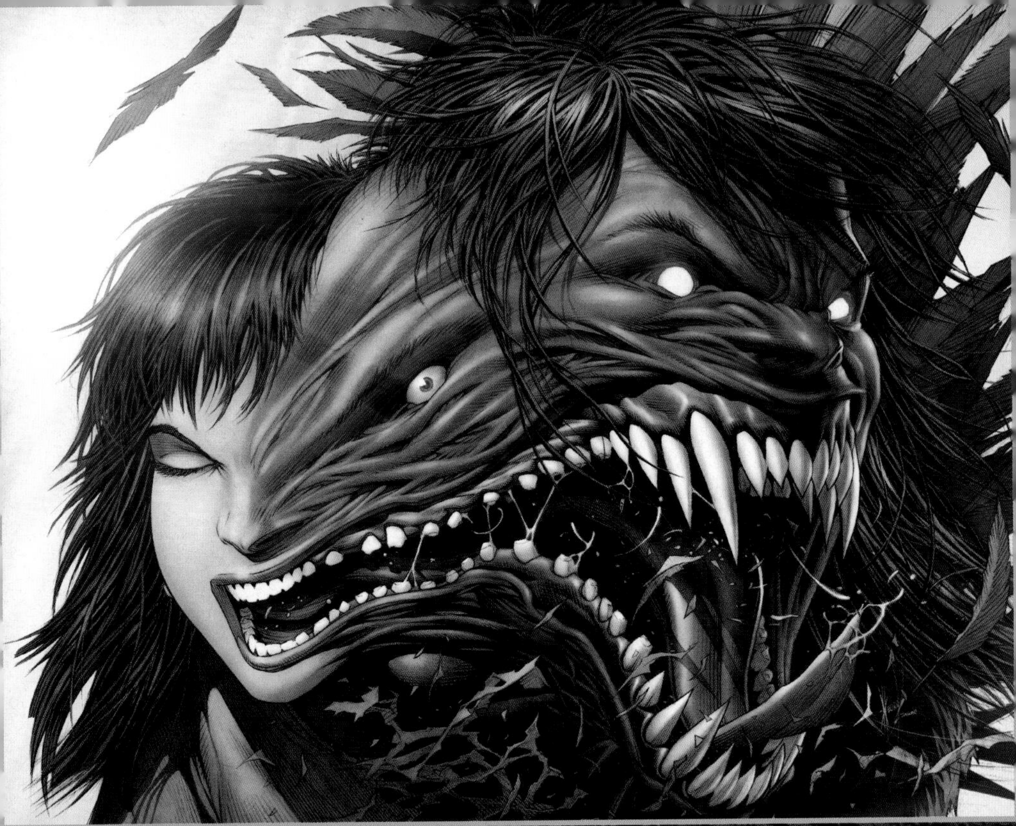

DALE KEOWN & JASON KEITH
#23 IMMORTAL VARIANT

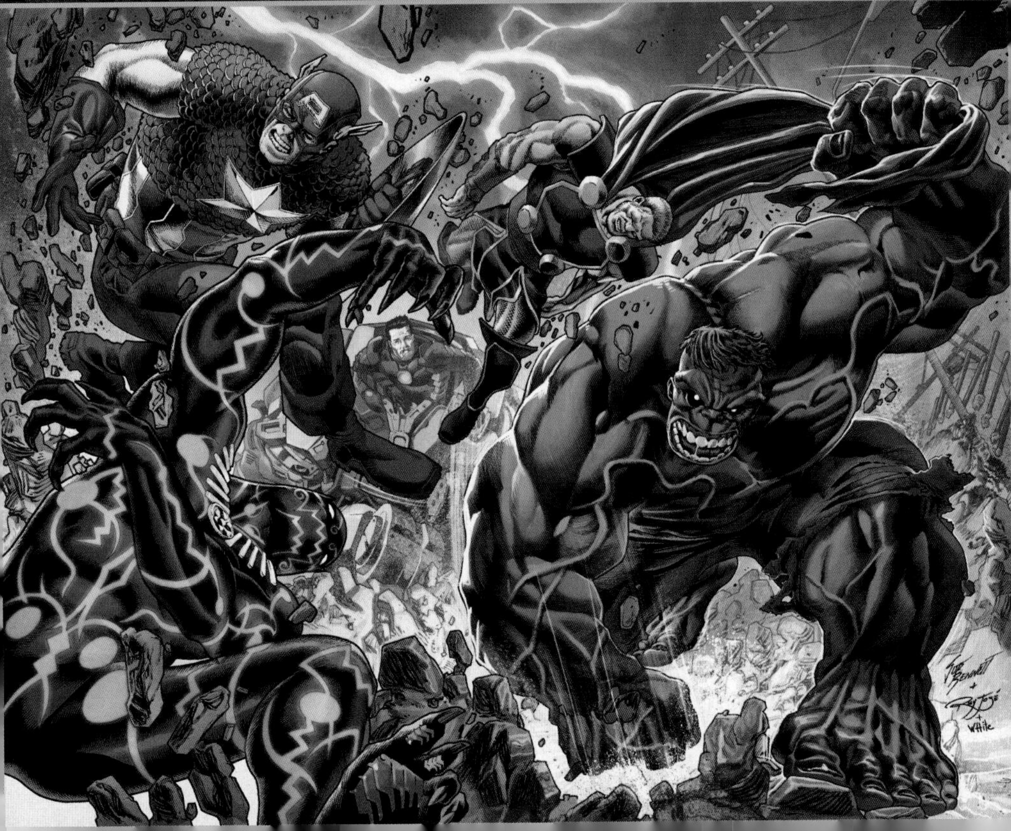

23

"LET YOUR

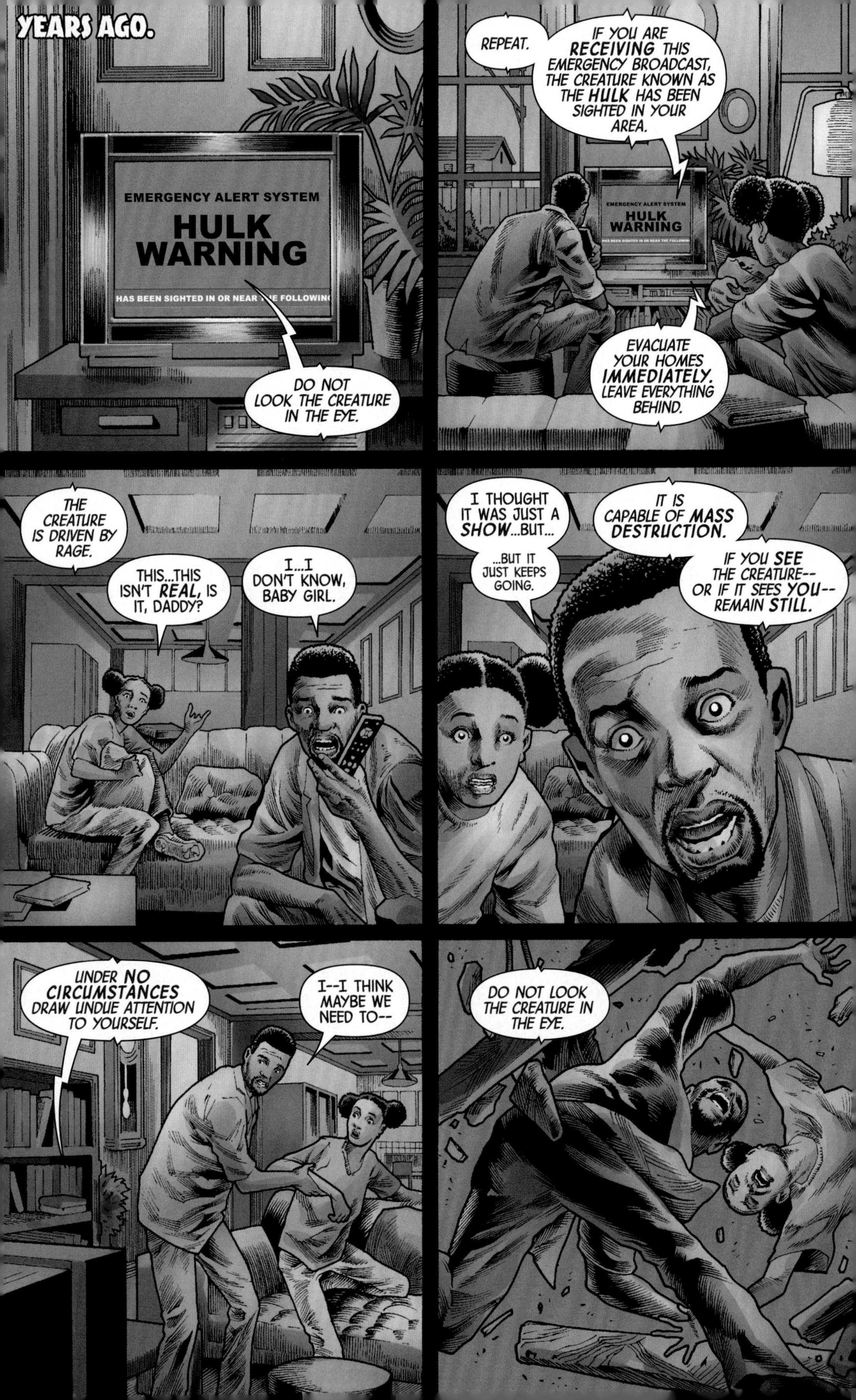
YEARS AGO.
EMERGENCY ALERT SYSTEM
HULK WARNING
HAS BEEN SIGHTED IN OR NEAR THE FOLLOWING
DO NOT LOOK THE CREATURE IN THE EYE.
REPEAT.
IF YOU ARE RECEIVING THIS EMERGENCY BROADCAST, THE CREATURE KNOWN AS THE HULK HAS BEEN SIGHTED IN YOUR AREA.
EVACUATE YOUR HOMES IMMEDIATELY. LEAVE EVERYTHING BEHIND.
THE CREATURE IS DRIVEN BY RAGE.
THIS...THIS ISN'T REAL, IS IT, DADDY?
I...I DON'T KNOW, BABY GIRL.
I THOUGHT IT WAS JUST A SHOW...BUT...
...BUT IT JUST KEEPS GOING.
IT IS CAPABLE OF MASS DESTRUCTION.
IF YOU SEE THE CREATURE-- OR IF IT SEES YOU-- REMAIN STILL.
UNDER NO CIRCUMSTANCES DRAW UNDUE ATTENTION TO YOURSELF.
I--I THINK MAYBE WE NEED TO--
DO NOT LOOK THE CREATURE IN THE EYE.

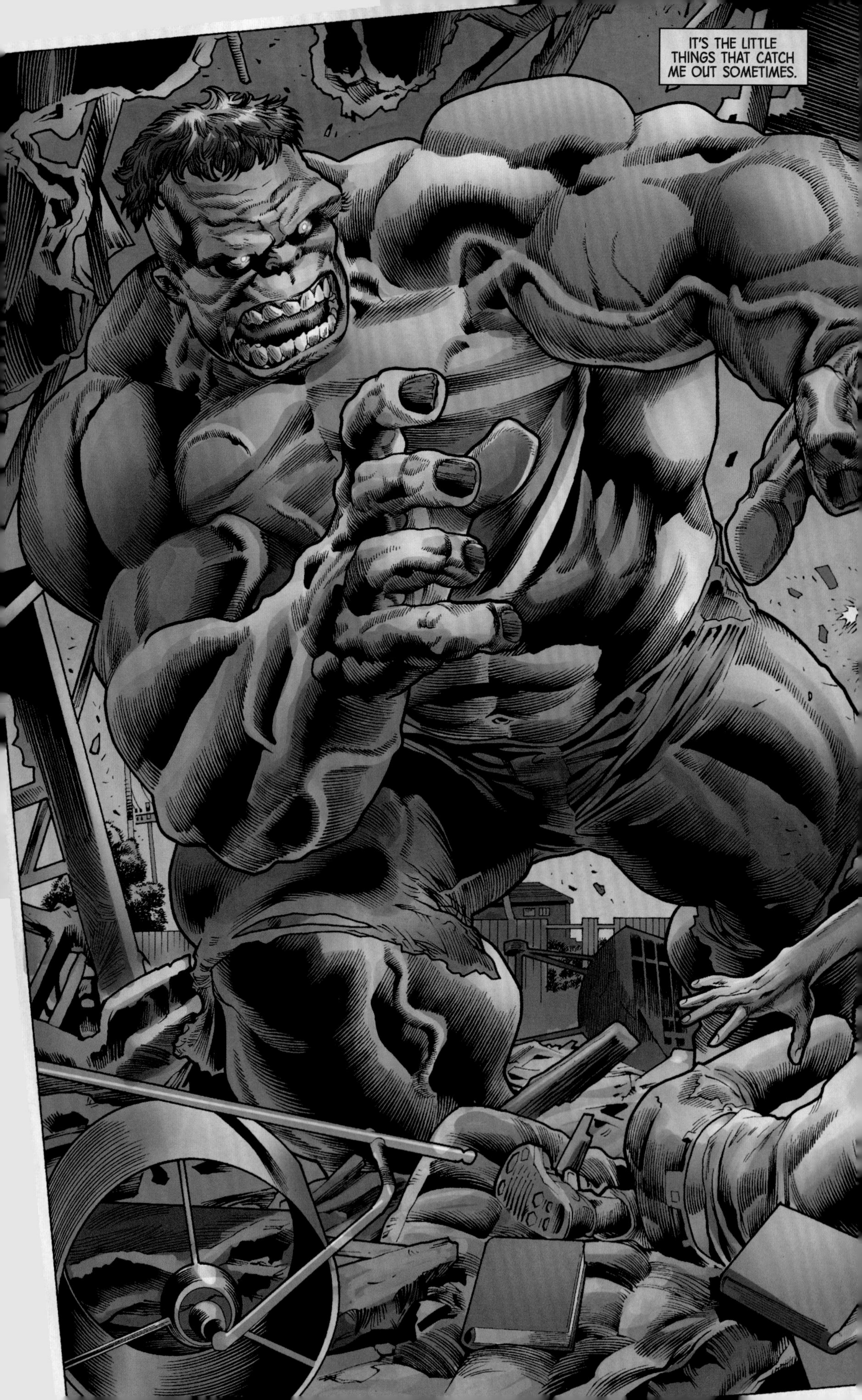
IT'S THE LITTLE THINGS THAT CATCH ME OUT SOMETIMES.

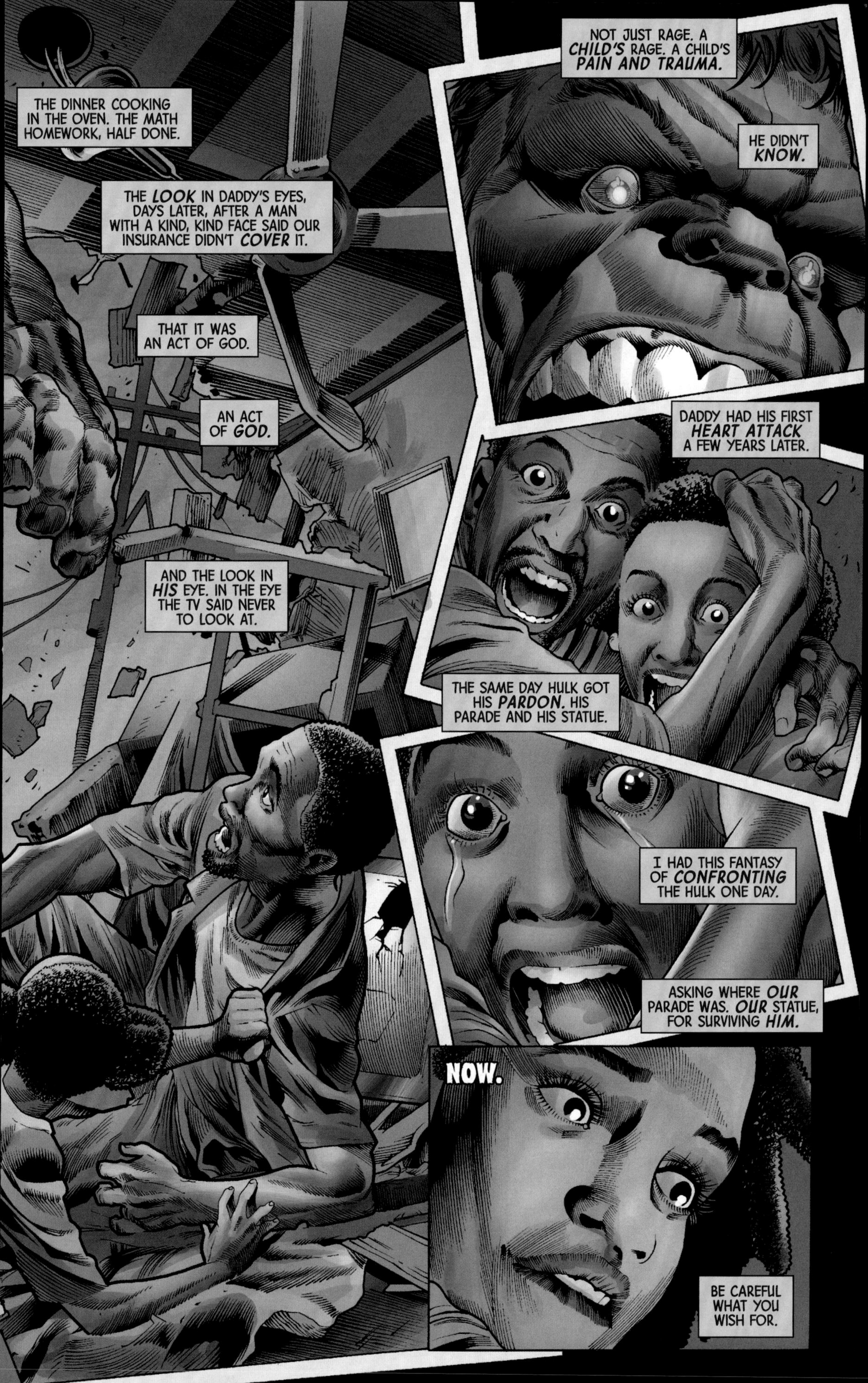
THE DINNER COOKING IN THE OVEN. THE MATH HOMEWORK, HALF DONE.
THE LOOK IN DADDY'S EYES, DAYS LATER, AFTER A MAN WITH A KIND, KIND FACE SAID OUR INSURANCE DIDN'T COVER IT.
THAT IT WAS AN ACT OF GOD.
AN ACT OF GOD.
AND THE LOOK IN HIS EYE. IN THE EYE THE TV SAID NEVER TO LOOK AT.
NOT JUST RAGE. A CHILD'S RAGE. A CHILD'S PAIN AND TRAUMA.
HE DIDN'T KNOW.
DADDY HAD HIS FIRST HEART ATTACK A FEW YEARS LATER.
THE SAME DAY HULK GOT HIS PARDON. HIS PARADE AND HIS STATUE.
I HAD THIS FANTASY OF CONFRONTING THE HULK ONE DAY.
ASKING WHERE OUR PARADE WAS. OUR STATUE, FOR SURVIVING HIM.
NOW.
BE CAREFUL WHAT YOU WISH FOR.

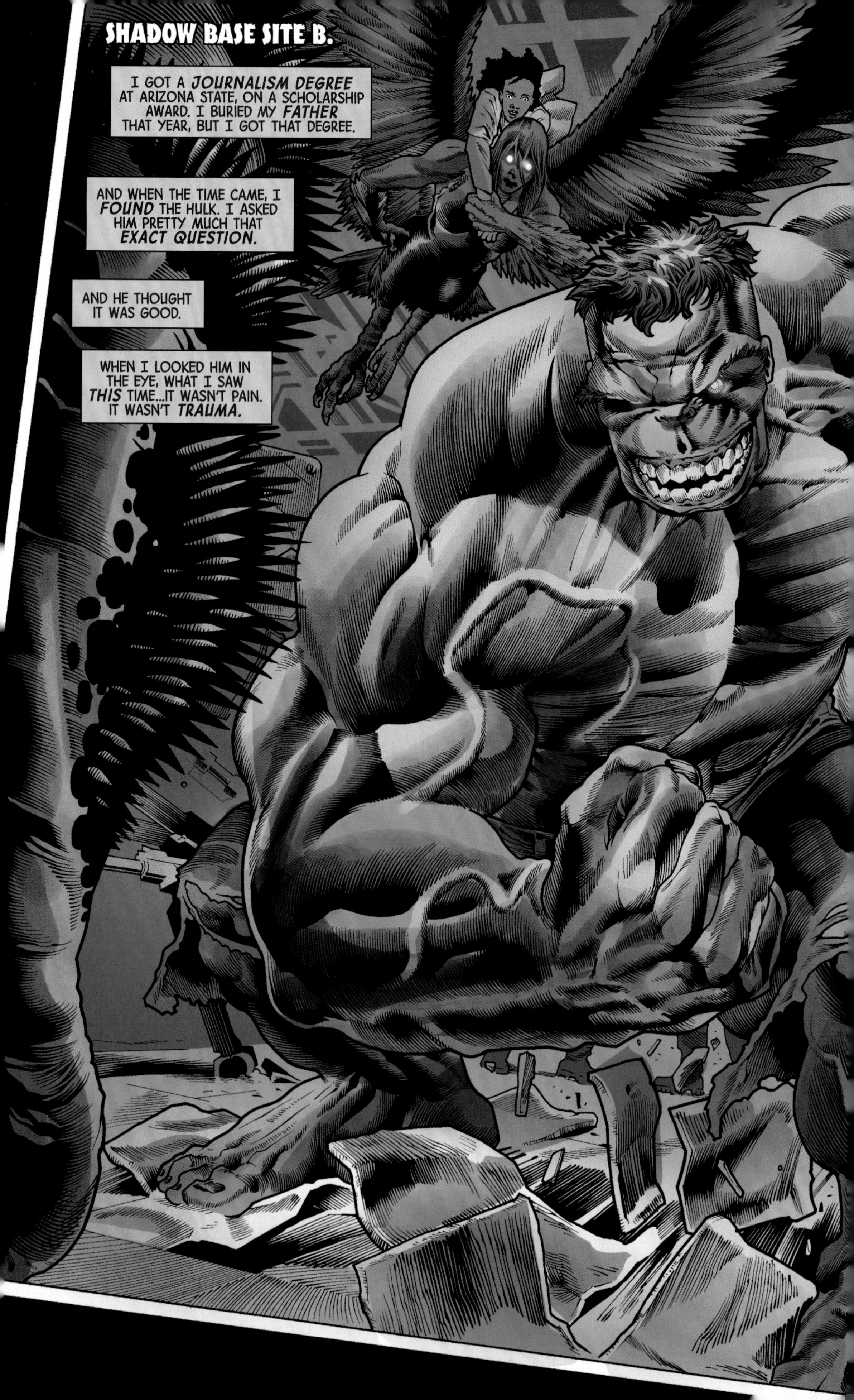
SHADOW BASE SITE B.
I GOT A JOURNALISM DEGREE AT ARIZONA STATE, ON A SCHOLARSHIP AWARD. I BURIED MY FATHER THAT YEAR, BUT I GOT THAT DEGREE.
AND WHEN THE TIME CAME, I FOUND THE HULK. I ASKED HIM PRETTY MUCH THAT EXACT QUESTION.
AND HE THOUGHT IT WAS GOOD.
WHEN I LOOKED HIM IN THE EYE, WHAT I SAW THIS TIME...IT WASN'T PAIN. IT WASN'T TRAUMA.

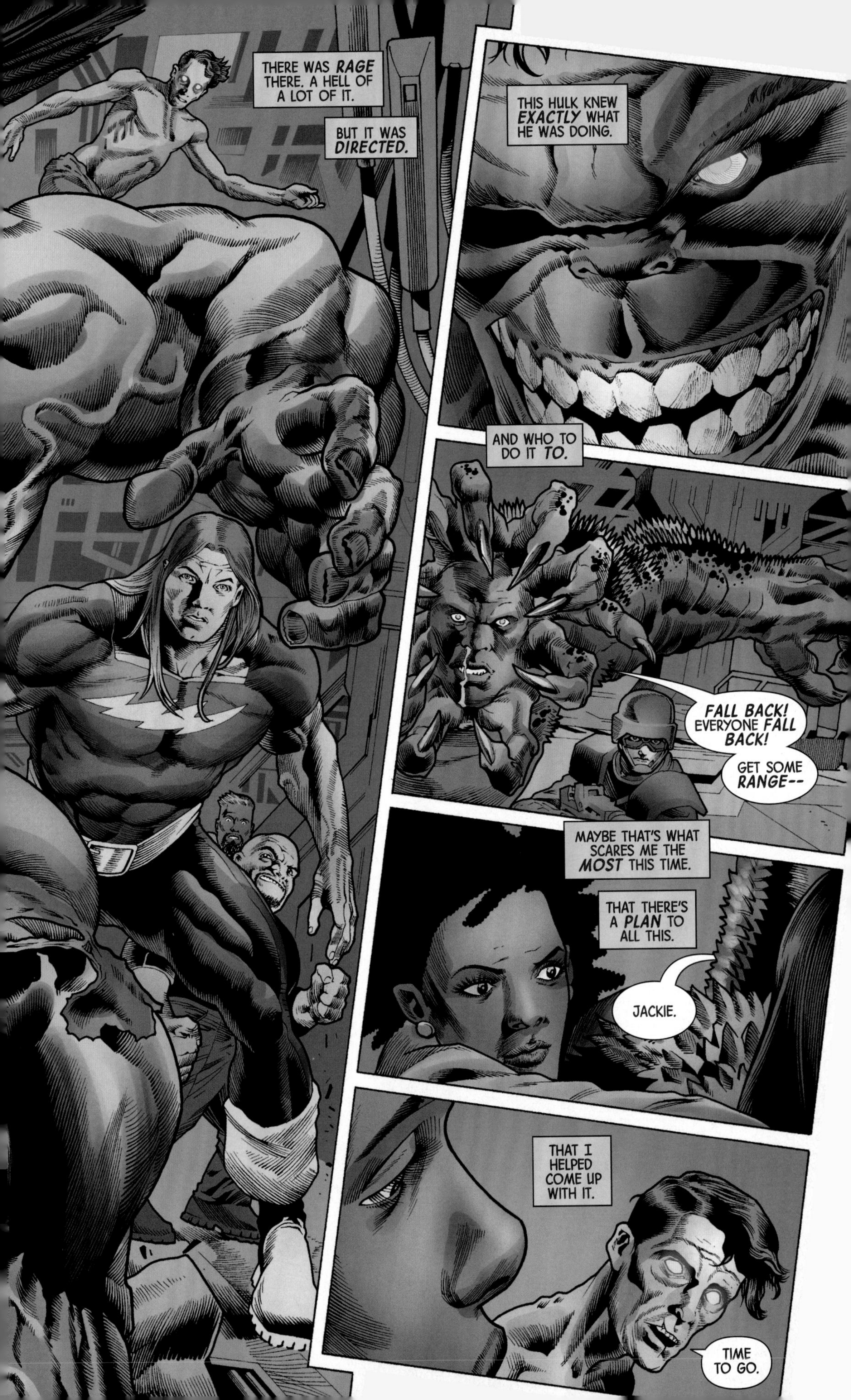
THERE WAS RAGE THERE. A HELL OF A LOT OF IT.
BUT IT WAS DIRECTED.
THIS HULK KNEW EXACTLY WHAT HE WAS DOING.
AND WHO TO DO IT TO.
FALL BACK! EVERYONE FALL BACK!
GET SOME RANGE--
MAYBE THAT'S WHAT SCARES ME THE MOST THIS TIME.
THAT THERE'S A PLAN TO ALL THIS.
JACKIE.
THAT I HELPED COME UP WITH IT.
TIME TO GO.

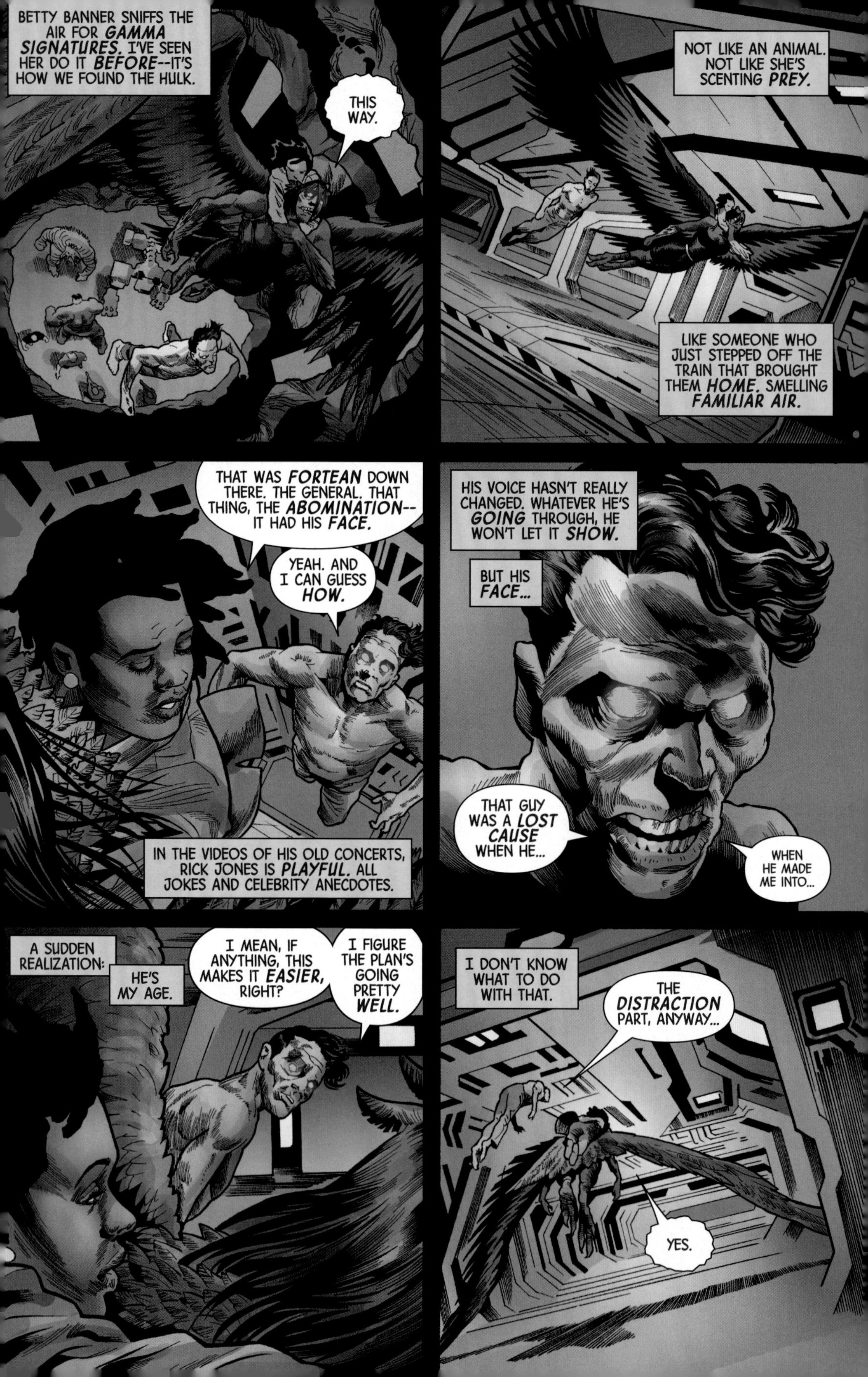
BETTY BANNER SNIFFS THE AIR FOR GAMMA SIGNATURES. I'VE SEEN HER DO IT BEFORE--IT'S HOW WE FOUND THE HULK.
THIS WAY.
NOT LIKE AN ANIMAL. NOT LIKE SHE'S SCENTING PREY.
LIKE SOMEONE WHO JUST STEPPED OFF THE TRAIN THAT BROUGHT THEM HOME. SMELLING FAMILIAR AIR.
THAT WAS FORTEAN DOWN THERE. THE GENERAL. THAT THING, THE ABOMINATION-- IT HAD HIS FACE.
YEAH. AND I CAN GUESS HOW.
IN THE VIDEOS OF HIS OLD CONCERTS, RICK JONES IS PLAYFUL. ALL JOKES AND CELEBRITY ANECDOTES.
HIS VOICE HASN'T REALLY CHANGED. WHATEVER HE'S GOING THROUGH, HE WON'T LET IT SHOW.
BUT HIS FACE...
THAT GUY WAS A LOST CAUSE WHEN HE...
WHEN HE MADE ME INTO...
A SUDDEN REALIZATION:
HE'S MY AGE.
I MEAN, IF ANYTHING, THIS MAKES IT EASIER, RIGHT?
I FIGURE THE PLAN'S GOING PRETTY WELL.
I DON'T KNOW WHAT TO DO WITH THAT.
THE DISTRACTION PART, ANYWAY...
YES.

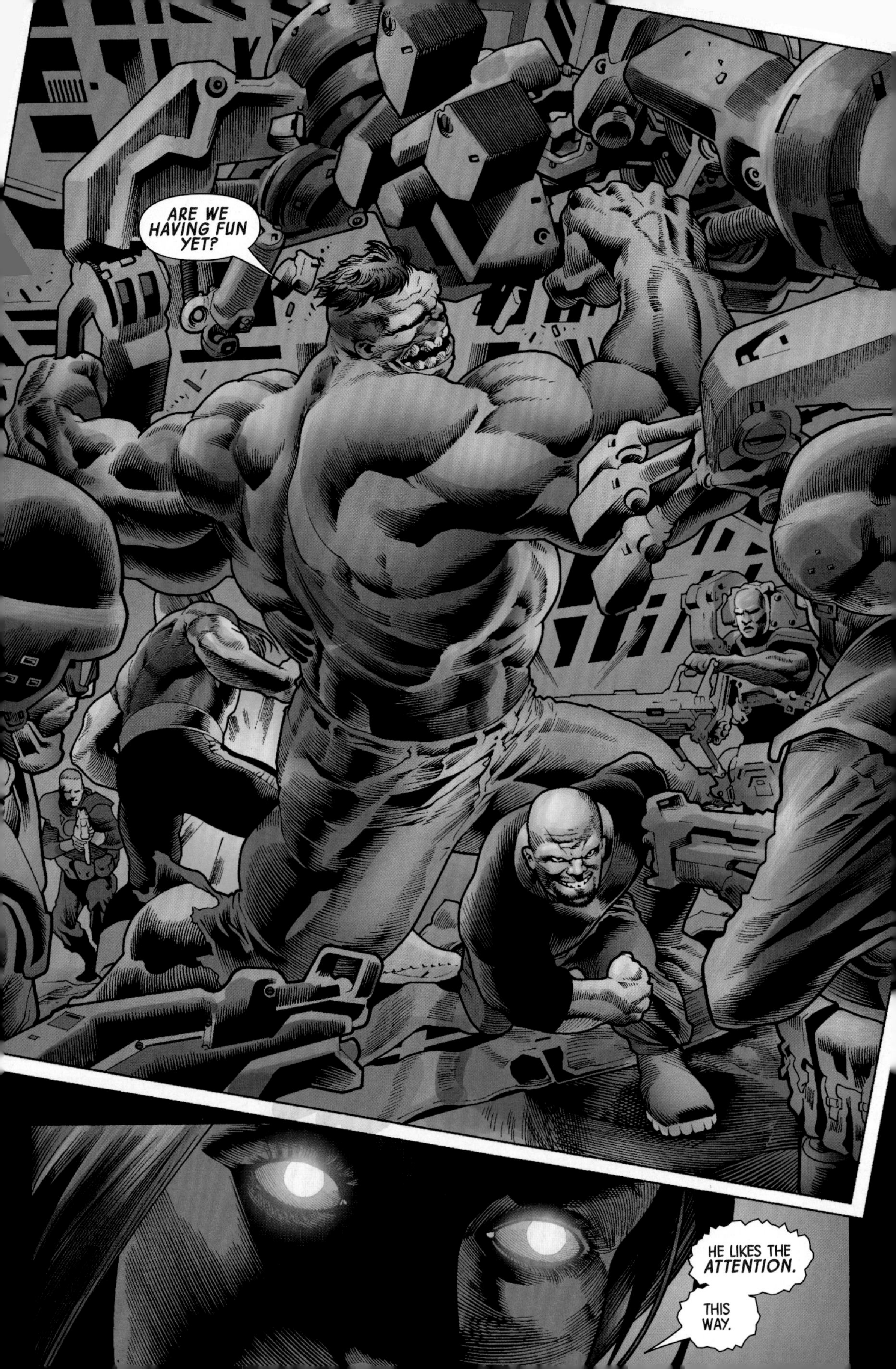
ARE WE HAVING FUN YET?
HE LIKES THE ATTENTION.
THIS WAY.

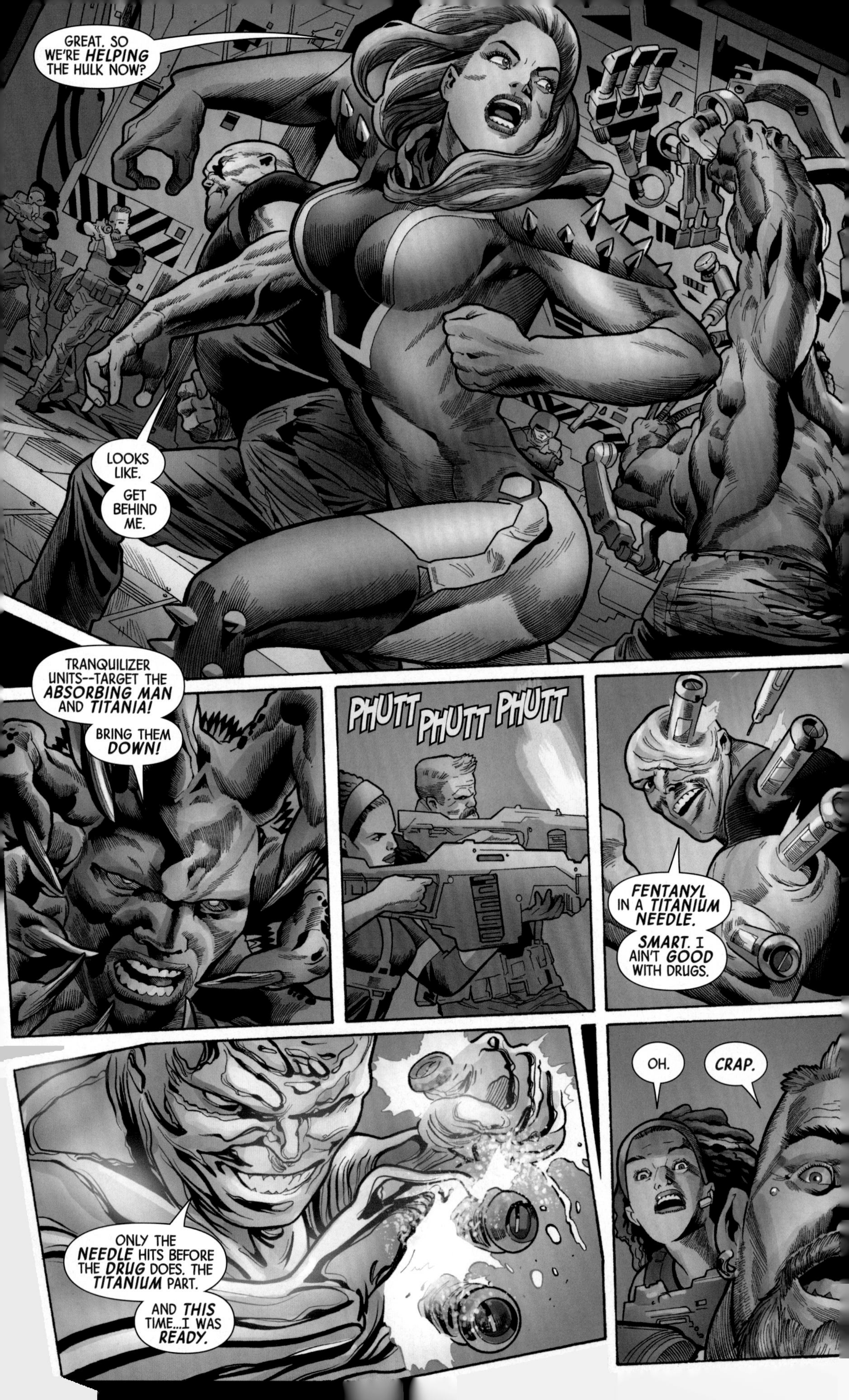
GREAT. SO WE'RE HELPING THE HULK NOW?
LOOKS LIKE.
GET BEHIND ME.
TRANQUILIZER UNITS--TARGET THE ABSORBING MAN AND TITANIA!
BRING THEM DOWN!
PHUTT PHUTT PHUTT
FENTANYL IN A TITANIUM NEEDLE.
SMART. I AIN'T GOOD WITH DRUGS.
ONLY THE NEEDLE HITS BEFORE THE DRUG DOES. THE TITANIUM PART.
AND THIS TIME...I WAS READY.
OH.
CRAP.

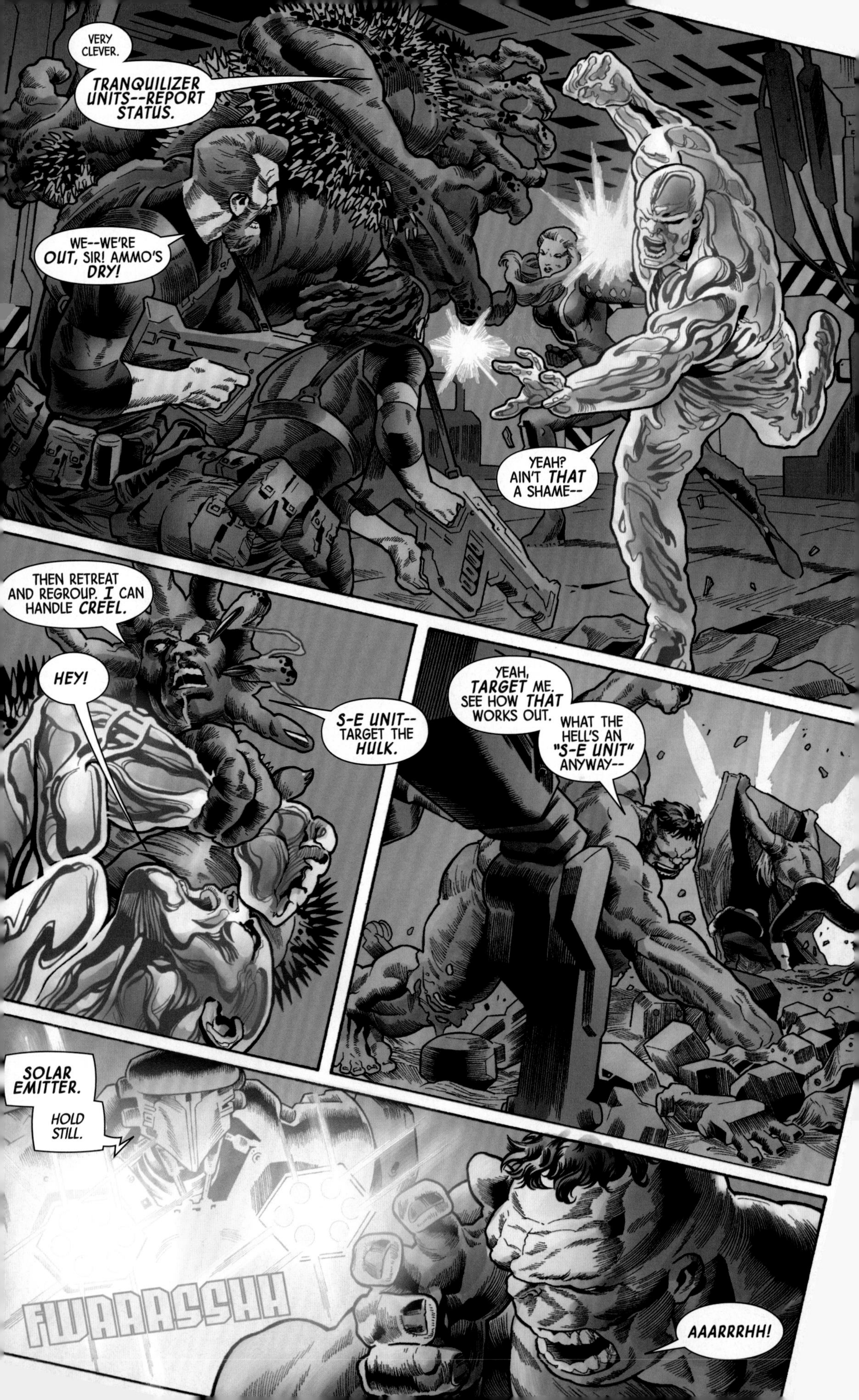
VERY CLEVER.
TRANQUILIZER UNITS--REPORT STATUS.
WE--WE'RE OUT, SIR! AMMO'S DRY!
YEAH? AIN'T THAT A SHAME--
THEN RETREAT AND REGROUP. I CAN HANDLE CREEL.
HEY!
S-E UNIT--TARGET THE HULK.
YEAH, TARGET ME. SEE HOW THAT WORKS OUT.
WHAT THE HELL'S AN "S-E UNIT" ANYWAY--
SOLAR EMITTER.
HOLD STILL.
FWAAASSHH
AAARRRHH!

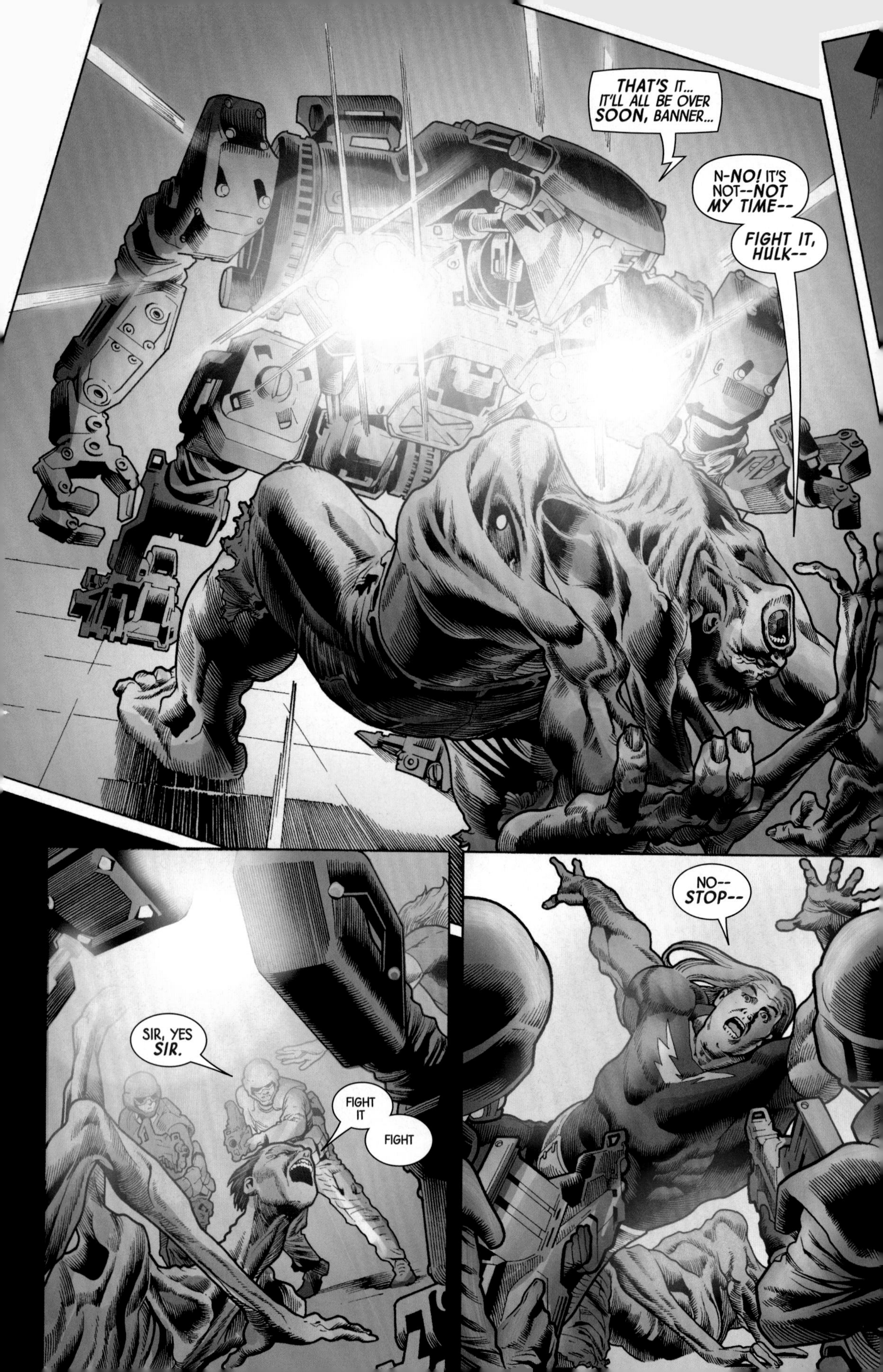

THAT'S IT... IT'LL ALL BE OVER SOON, BANNER...
N-NO! IT'S NOT--NOT MY TIME--
FIGHT IT, HULK--
SIR, YES SIR.
FIGHT IT
FIGHT
NO-- STOP--

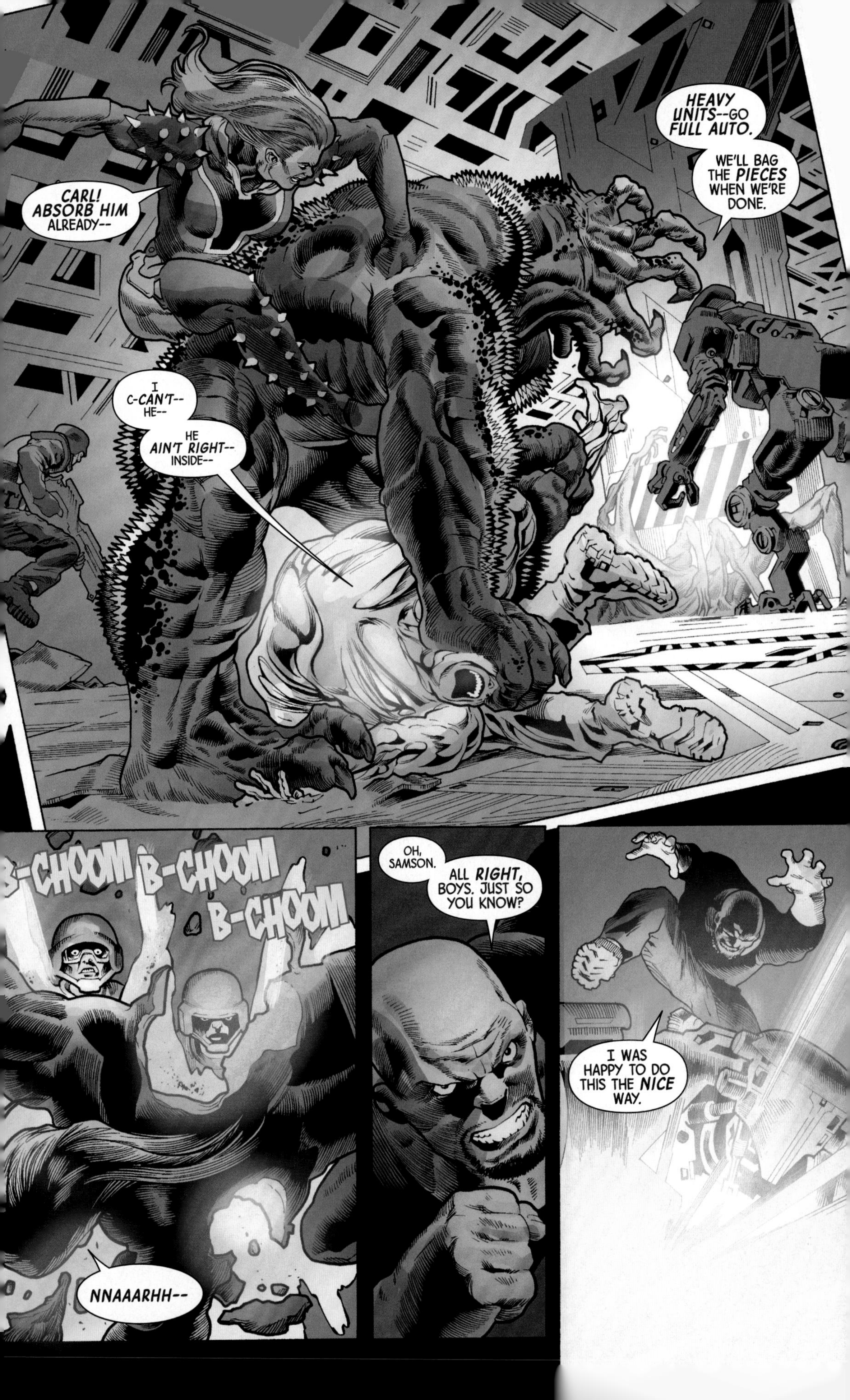
CARL! ABSORB HIM ALREADY--
HEAVY UNITS--GO FULL AUTO.
WE'LL BAG THE PIECES WHEN WE'RE DONE.
I C-CAN'T-- HE--
HE AIN'T RIGHT-- INSIDE--
B-CHOOM B-CHOOM B-CHOOM
NNAAARHH--
OH, SAMSON.
ALL RIGHT, BOYS. JUST SO YOU KNOW?
I WAS HAPPY TO DO THIS THE NICE WAY.

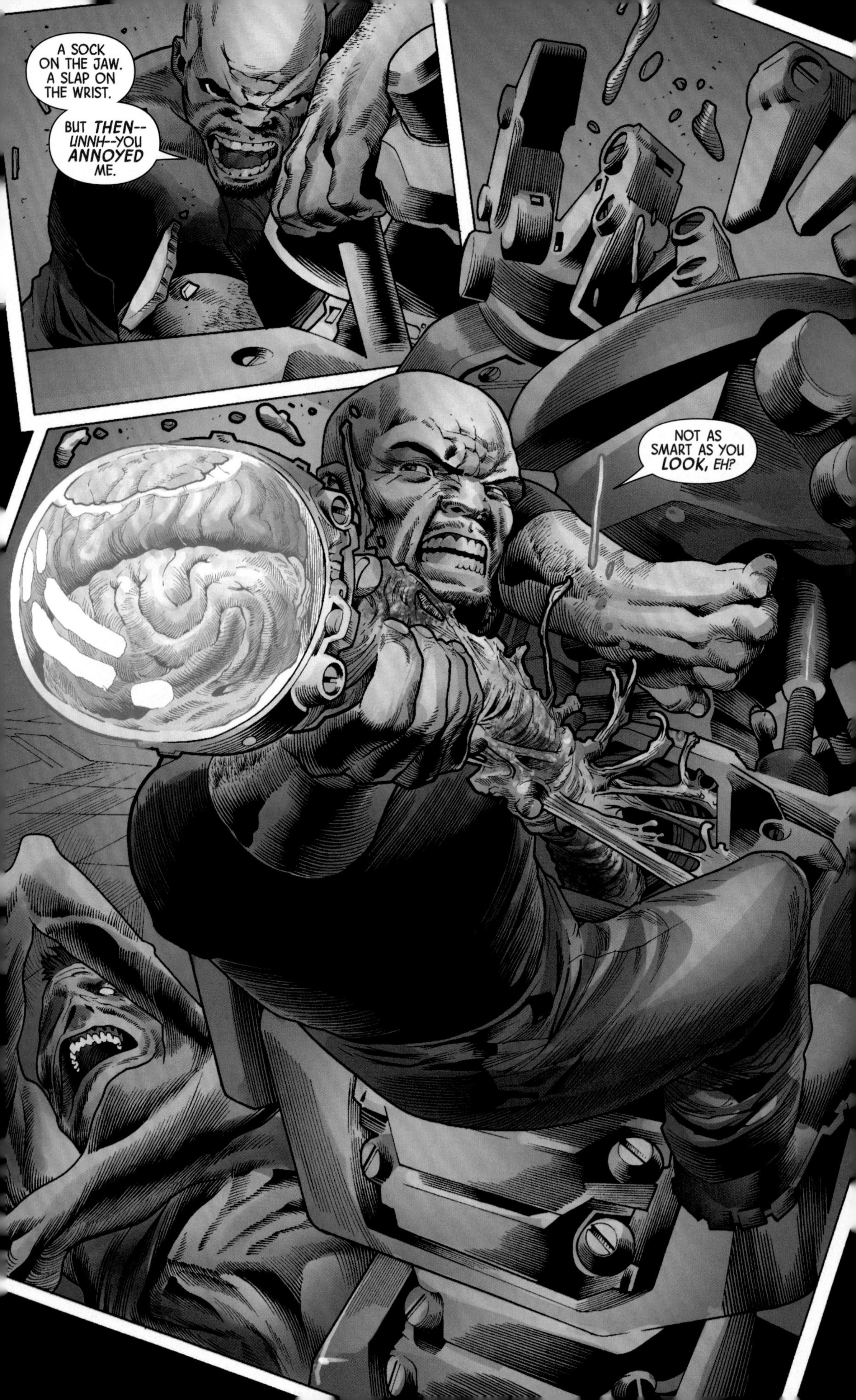
A SOCK ON THE JAW. A SLAP ON THE WRIST.
BUT THEN-- UNNH--YOU ANNOYED ME.
NOT AS SMART AS YOU LOOK, EH?

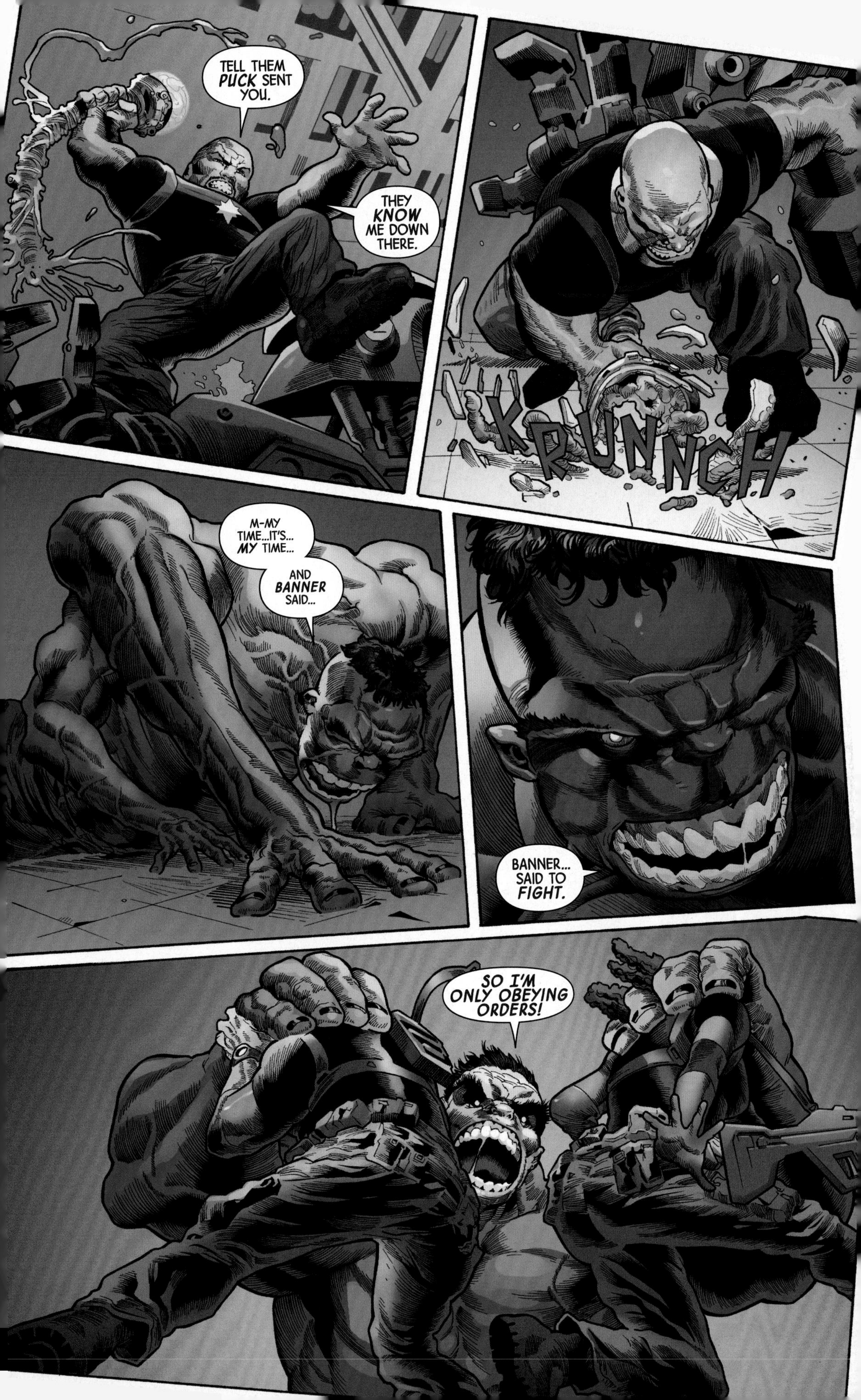
TELL THEM PUCK SENT YOU.
THEY KNOW ME DOWN THERE.
KRUNNCH
M-MY TIME...IT'S... MY TIME...
AND BANNER SAID...
BANNER... SAID TO FIGHT.
SO I'M ONLY OBEYING ORDERS!

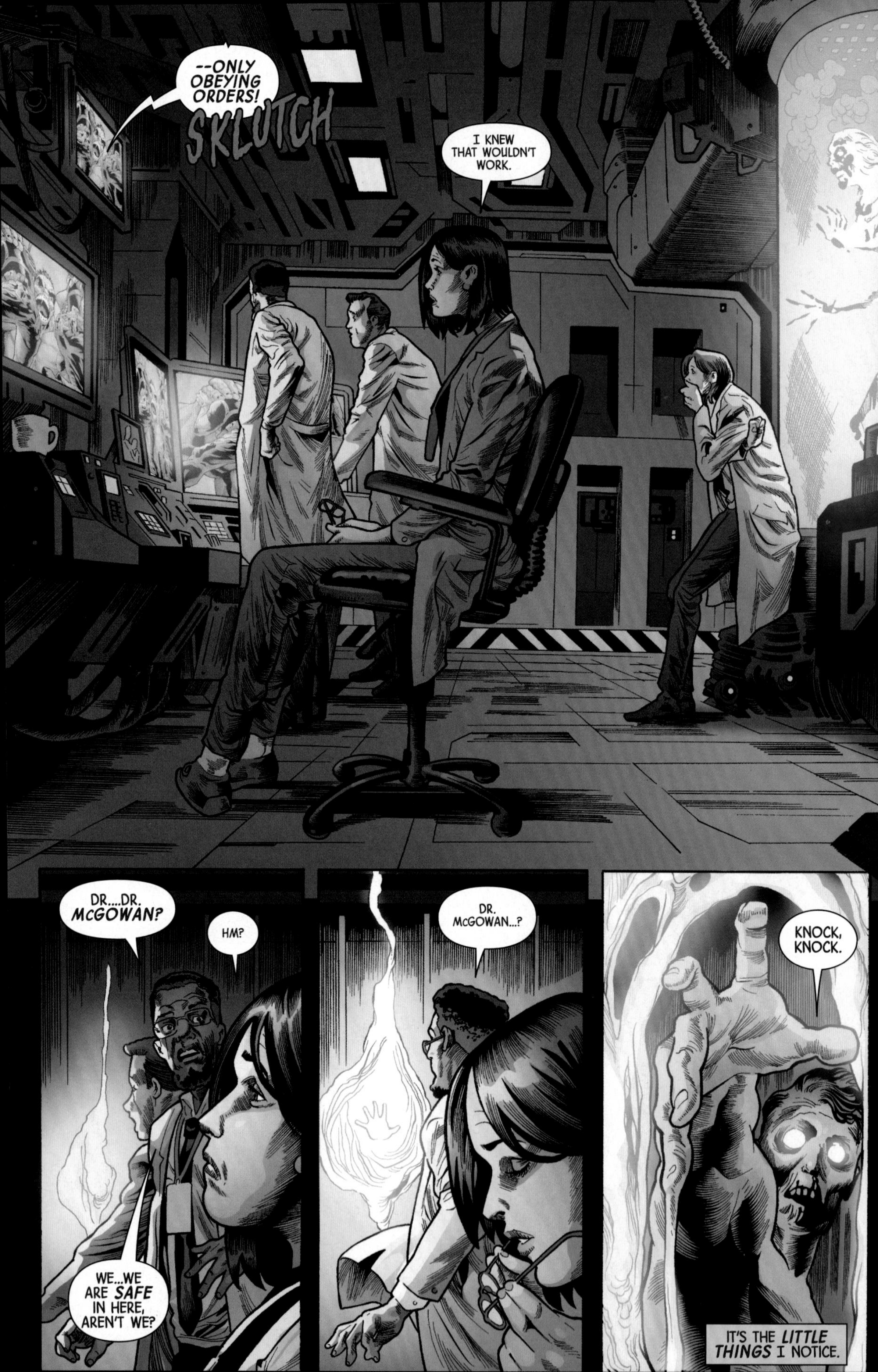
--ONLY OBEYING ORDERS!
SKLUTCH
I KNEW THAT WOULDN'T WORK.
DR....DR. McGOWAN?
HM?
WE...WE ARE SAFE IN HERE, AREN'T WE?
DR. McGOWAN...?
KNOCK, KNOCK.
IT'S THE LITTLE THINGS I NOTICE.

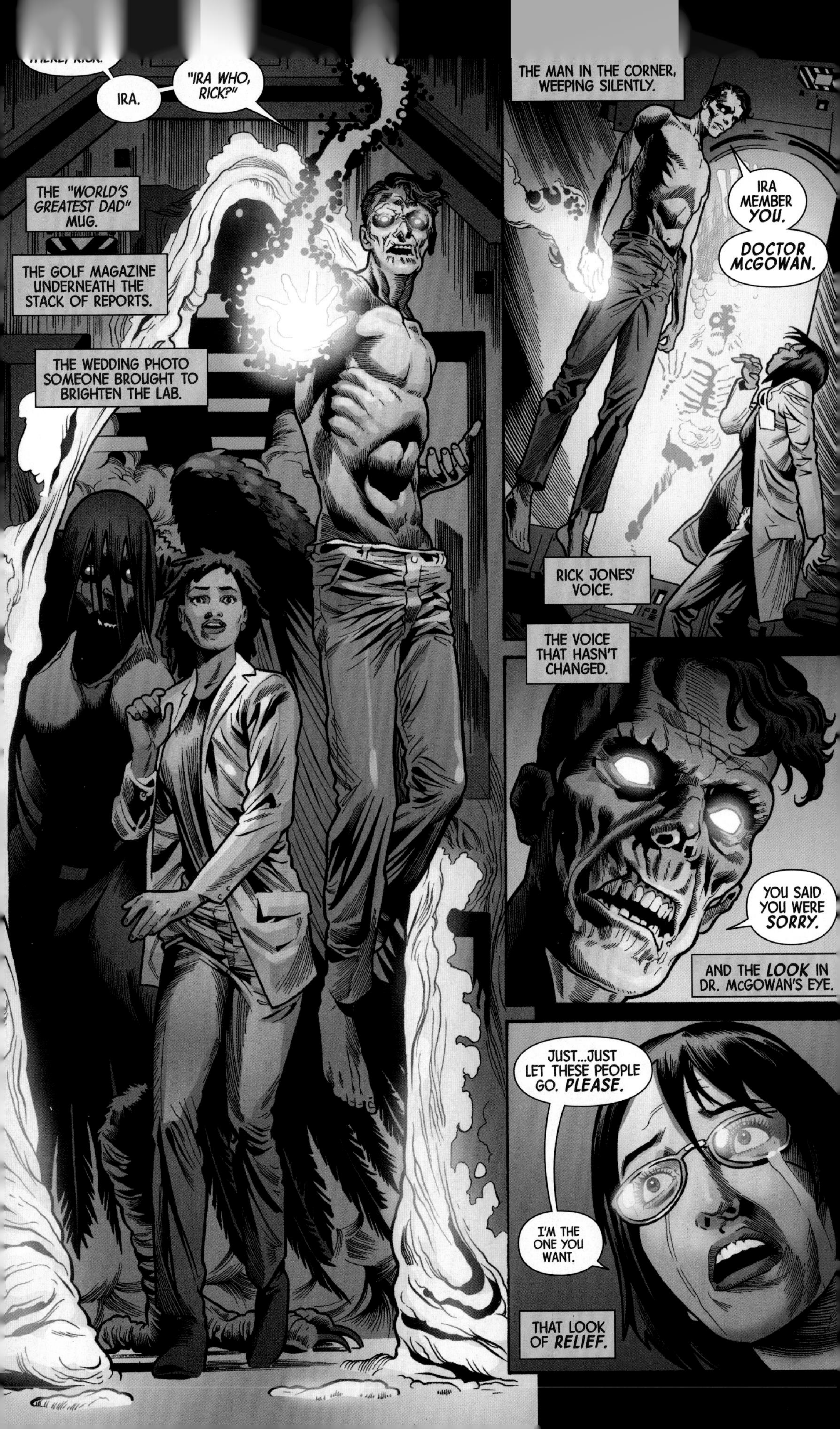
IRA.
"IRA WHO, RICK?"
THE "WORLD'S GREATEST DAD" MUG.
THE GOLF MAGAZINE UNDERNEATH THE STACK OF REPORTS.
THE WEDDING PHOTO SOMEONE BROUGHT TO BRIGHTEN THE LAB.
THE MAN IN THE CORNER, WEEPING SILENTLY.
IRA MEMBER YOU.
DOCTOR McGOWAN.
RICK JONES' VOICE.
THE VOICE THAT HASN'T CHANGED.
YOU SAID YOU WERE SORRY.
AND THE LOOK IN DR. McGOWAN'S EYE.
JUST...JUST LET THESE PEOPLE GO. PLEASE.
I'M THE ONE YOU WANT.
THAT LOOK OF RELIEF.

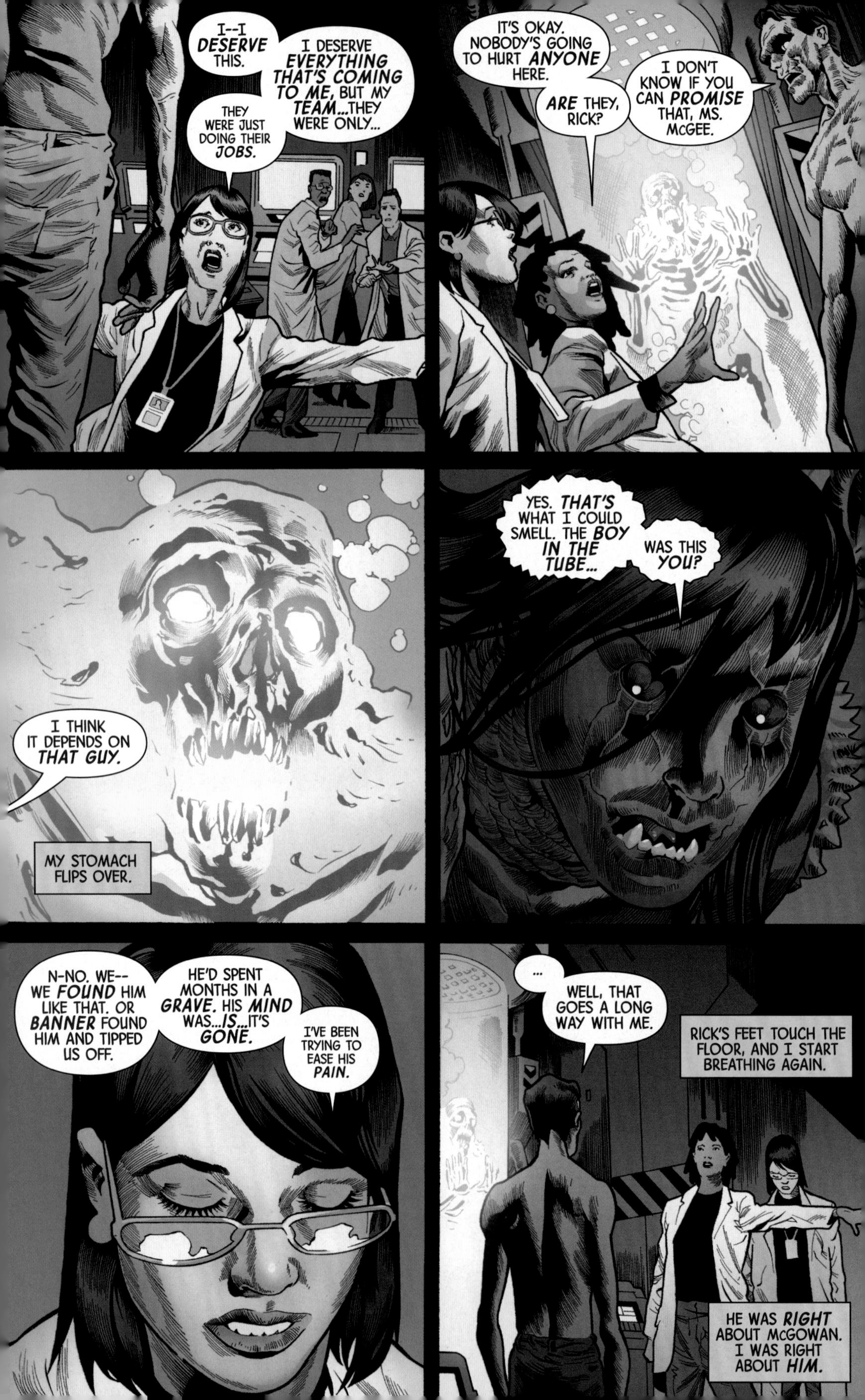

I--I DESERVE THIS.
I DESERVE EVERYTHING THAT'S COMING TO ME, BUT MY TEAM...THEY WERE ONLY...
THEY WERE JUST DOING THEIR JOBS.
IT'S OKAY. NOBODY'S GOING TO HURT ANYONE HERE.
ARE THEY, RICK?
I DON'T KNOW IF YOU CAN PROMISE THAT, MS. McGEE.
I THINK IT DEPENDS ON THAT GUY.
MY STOMACH FLIPS OVER.
YES. THAT'S WHAT I COULD SMELL. THE BOY IN THE TUBE...
WAS THIS YOU?
N-NO. WE--WE FOUND HIM LIKE THAT. OR BANNER FOUND HIM AND TIPPED US OFF.
HE'D SPENT MONTHS IN A GRAVE. HIS MIND WAS...IS...IT'S GONE.
I'VE BEEN TRYING TO EASE HIS PAIN.
...
WELL, THAT GOES A LONG WAY WITH ME.
RICK'S FEET TOUCH THE FLOOR, AND I START BREATHING AGAIN.
HE WAS RIGHT ABOUT McGOWAN. I WAS RIGHT ABOUT HIM.

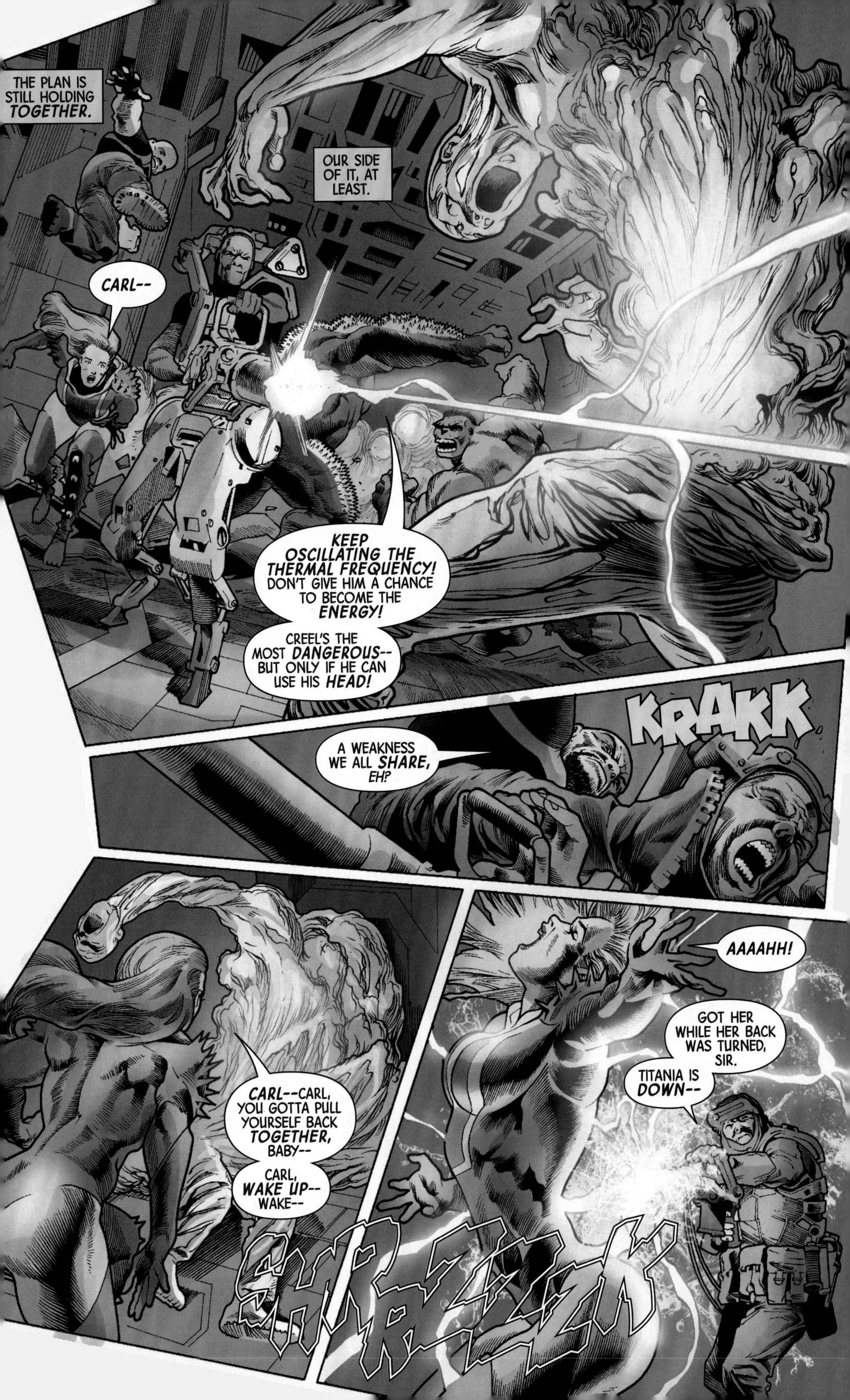

THE PLAN IS STILL HOLDING TOGETHER.
OUR SIDE OF IT, AT LEAST.
CARL--
KEEP OSCILLATING THE THERMAL FREQUENCY! DON'T GIVE HIM A CHANCE TO BECOME THE ENERGY!
CREEL'S THE MOST DANGEROUS-- BUT ONLY IF HE CAN USE HIS HEAD!
KRAKK
A WEAKNESS WE ALL SHARE, EH?
CARL--CARL, YOU GOTTA PULL YOURSELF BACK TOGETHER, BABY--
CARL, WAKE UP-- WAKE--
SHRZZZK
AAAAHH!
GOT HER WHILE HER BACK WAS TURNED, SIR.
TITANIA IS DOWN--

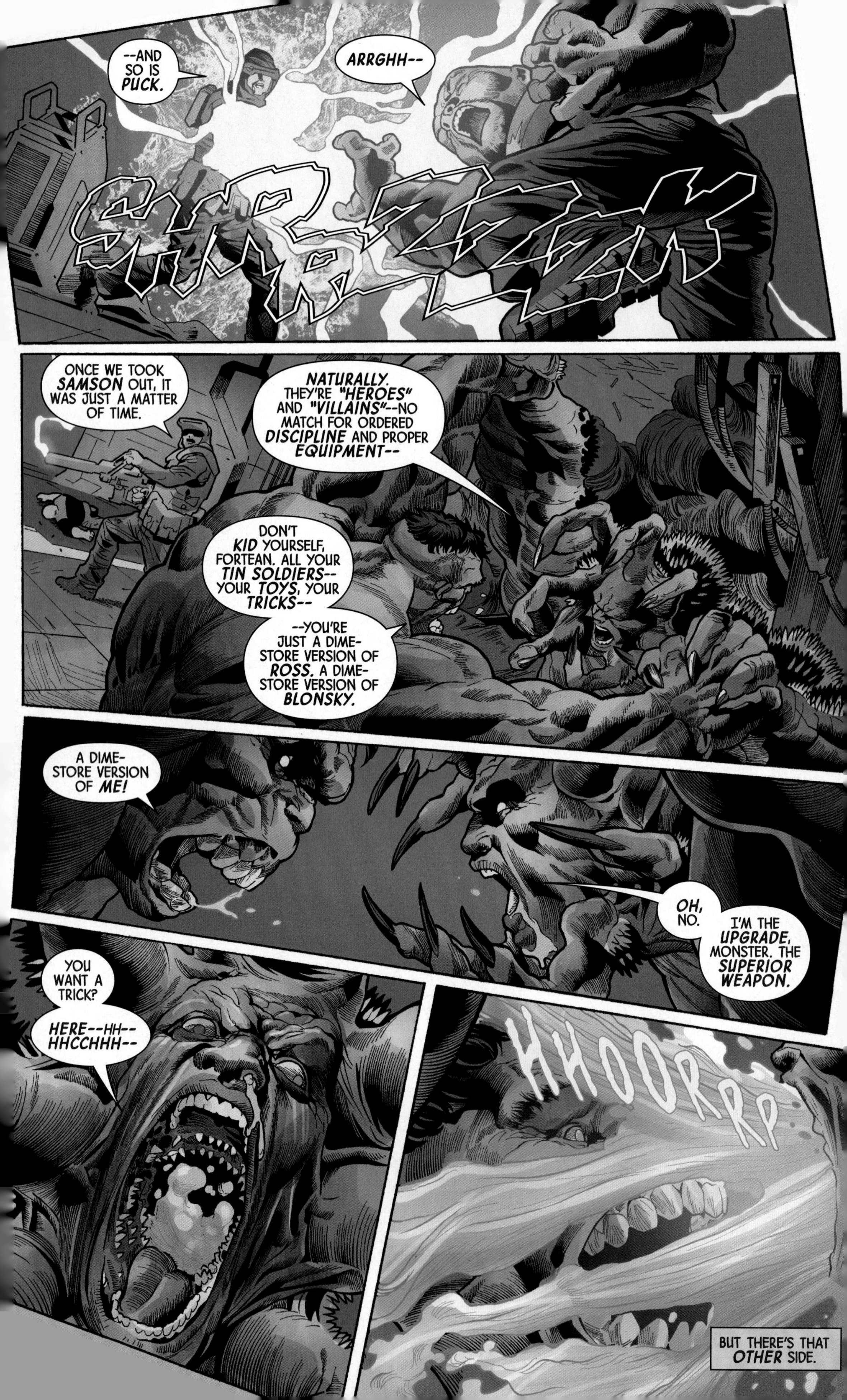
--AND SO IS PUCK.
ARRGHH--
SHRZZZZK
ONCE WE TOOK SAMSON OUT, IT WAS JUST A MATTER OF TIME.
NATURALLY. THEY'RE "HEROES" AND "VILLAINS"--NO MATCH FOR ORDERED DISCIPLINE AND PROPER EQUIPMENT--
DON'T KID YOURSELF, FORTEAN. ALL YOUR TIN SOLDIERS--YOUR TOYS, YOUR TRICKS--
--YOU'RE JUST A DIME-STORE VERSION OF ROSS. A DIME-STORE VERSION OF BLONSKY.
A DIME-STORE VERSION OF ME!
OH, NO.
I'M THE UPGRADE, MONSTER. THE SUPERIOR WEAPON.
YOU WANT A TRICK?
HERE--HH--HHCCHHH--
HHOORRP
BUT THERE'S THAT OTHER SIDE.

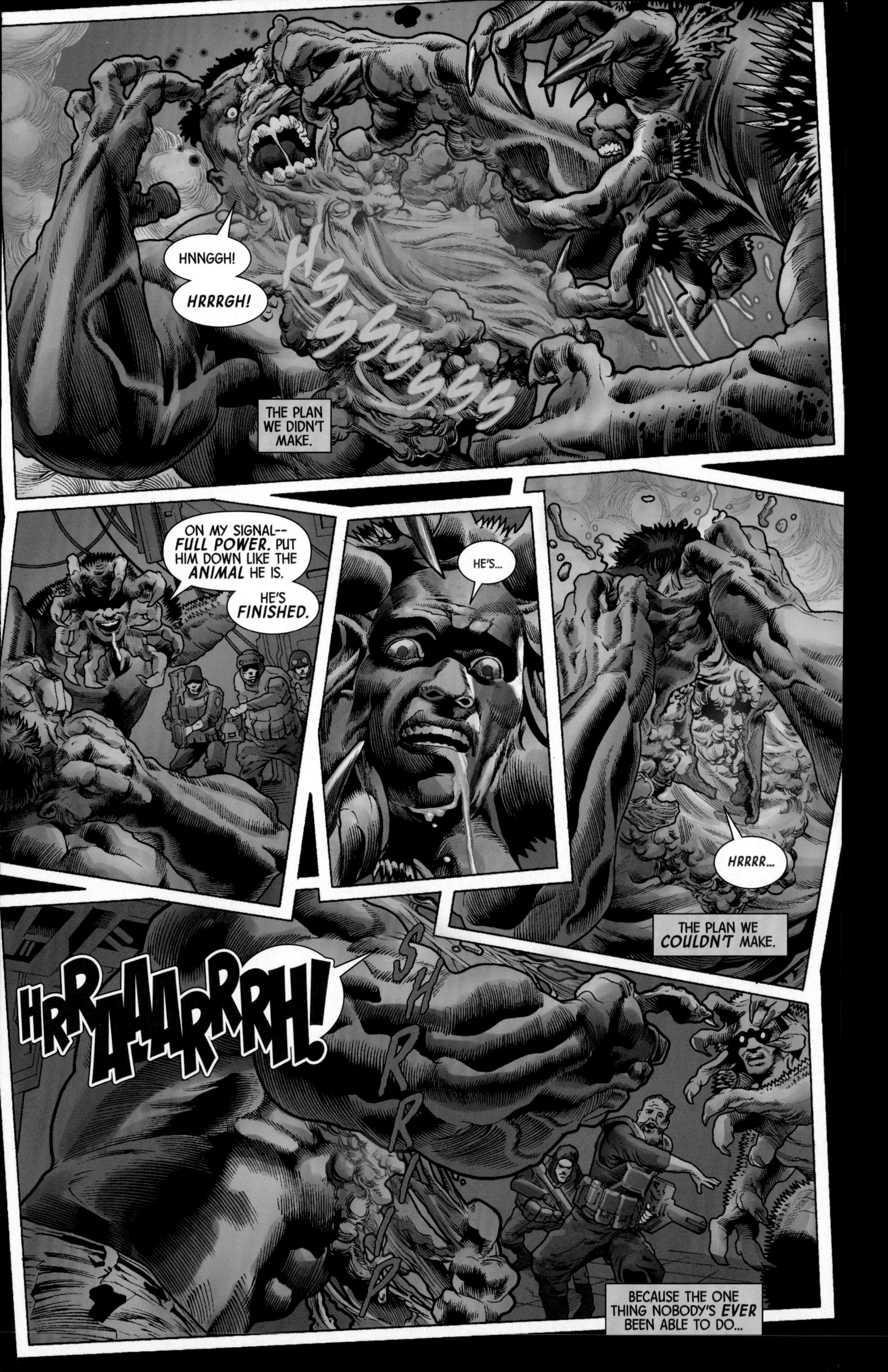
HNNGGH!
HRRRGH!
HSSSSSSSS
THE PLAN WE DIDN'T MAKE.
ON MY SIGNAL-- FULL POWER. PUT HIM DOWN LIKE THE ANIMAL HE IS.
HE'S FINISHED.
HE'S...
HRRRR...
THE PLAN WE COULDN'T MAKE.
HRRAAARRRH!
SHRRIP
BECAUSE THE ONE THING NOBODY'S EVER BEEN ABLE TO DO...

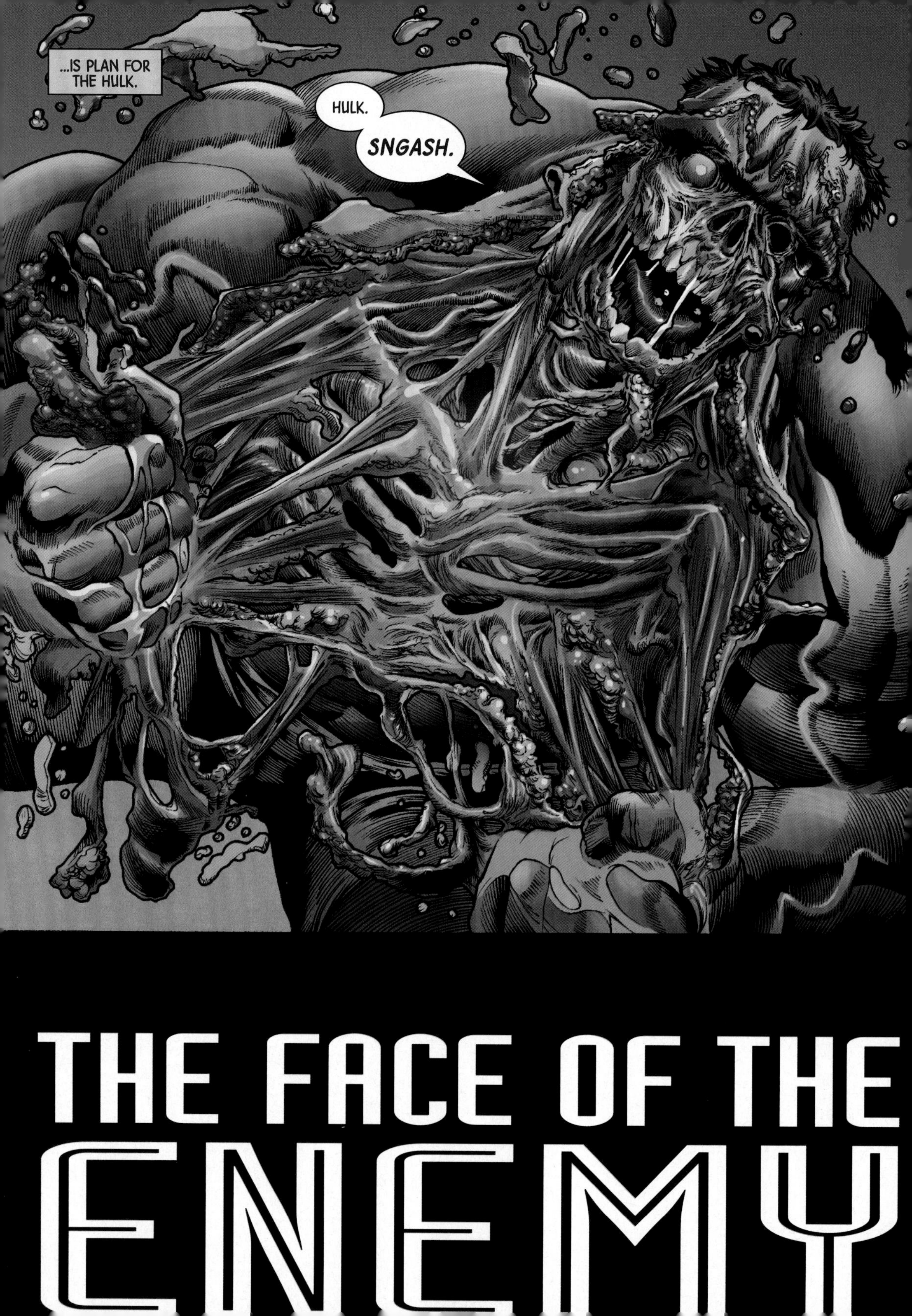
...IS PLAN FOR THE HULK.
HULK.
SNGASH.

THE FACE OF THE ENEMY

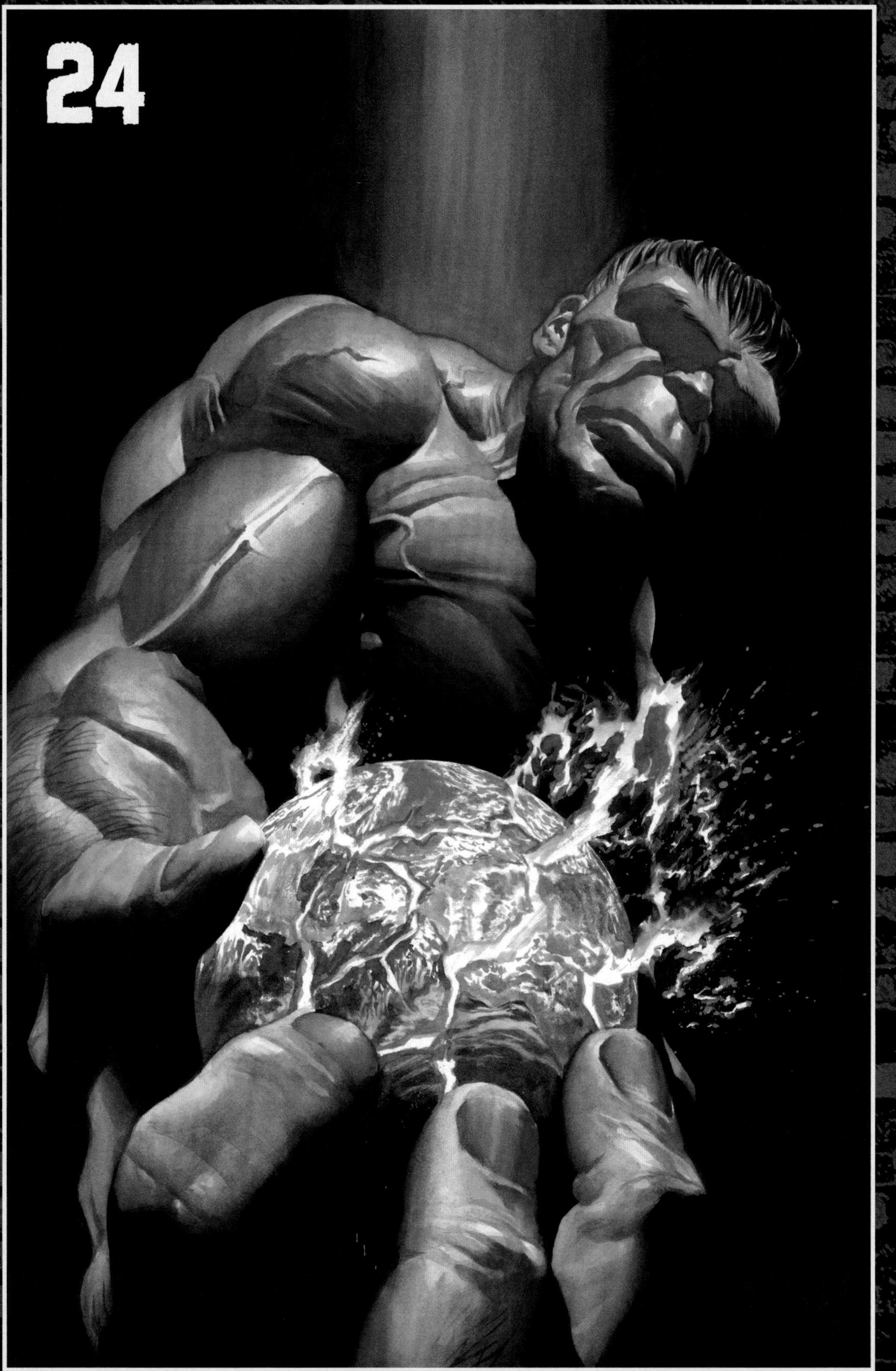
24

"THEY WISHED -- THEY PRAYED -- AND THEN THEY FOUND FULFILLMENT -- AS THE FIRST COSMIC-RAY BURST INUNDATED THE STAR-CROSSED SHIP -- !"

- STAN LEE & JACK KIRBY, "GALACTUS: THE ORIGIN"

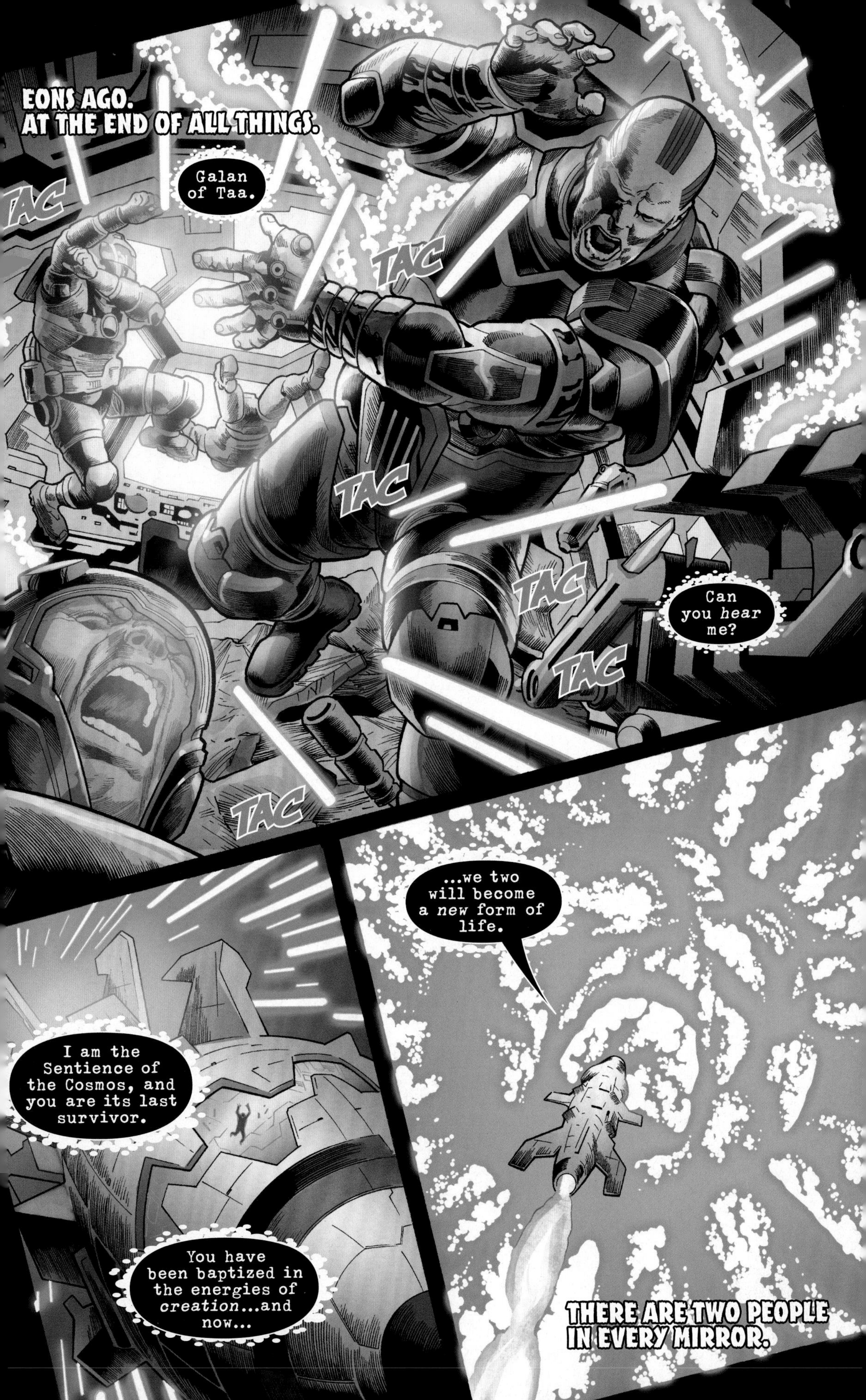
EONS AGO.
AT THE END OF ALL THINGS.
Galan of Taa.
TAC
TAC
TAC
TAC
Can you *hear* me?
TAC
TAC
I am the Sentience of the Cosmos, and you are its last survivor.
You have been baptized in the energies of *creation*...and now...
...we two will become a *new* form of life.
THERE ARE TWO PEOPLE IN EVERY MIRROR.

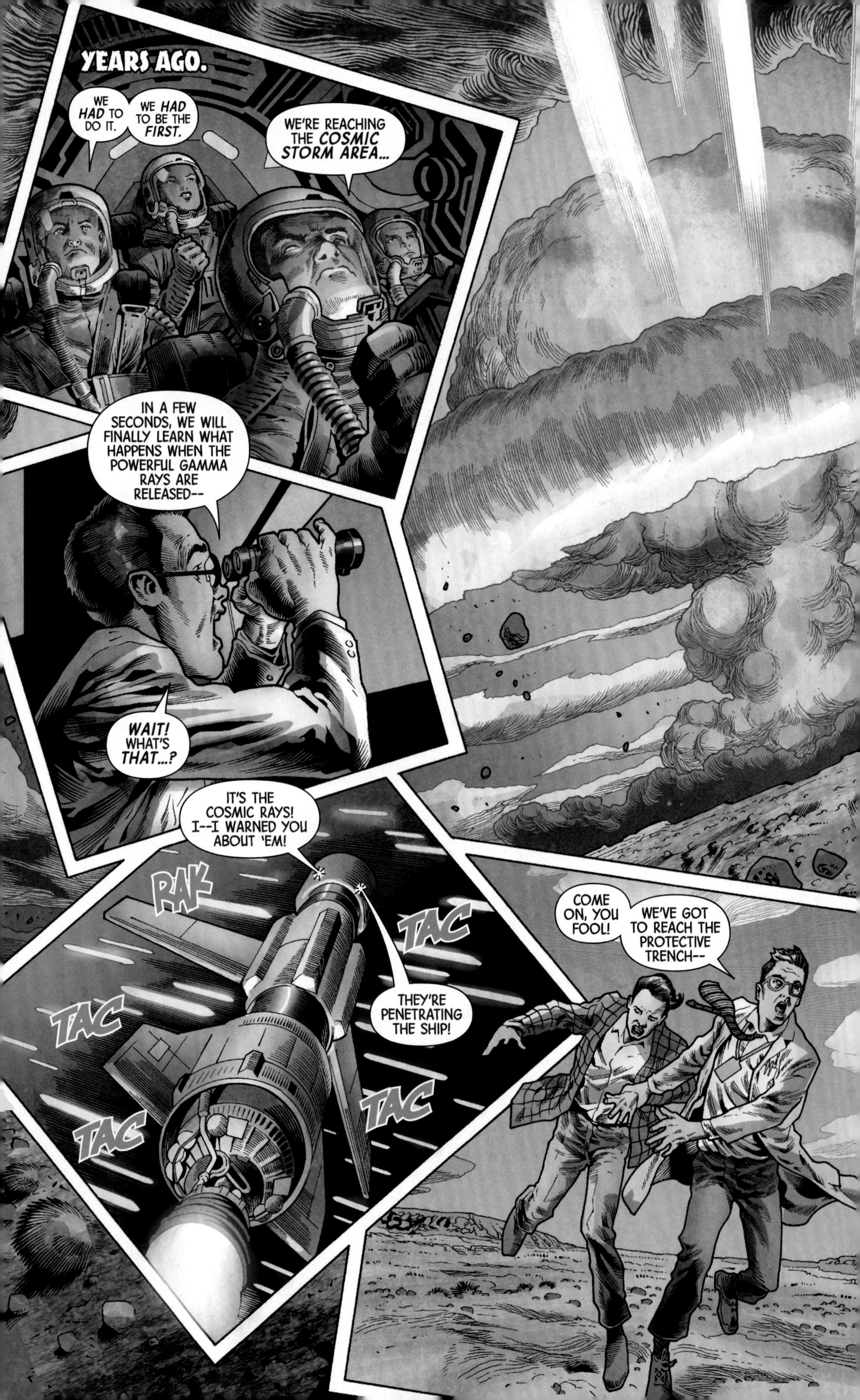

YEARS AGO.
WE HAD TO DO IT.
WE HAD TO BE THE FIRST.
WE'RE REACHING THE COSMIC STORM AREA...
IN A FEW SECONDS, WE WILL FINALLY LEARN WHAT HAPPENS WHEN THE POWERFUL GAMMA RAYS ARE RELEASED--
WAIT! WHAT'S THAT...?
IT'S THE COSMIC RAYS! I--I WARNED YOU ABOUT 'EM!
RAK
TAC
THEY'RE PENETRATING THE SHIP!
TAC
TAC
TAC
COME ON, YOU FOOL!
WE'VE GOT TO REACH THE PROTECTIVE TRENCH--

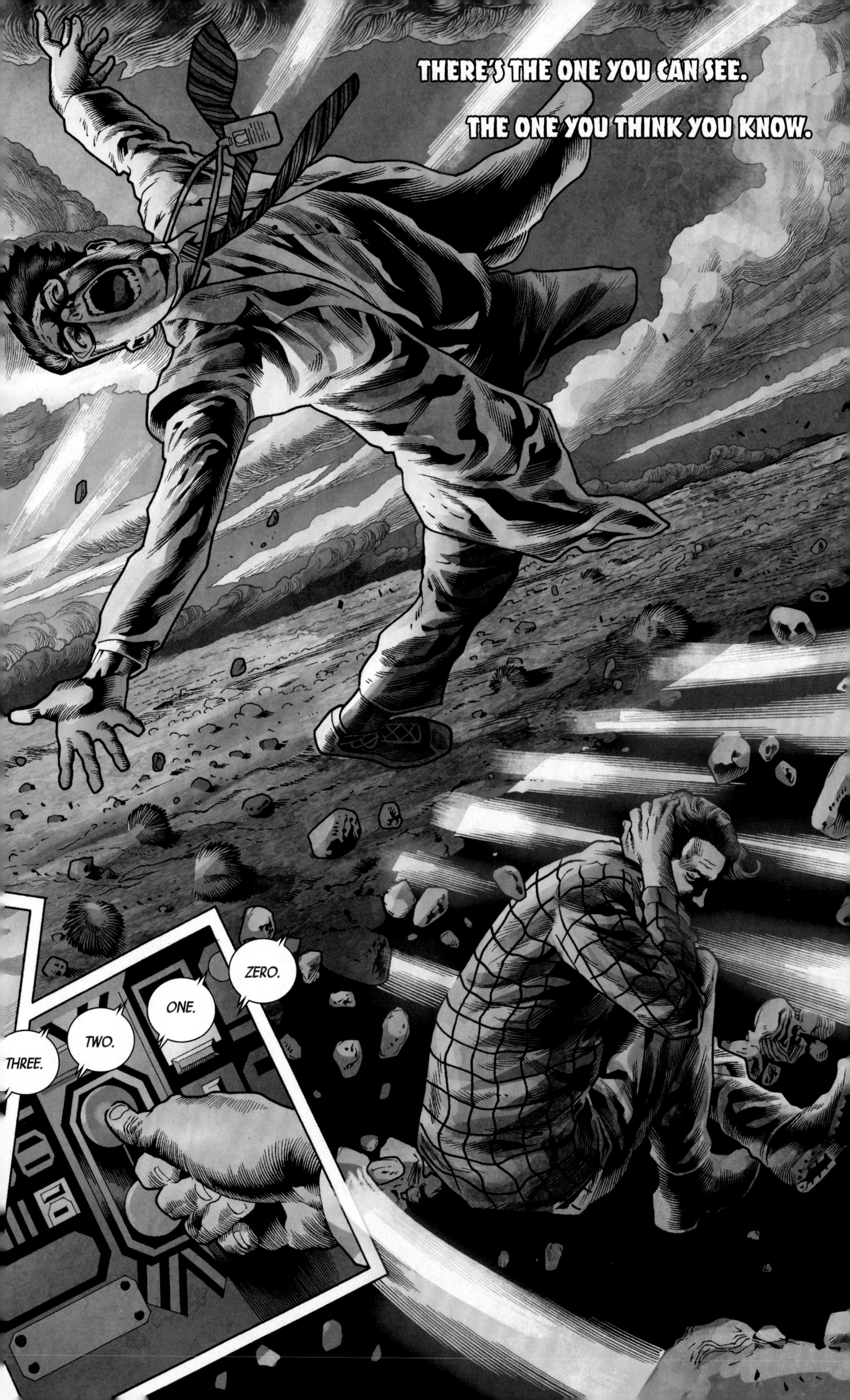
THERE'S THE ONE YOU CAN SEE.
THE ONE YOU THINK YOU KNOW.
THREE.
TWO.
ONE.
ZERO.

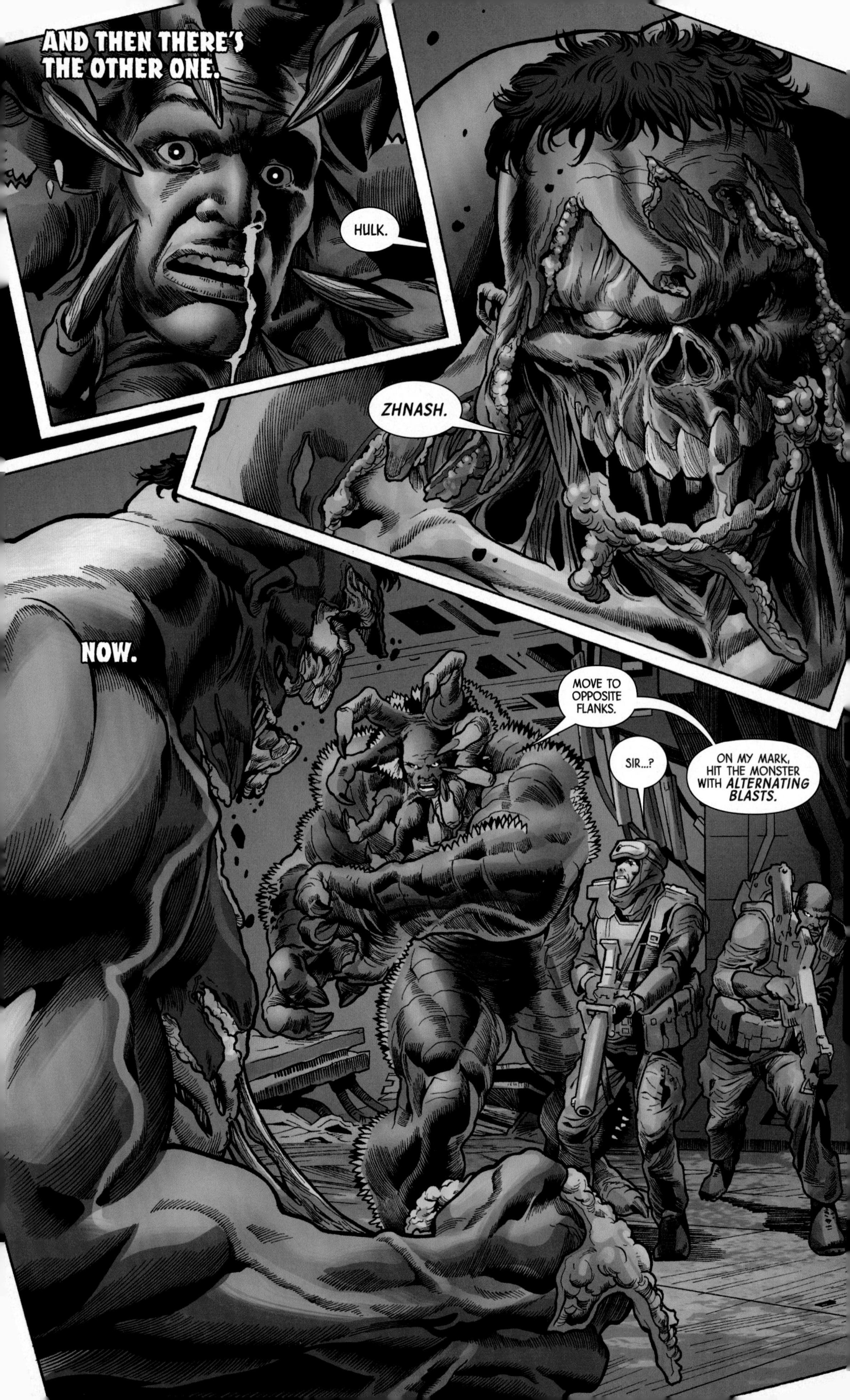
AND THEN THERE'S THE OTHER ONE.
HULK.
ZHNASH.
NOW.
MOVE TO OPPOSITE FLANKS.
SIR...?
ON MY MARK, HIT THE MONSTER WITH ALTERNATING BLASTS.

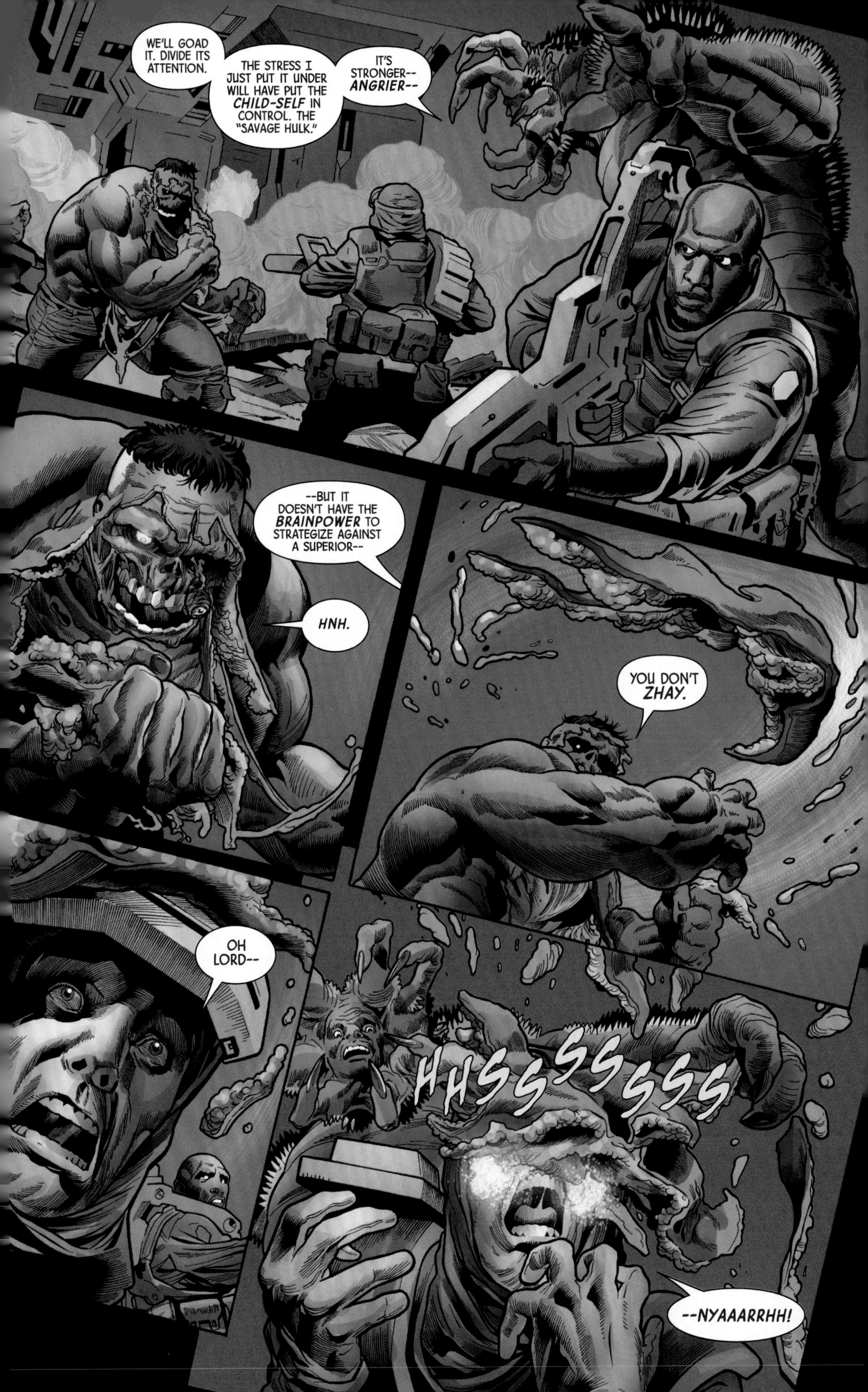
WE'LL GOAD IT. DIVIDE ITS ATTENTION.
THE STRESS I JUST PUT IT UNDER WILL HAVE PUT THE CHILD-SELF IN CONTROL. THE "SAVAGE HULK."
IT'S STRONGER-- ANGRIER--
--BUT IT DOESN'T HAVE THE BRAINPOWER TO STRATEGIZE AGAINST A SUPERIOR--
HNH.
YOU DON'T ZHAY.
OH LORD--
HHSSSSSSSS
--NYAAARRHH!

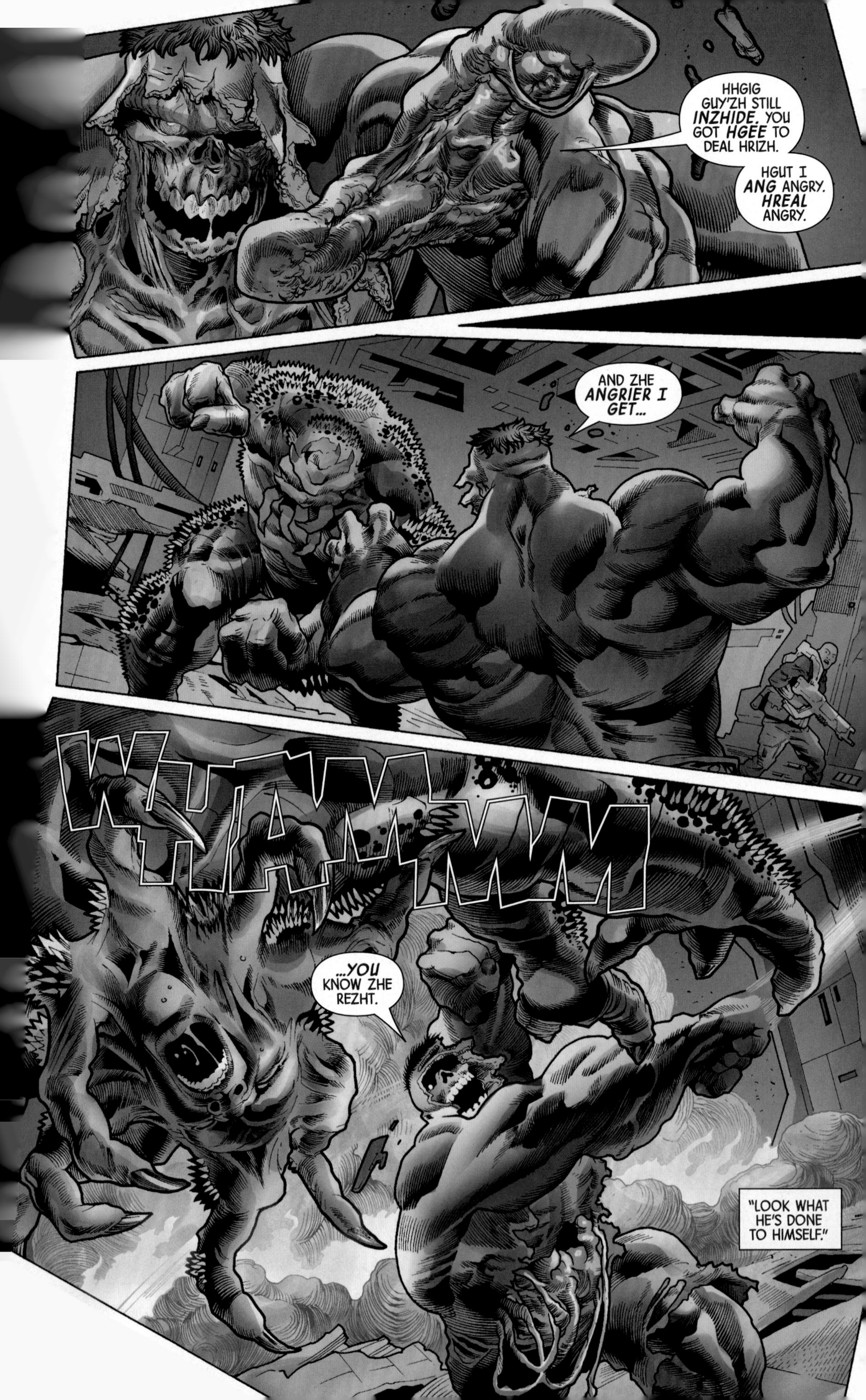
HHGIG GUY'ZH STILL INZHIDE. YOU GOT HGEE TO DEAL HRIZH.
HGUT I ANG ANGRY. HREAL ANGRY.
AND ZHE ANGRIER I GET...
WHAMMM
...YOU KNOW ZHE REZHT.
"LOOK WHAT HE'S DONE TO HIMSELF."

HE'S *DESTROYED* HIMSELF. AND NOW YOU WANT ME TO DESTROY HIM *AGAIN*?

I DON'T KNOW IF I CAN DO THAT.

WHEN THE GENERAL *FOUND* US-- THE SCIENCE TEAM, THE OPS TEAM, THE MONITORS, *ALL* OF US--

--HE PULLED US OUT OF SOME *BAD SITUATIONS*. BAD *DECISIONS*.

I...WAS FIRED FROM *CALTECH*. DRINK AND DRUGS. I ENDED UP WORKING IN AN *MGH* LAB.

IT WAS *UGLY* WORK, BUT...ONCE YOU'RE *IN*, THERE'S NO OUT.

THEN *DAREDEVIL* HAPPENED, AND I WENT TO *JAIL*.

AND...AND IF NOT FOR *REG FORTEAN*...

I GET IT.

FORTEAN HAD YOUR *BACK*. HE GAVE YOU A *LIFE* AGAIN.

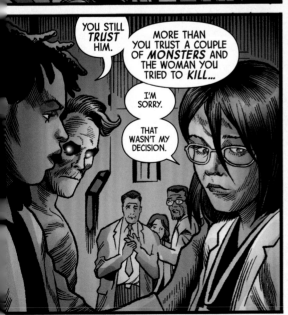

YOU STILL *TRUST* HIM.

MORE THAN YOU TRUST A COUPLE OF *MONSTERS* AND THE WOMAN YOU TRIED TO *KILL*...

I'M SORRY.

THAT WASN'T MY DECISION.

NO.

IT WAS *REG FORTEAN'S*.

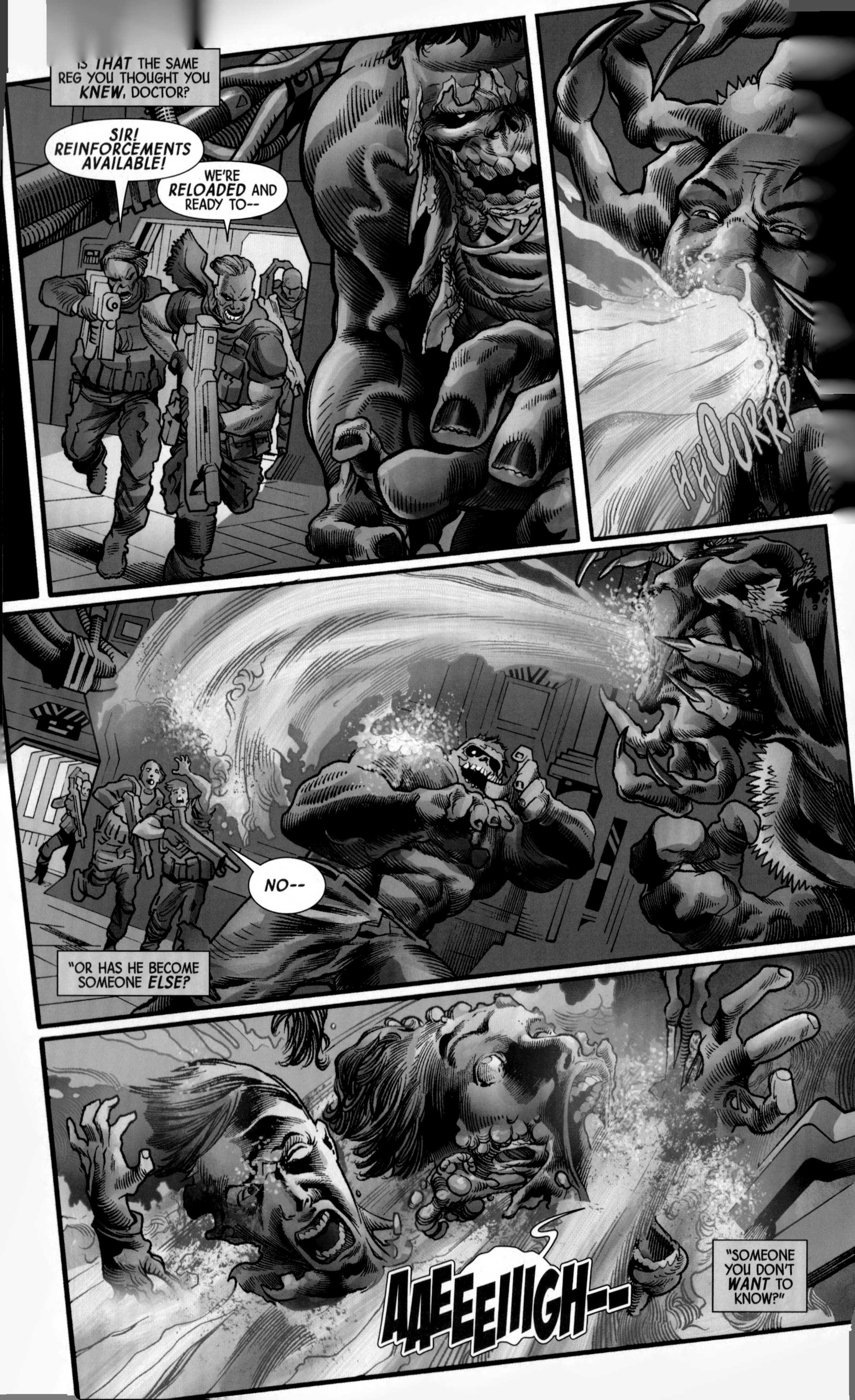
IS THAT THE SAME REG YOU THOUGHT YOU KNEW, DOCTOR?
SIR! REINFORCEMENTS AVAILABLE!
WE'RE RELOADED AND READY TO--
HHOORRP
NO--
"OR HAS HE BECOME SOMEONE ELSE?
AAEEEIIIGH--
"SOMEONE YOU DON'T WANT TO KNOW?"

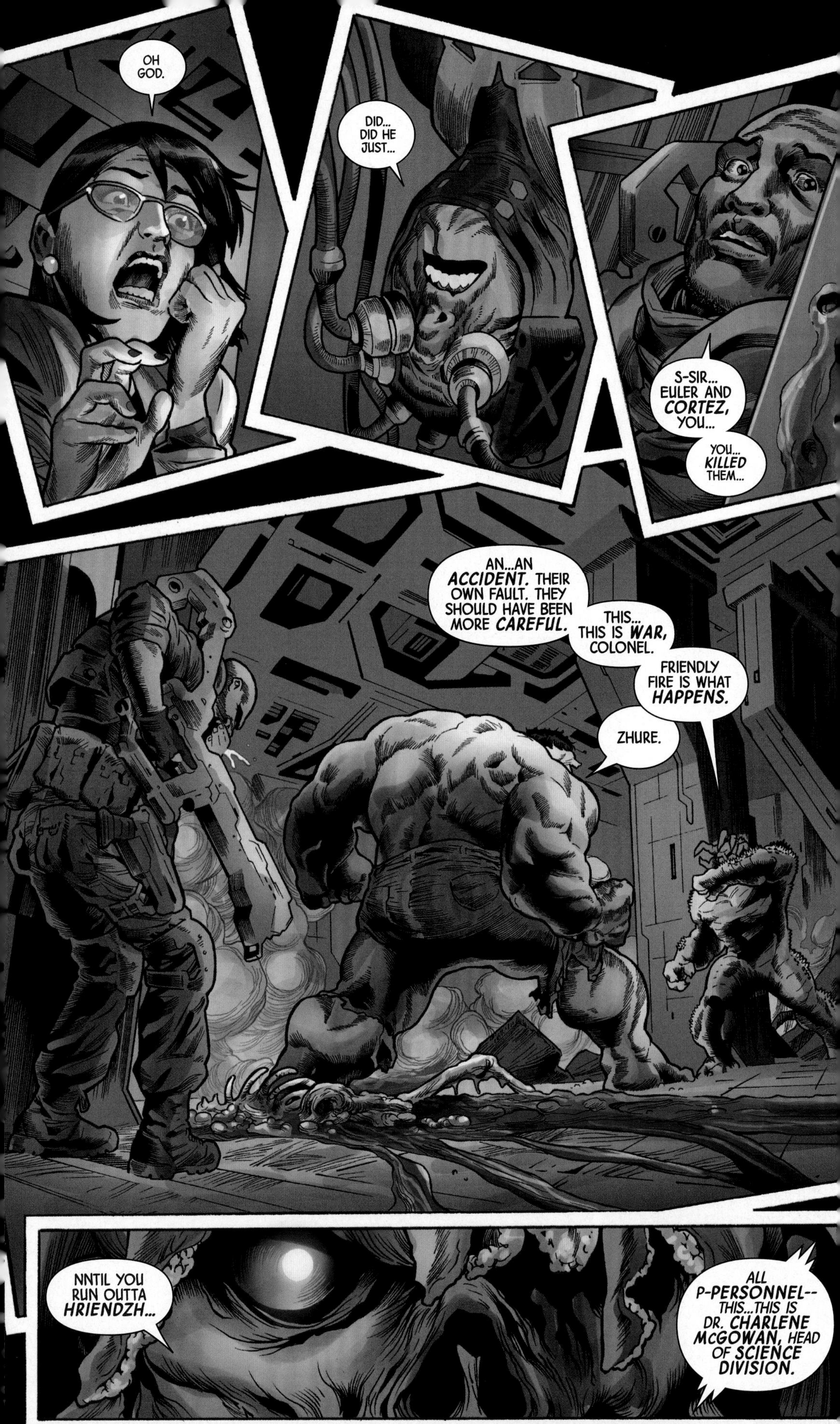
OH GOD.
DID... DID HE JUST...
S-SIR... EULER AND CORTEZ, YOU...
YOU... KILLED THEM...
AN...AN ACCIDENT. THEIR OWN FAULT. THEY SHOULD HAVE BEEN MORE CAREFUL.
THIS... THIS IS WAR, COLONEL.
FRIENDLY FIRE IS WHAT HAPPENS.
ZHURE.
NNTIL YOU RUN OUTTA HRIENDZH...
ALL P-PERSONNEL-- THIS...THIS IS DR. CHARLENE McGOWAN, HEAD OF SCIENCE DIVISION.

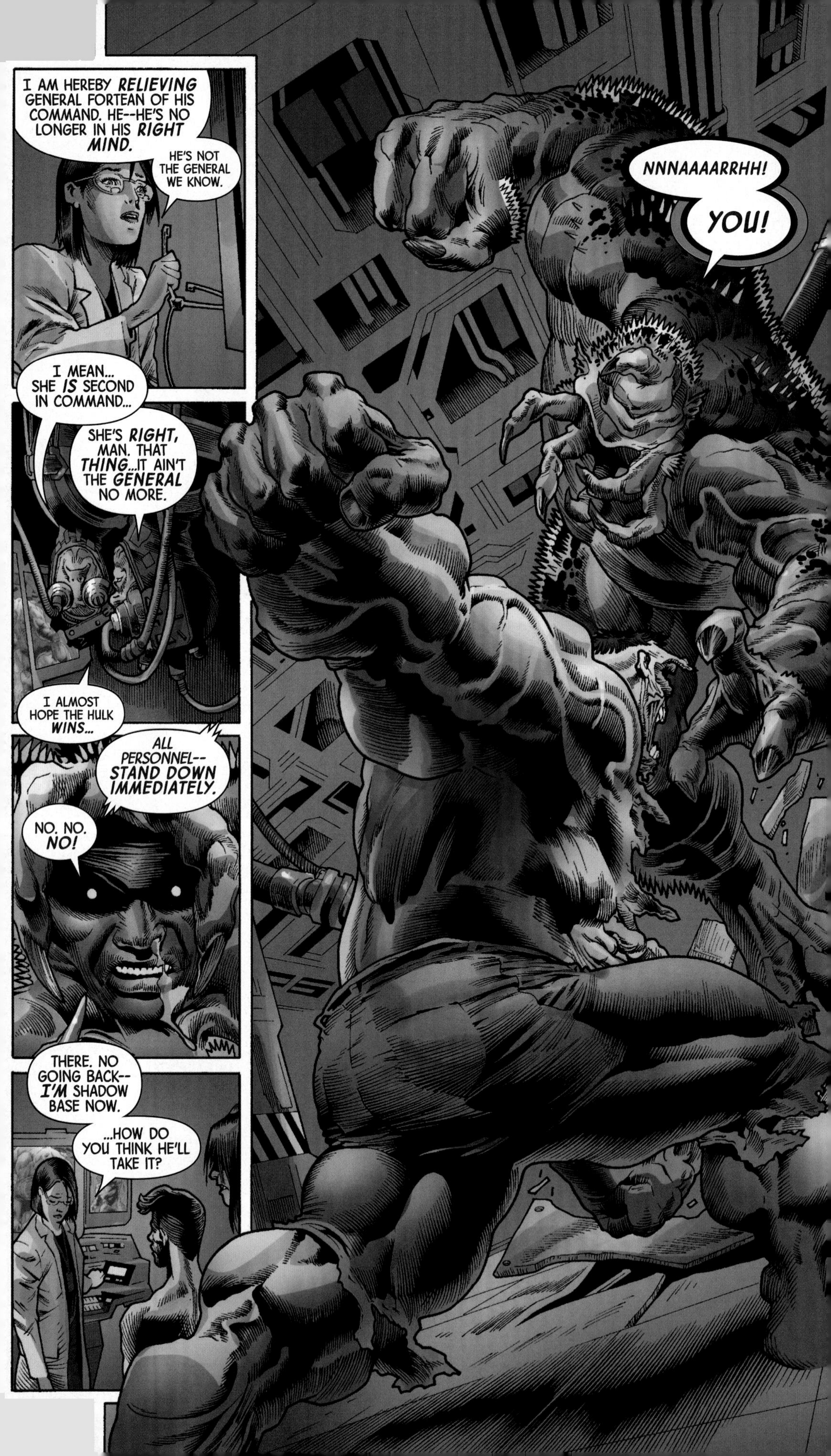

I AM HEREBY RELIEVING GENERAL FORTEAN OF HIS COMMAND. HE--HE'S NO LONGER IN HIS RIGHT MIND.
HE'S NOT THE GENERAL WE KNOW.
I MEAN... SHE IS SECOND IN COMMAND...
SHE'S RIGHT, MAN. THAT THING...IT AIN'T THE GENERAL NO MORE.
I ALMOST HOPE THE HULK WINS...
ALL PERSONNEL-- STAND DOWN IMMEDIATELY.
NO. NO. NO!
THERE. NO GOING BACK-- I'M SHADOW BASE NOW.
...HOW DO YOU THINK HE'LL TAKE IT?
NNNAAAARRHH!
YOU!

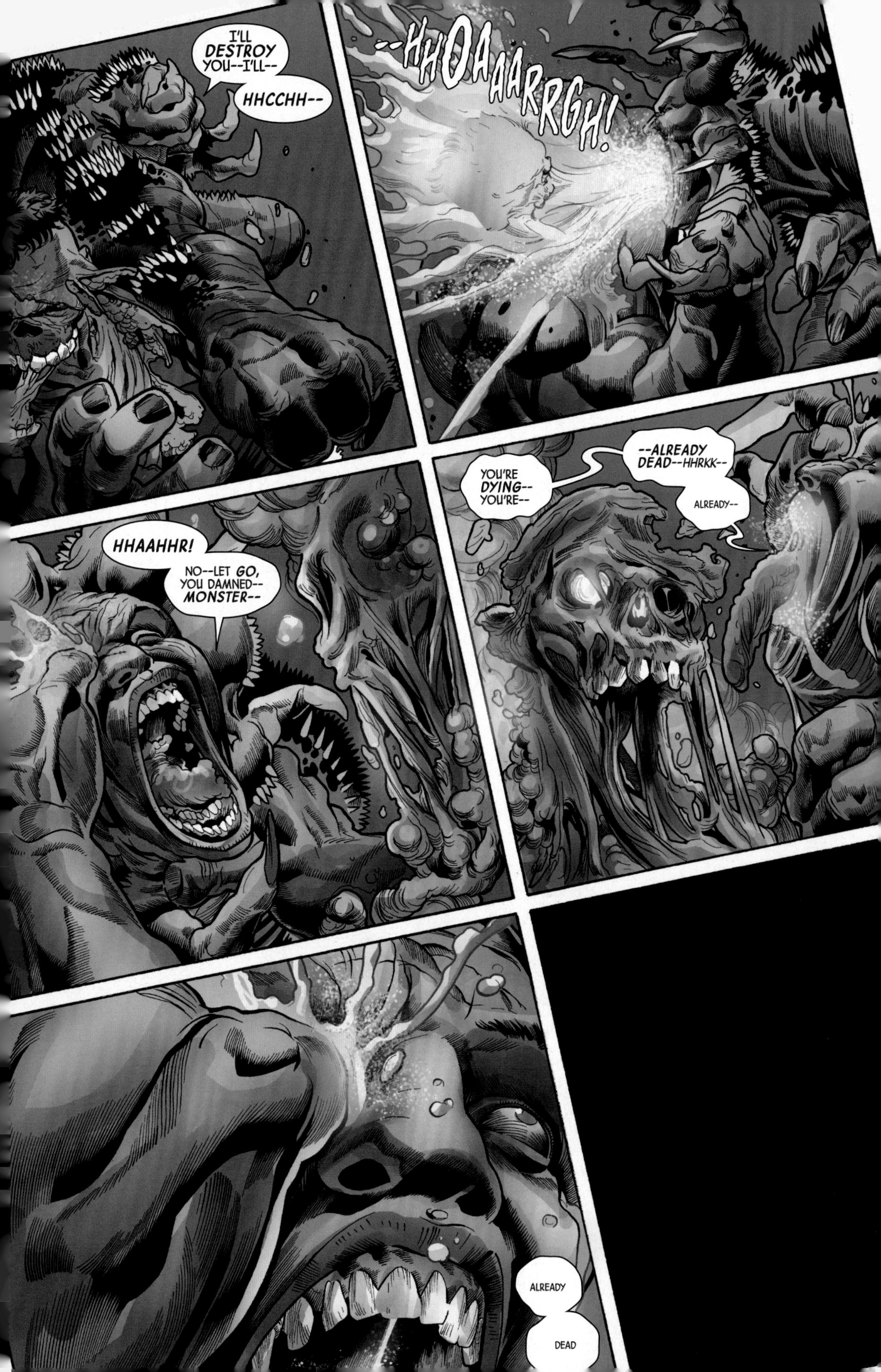
I'LL DESTROY YOU--I'LL--
HHCCHH--
--HHOAAARRGH!
HHAAAHHR!
NO--LET GO, YOU DAMNED--MONSTER--
YOU'RE DYING--YOU'RE--
--ALREADY DEAD--HHRKK--
ALREADY--
ALREADY
DEAD

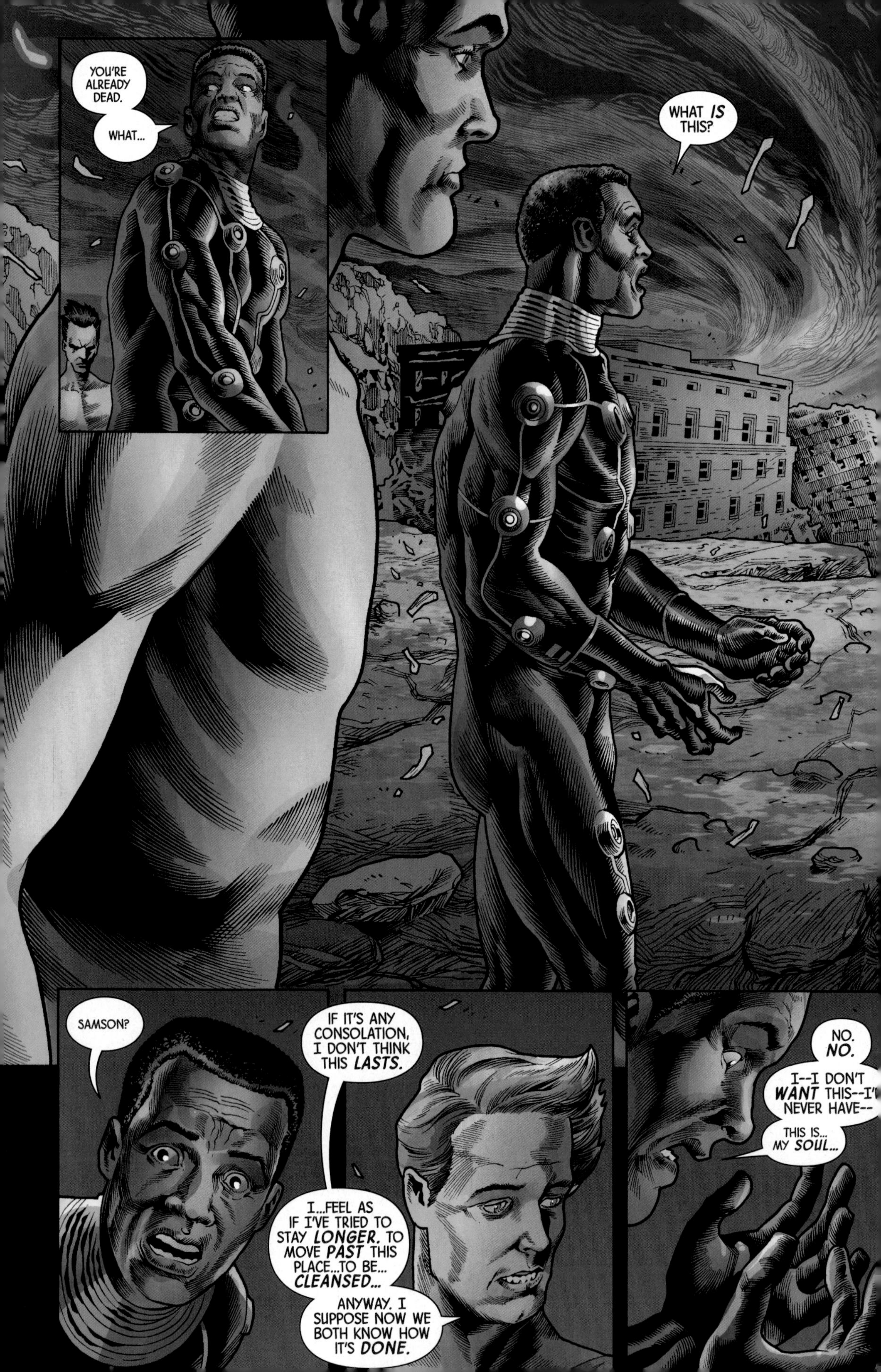
YOU'RE ALREADY DEAD.
WHAT...
WHAT *IS* THIS?
SAMSON?
IF IT'S ANY CONSOLATION, I DON'T THINK THIS *LASTS.*
I...FEEL AS IF I'VE TRIED TO STAY *LONGER.* TO MOVE *PAST* THIS PLACE...TO BE... *CLEANSED...*
ANYWAY. I SUPPOSE NOW WE BOTH KNOW HOW IT'S *DONE.*
NO. *NO.*
I--I DON'T *WANT* THIS--I'VE NEVER HAVE--
THIS IS... MY *SOUL...*

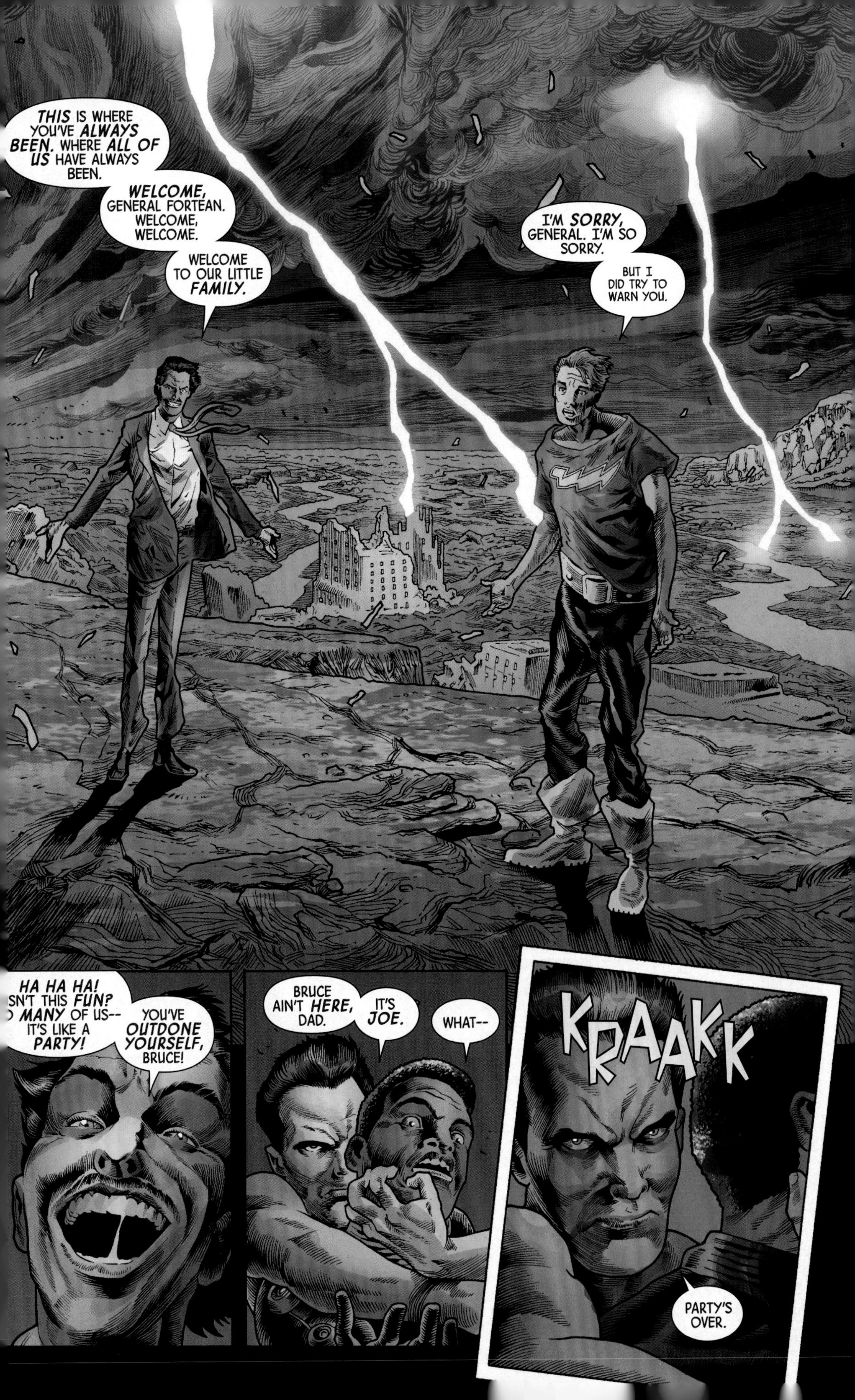
THIS IS WHERE YOU'VE ALWAYS BEEN. WHERE ALL OF US HAVE ALWAYS BEEN.
WELCOME, GENERAL FORTEAN. WELCOME, WELCOME.
WELCOME TO OUR LITTLE FAMILY.
I'M SORRY, GENERAL. I'M SO SORRY.
BUT I DID TRY TO WARN YOU.
HA HA HA! SN'T THIS FUN? MANY OF US-- IT'S LIKE A PARTY!
YOU'VE OUTDONE YOURSELF, BRUCE!
BRUCE AIN'T HERE, DAD.
IT'S JOE.
WHAT--
KRAAKK
PARTY'S OVER.

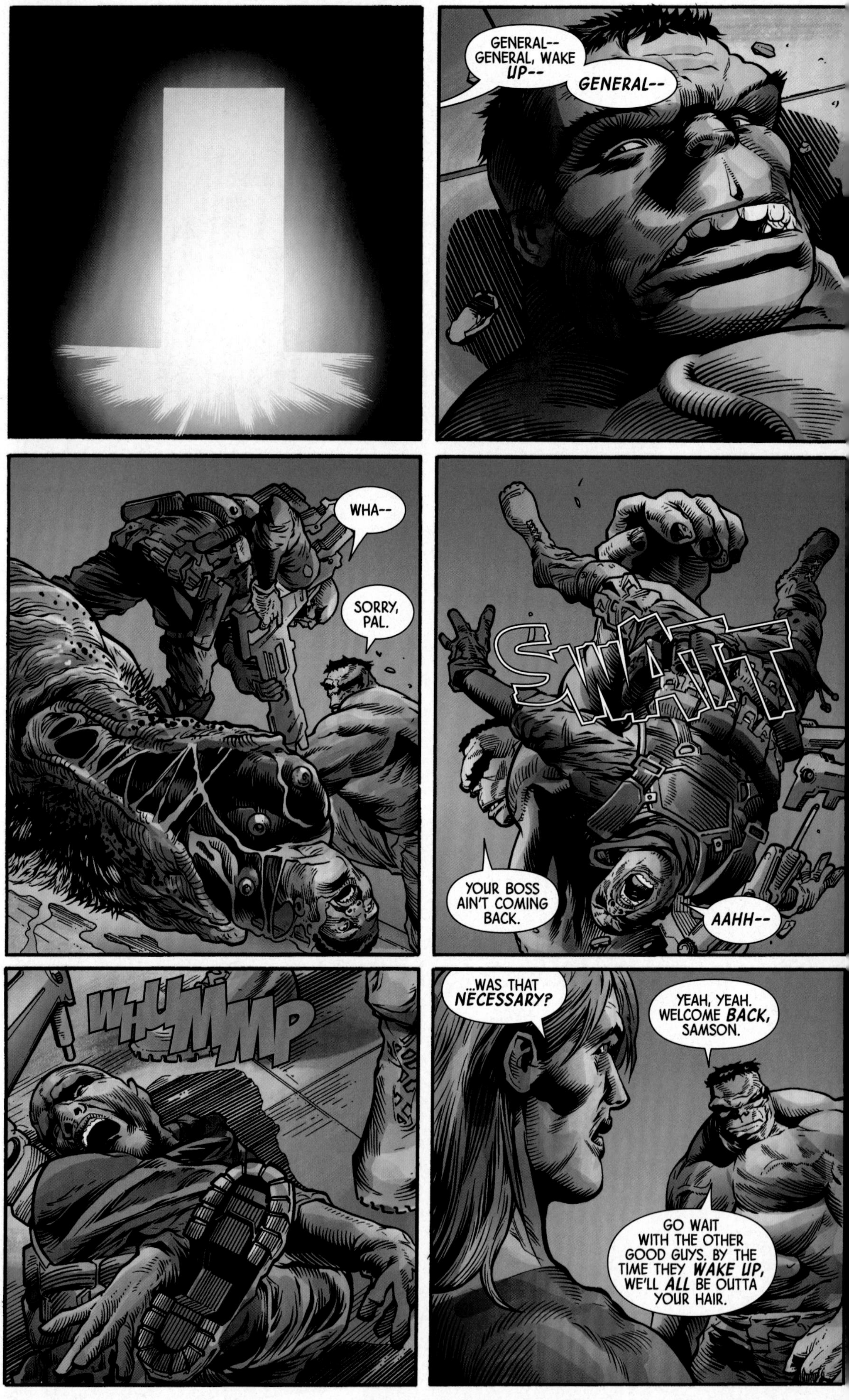
GENERAL-- GENERAL, WAKE *UP*--
GENERAL--
WHA--
SORRY, PAL.
SWAT
YOUR BOSS AIN'T COMING BACK.
AAHH--
WHUMMP
...WAS THAT *NECESSARY?*
YEAH, YEAH. WELCOME *BACK,* SAMSON.
GO WAIT WITH THE OTHER GOOD GUYS. BY THE TIME THEY *WAKE UP,* WE'LL *ALL* BE OUTTA YOUR HAIR.

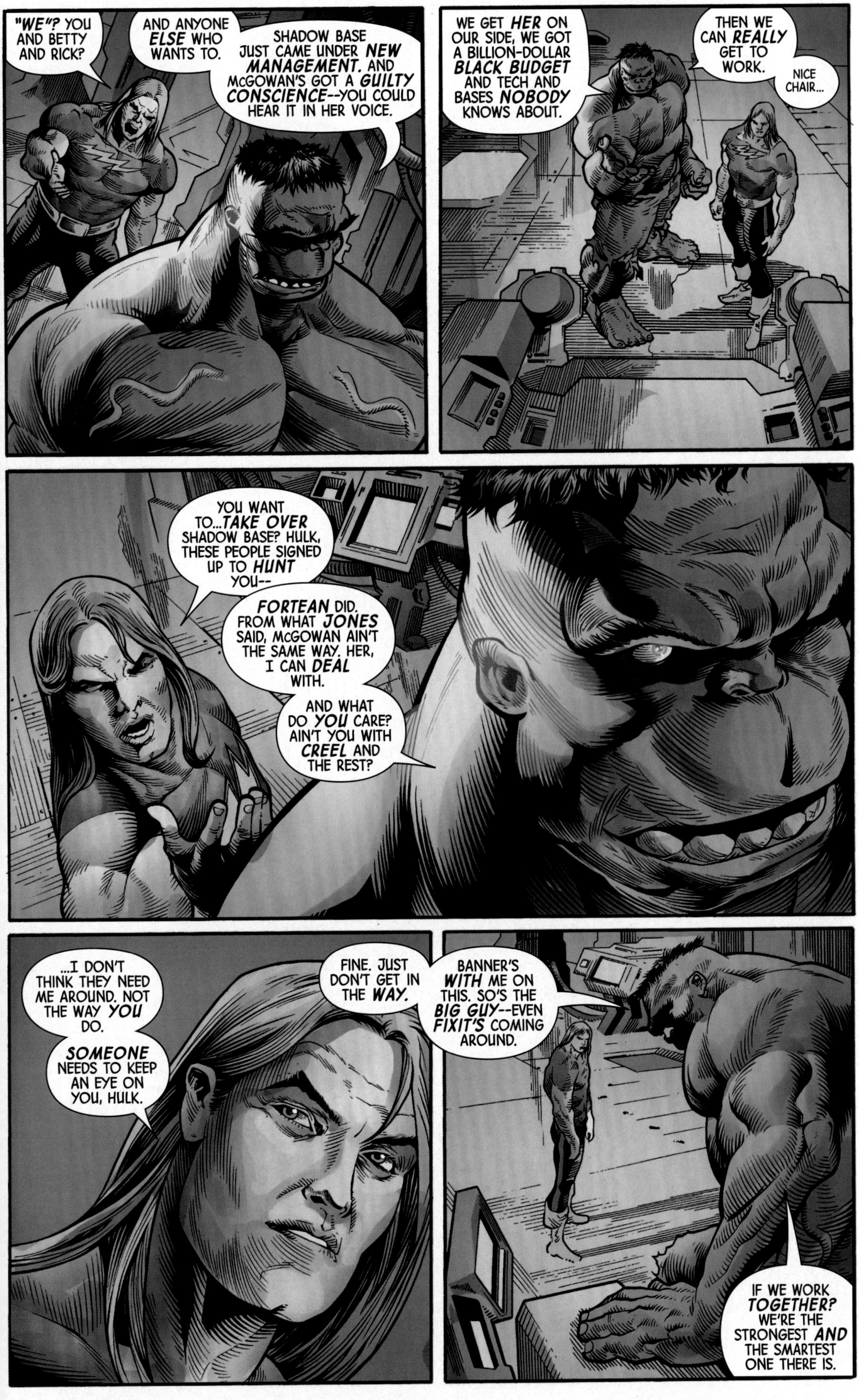
"WE"? YOU AND BETTY AND RICK?
AND ANYONE ELSE WHO WANTS TO.
SHADOW BASE JUST CAME UNDER NEW MANAGEMENT. AND McGOWAN'S GOT A GUILTY CONSCIENCE--YOU COULD HEAR IT IN HER VOICE.
WE GET HER ON OUR SIDE, WE GOT A BILLION-DOLLAR BLACK BUDGET AND TECH AND BASES NOBODY KNOWS ABOUT.
THEN WE CAN REALLY GET TO WORK.
NICE CHAIR...
YOU WANT TO...TAKE OVER SHADOW BASE? HULK, THESE PEOPLE SIGNED UP TO HUNT YOU--
FORTEAN DID. FROM WHAT JONES SAID, McGOWAN AIN'T THE SAME WAY. HER, I CAN DEAL WITH.
AND WHAT DO YOU CARE? AIN'T YOU WITH CREEL AND THE REST?
...I DON'T THINK THEY NEED ME AROUND. NOT THE WAY YOU DO.
SOMEONE NEEDS TO KEEP AN EYE ON YOU, HULK.
FINE. JUST DON'T GET IN THE WAY.
BANNER'S WITH ME ON THIS. SO'S THE BIG GUY--EVEN FIXIT'S COMING AROUND.
IF WE WORK TOGETHER? WE'RE THE STRONGEST AND THE SMARTEST ONE THERE IS.

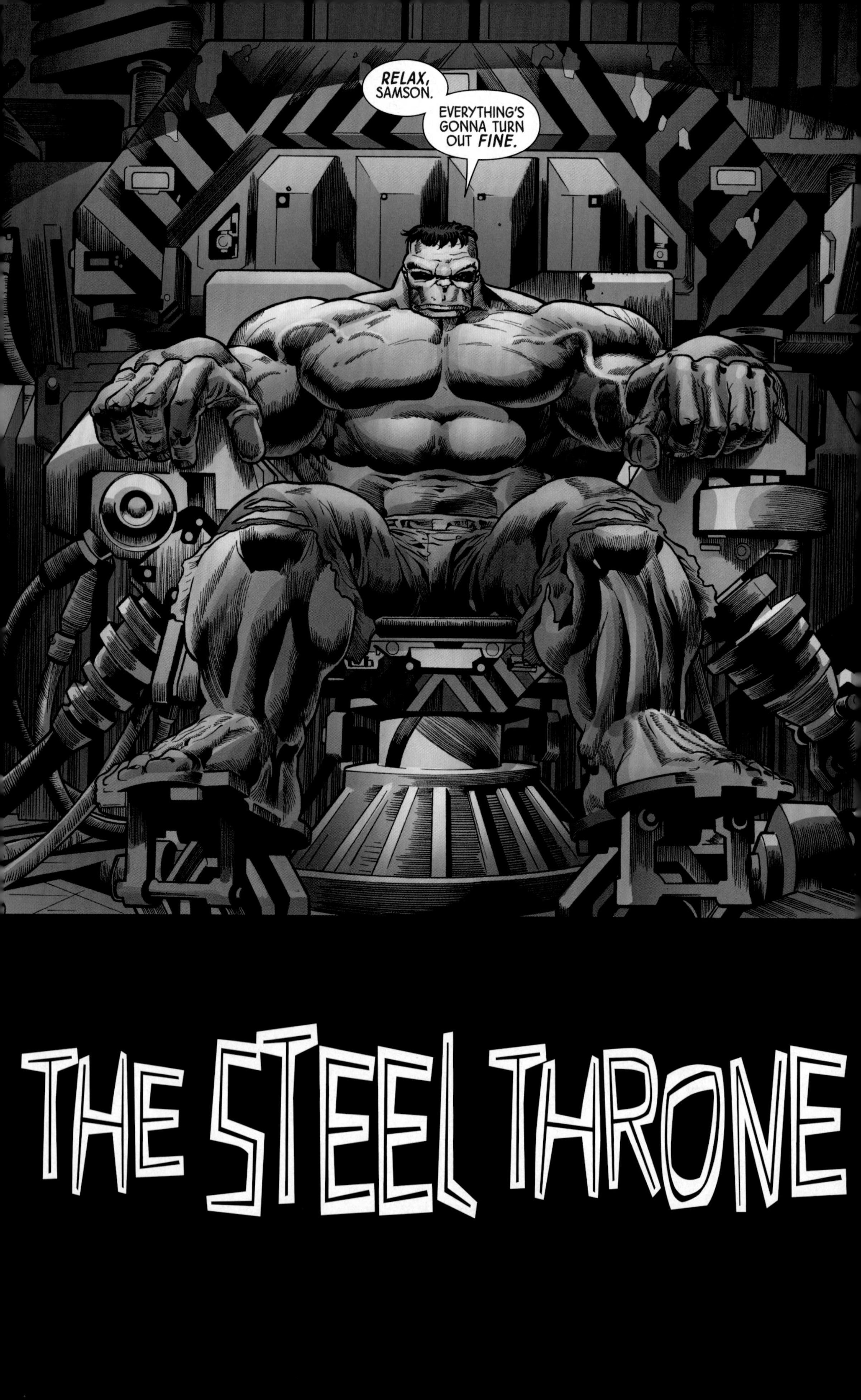
RELAX, SAMSON.
EVERYTHING'S GONNA TURN OUT FINE.
THE STEEL THRONE

EONS FROM NOW.

AT THE END OF ALL THINGS.

Bruce Banner
of Earth.

I am the
Sentience of the Cosmos...

...and you are its
last survivor.

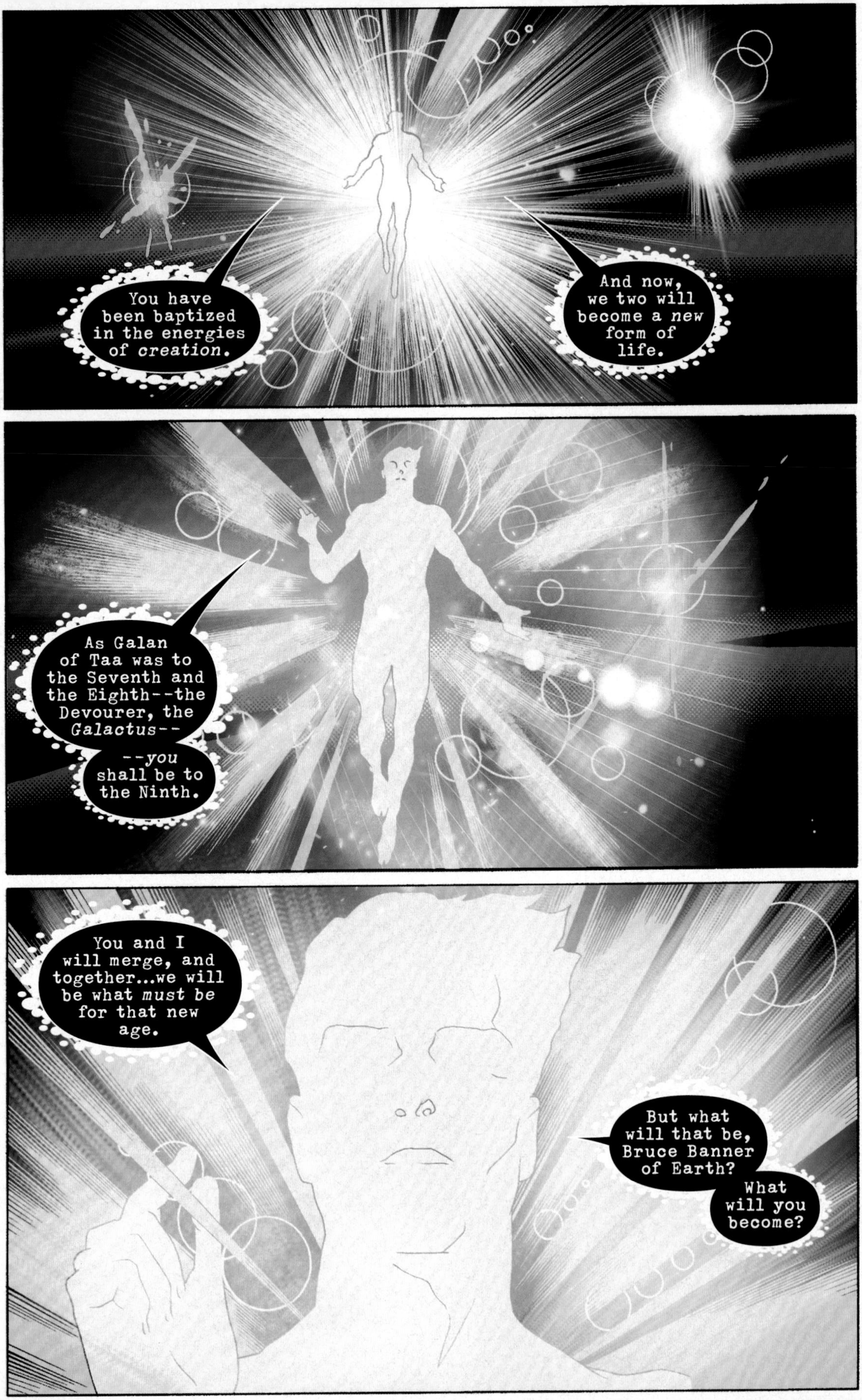
You have been baptized in the energies of *creation*.
And now, we two will become a *new* form of life.
As Galan of Taa was to the Seventh and the Eighth--the Devourer, the *Galactus*--
--*you* shall be to the Ninth.
You and I will merge, and together...we will be what *must be* for that new age.
But what will that be, Bruce Banner of Earth?
What will you become?

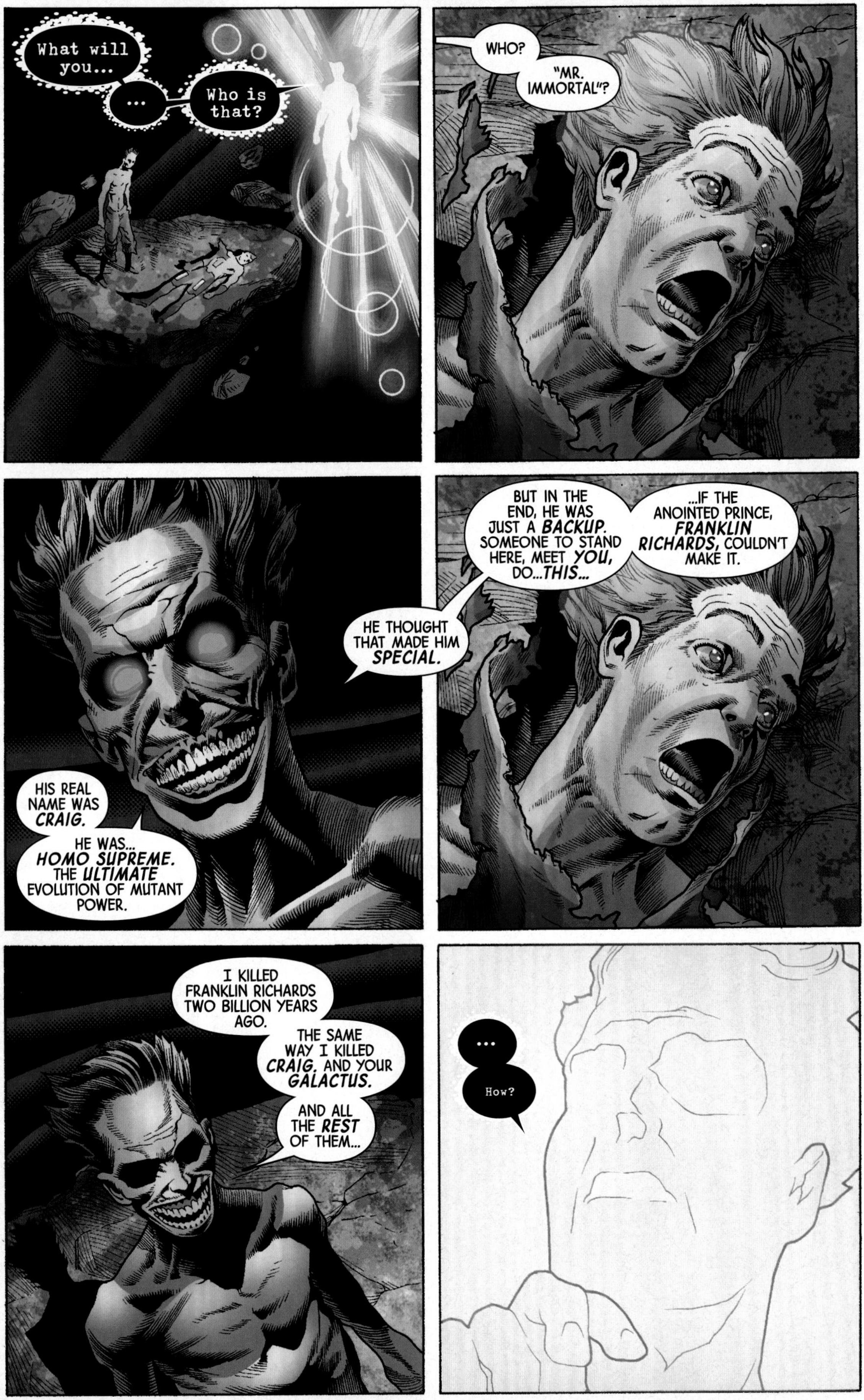
What will you...
...
Who is that?
WHO?
"MR. IMMORTAL"?
HIS REAL NAME WAS CRAIG.
HE WAS... HOMO SUPREME. THE ULTIMATE EVOLUTION OF MUTANT POWER.
HE THOUGHT THAT MADE HIM SPECIAL.
BUT IN THE END, HE WAS JUST A BACKUP. SOMEONE TO STAND HERE, MEET YOU, DO...THIS...
...IF THE ANOINTED PRINCE, FRANKLIN RICHARDS, COULDN'T MAKE IT.
I KILLED FRANKLIN RICHARDS TWO BILLION YEARS AGO.
THE SAME WAY I KILLED CRAIG. AND YOUR GALACTUS.
AND ALL THE REST OF THEM...
...
How?

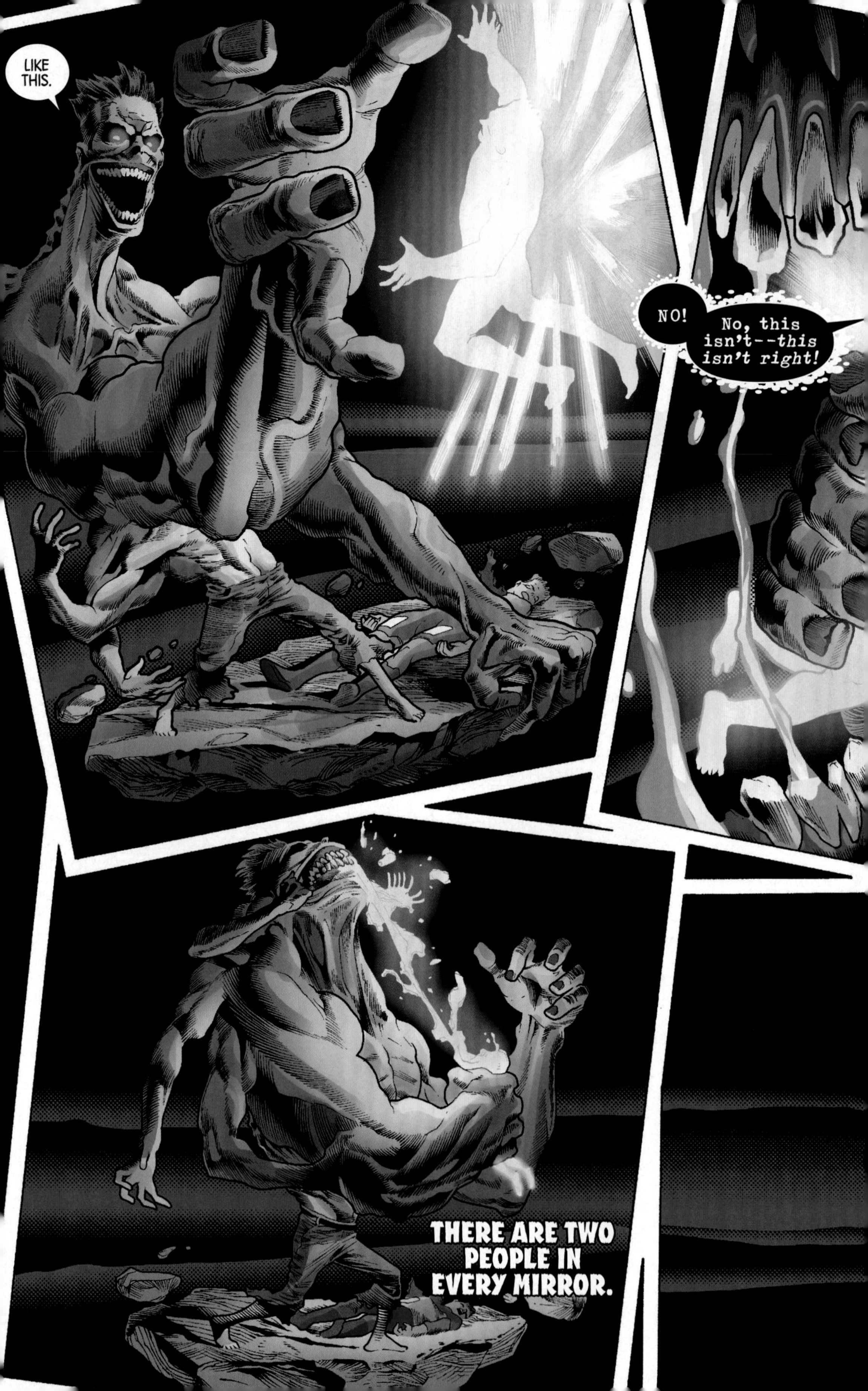
LIKE THIS.
NO!
No, this isn't--this isn't right!
THERE ARE TWO PEOPLE IN EVERY MIRROR.

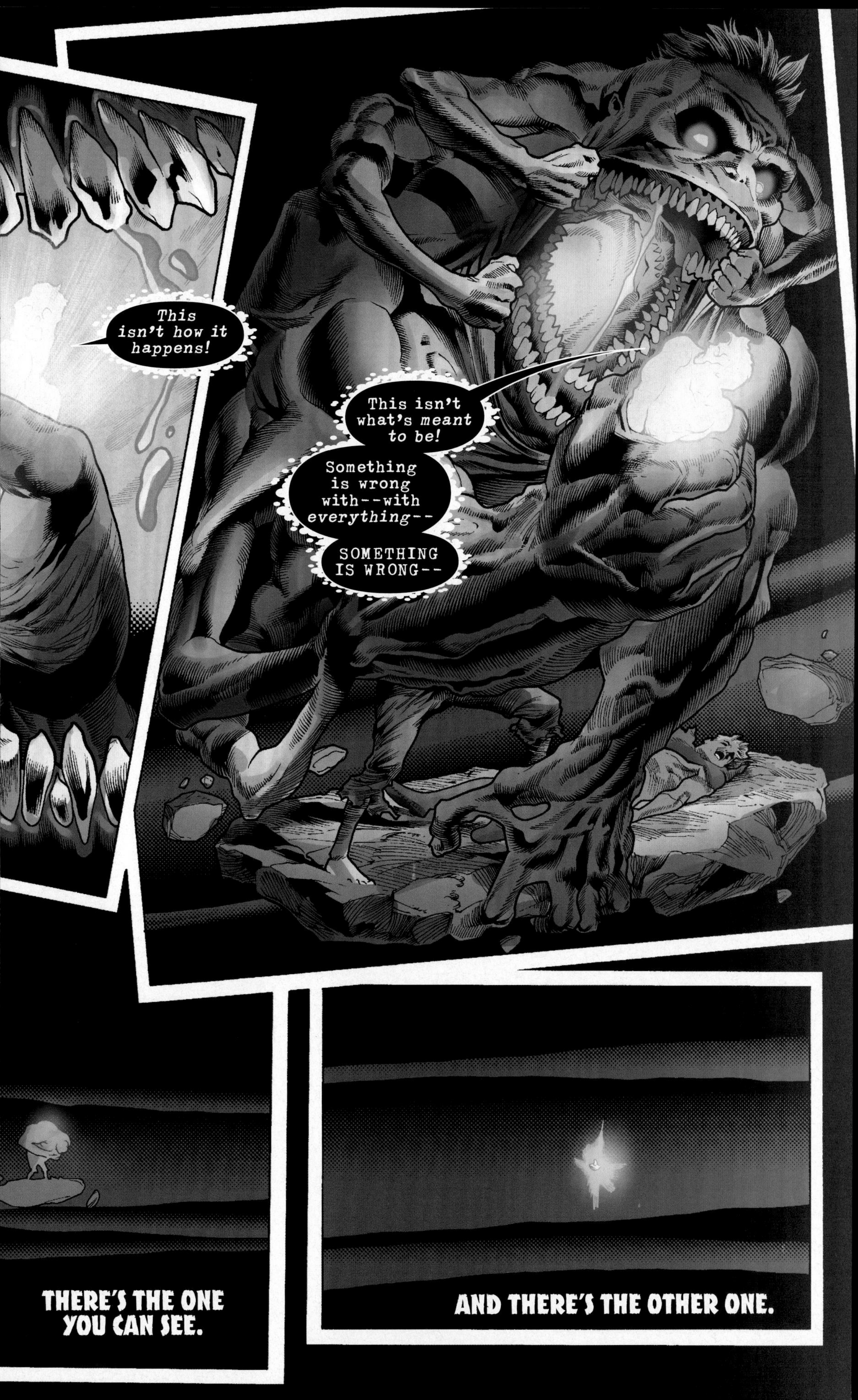

This isn't how it happens!
This isn't what's *meant* to be!
Something is wrong with--with *everything*--
SOMETHING IS WRONG--
THERE'S THE ONE YOU CAN SEE.
AND THERE'S THE OTHER ONE.

THE ONE YOU DON'T WANT TO.

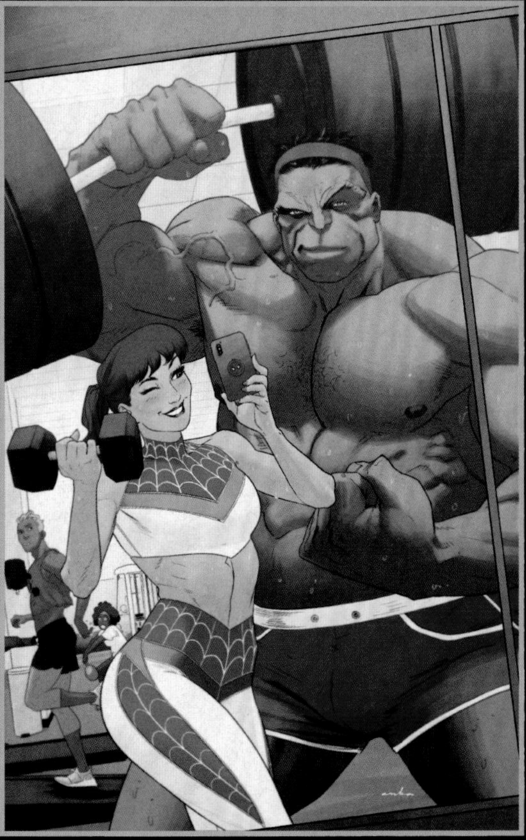

KRIS ANKA
#25 AMAZING MARY JANE VARIANT

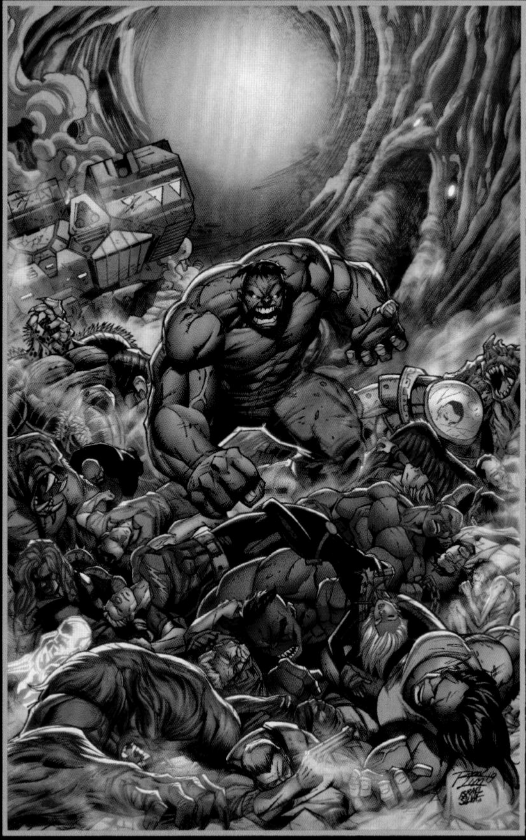

RON LIM & ISRAEL SILVA
#25 VARIANT

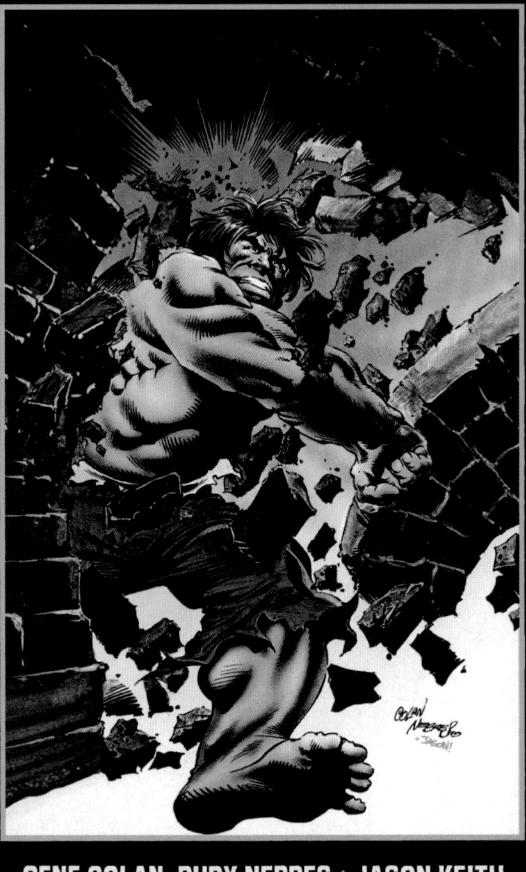

GENE COLAN, RUDY NEBRES & JASON KEITH
#25 HIDDEN GEM VARIANT

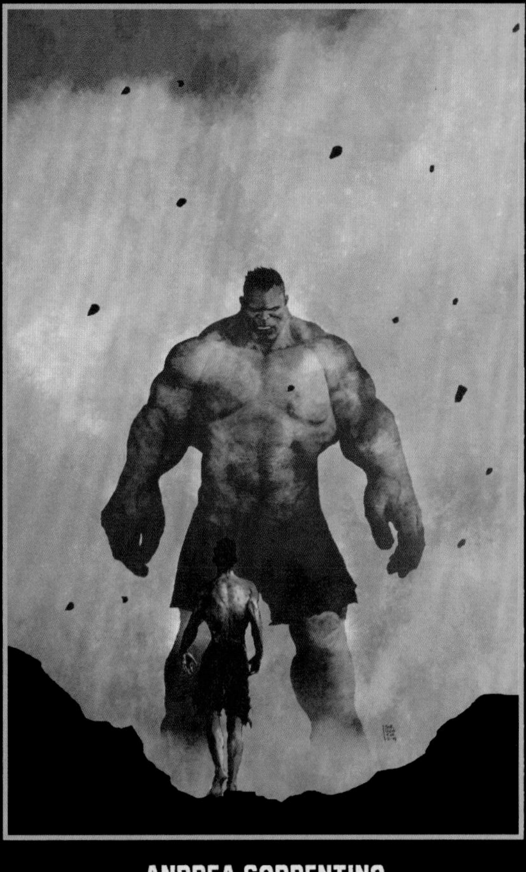

ANDREA SORRENTINO
#25 VARIANT

25

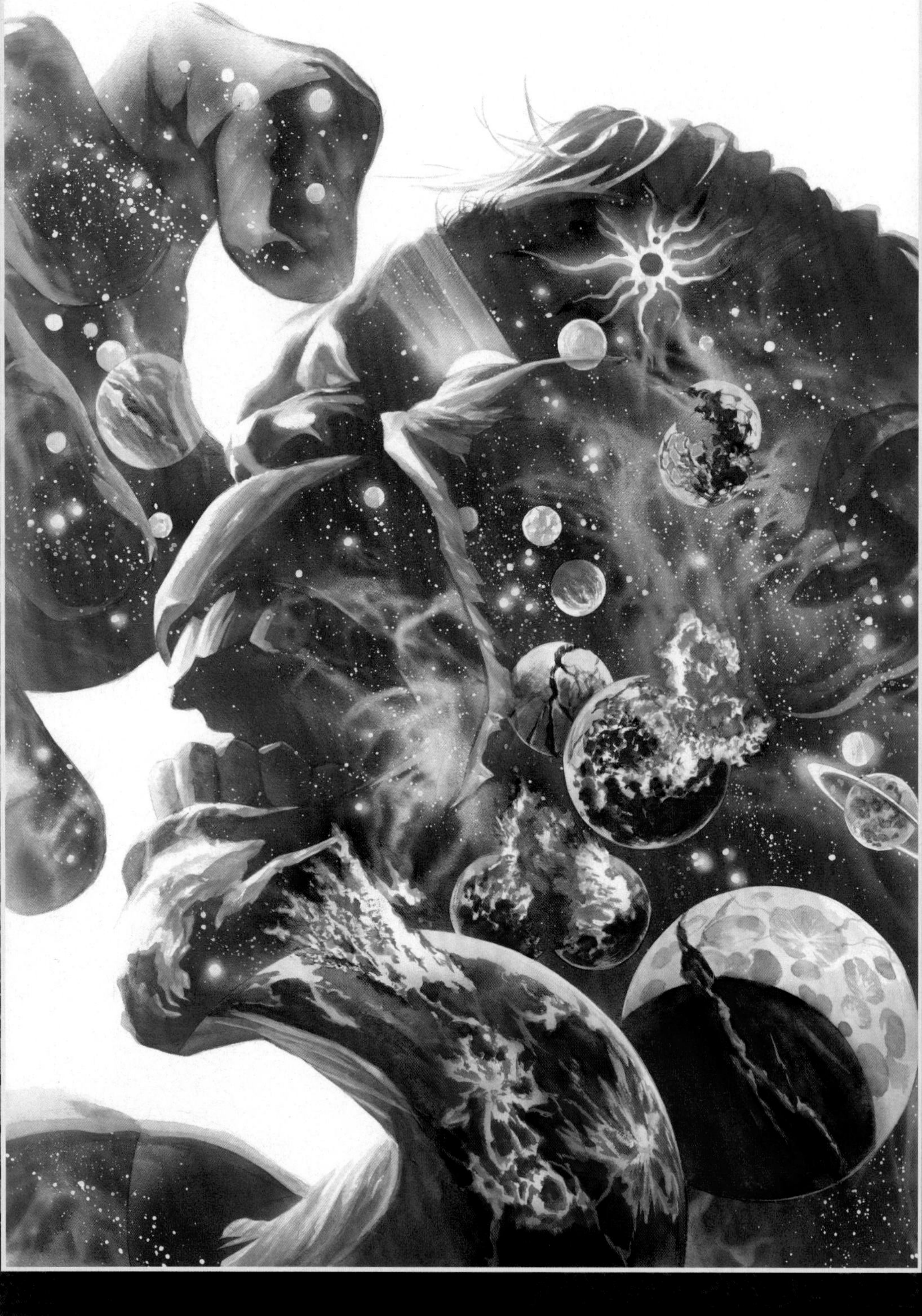

"IT IS A FEARFUL THING TO FALL INTO THE HANDS OF THE LIVING GOD."

- *HEBREWS 10:31*

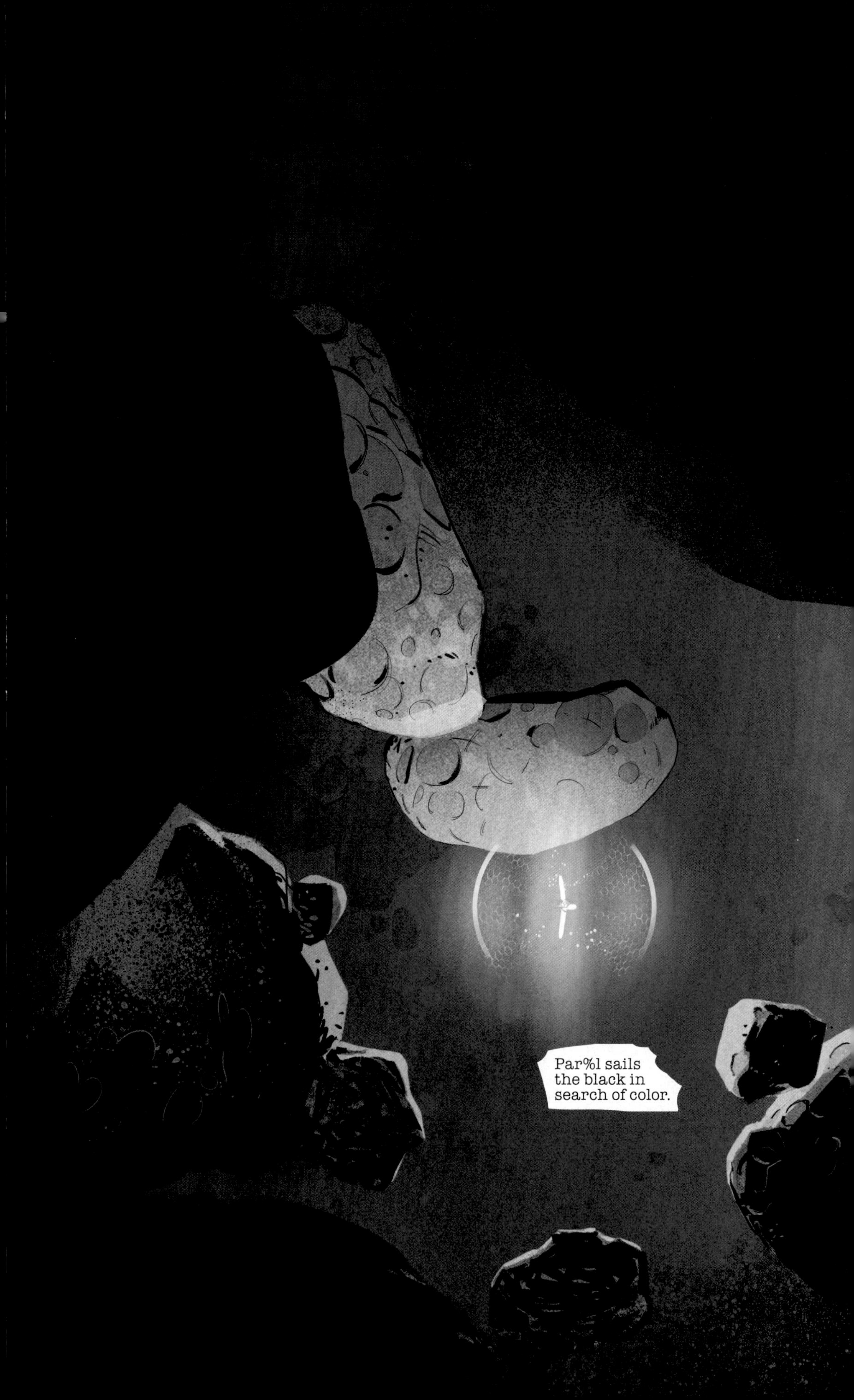
Par%l sails the black in search of color.

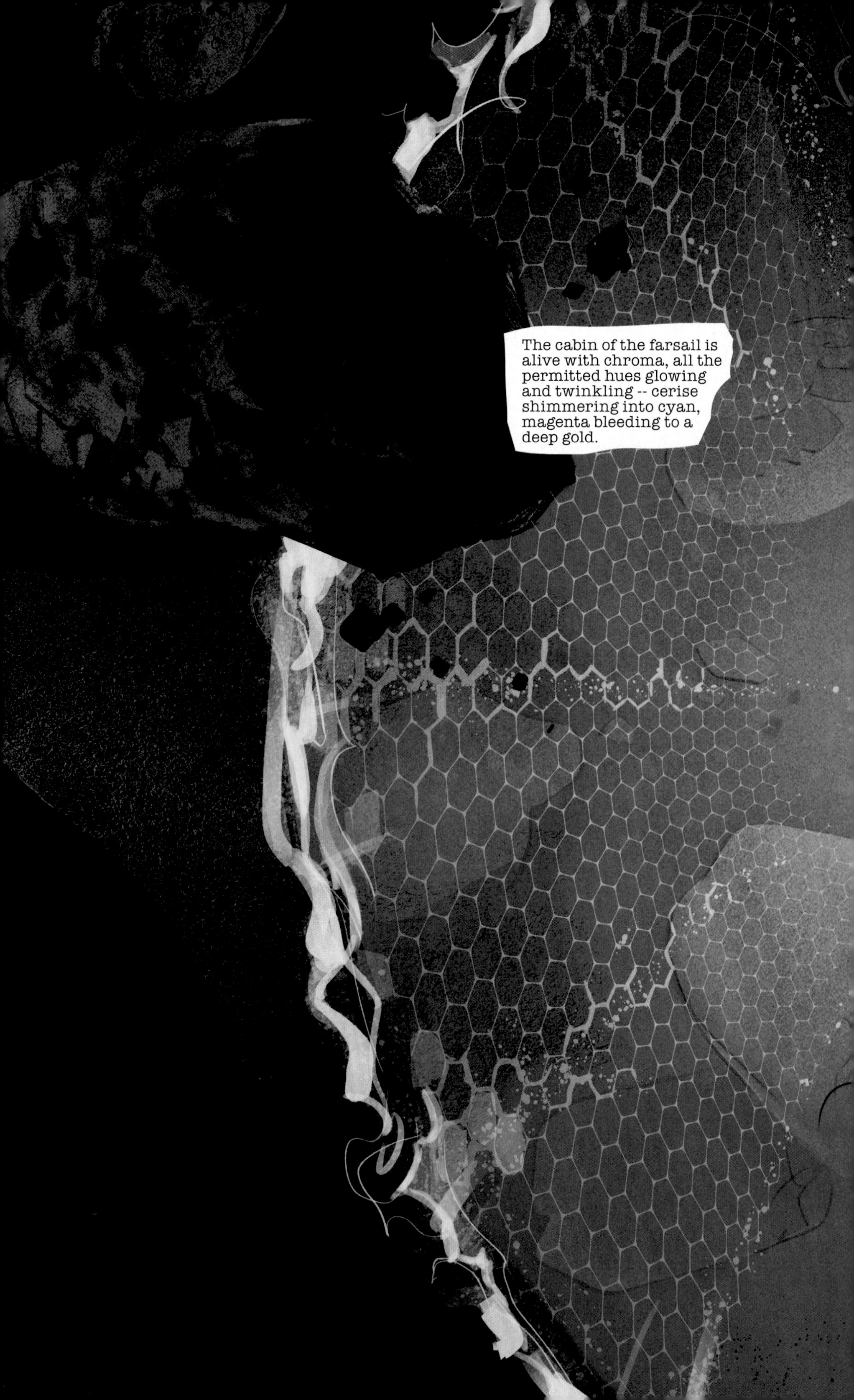
The cabin of the farsail is alive with chroma, all the permitted hues glowing and twinkling -- cerise shimmering into cyan, magenta bleeding to a deep gold.

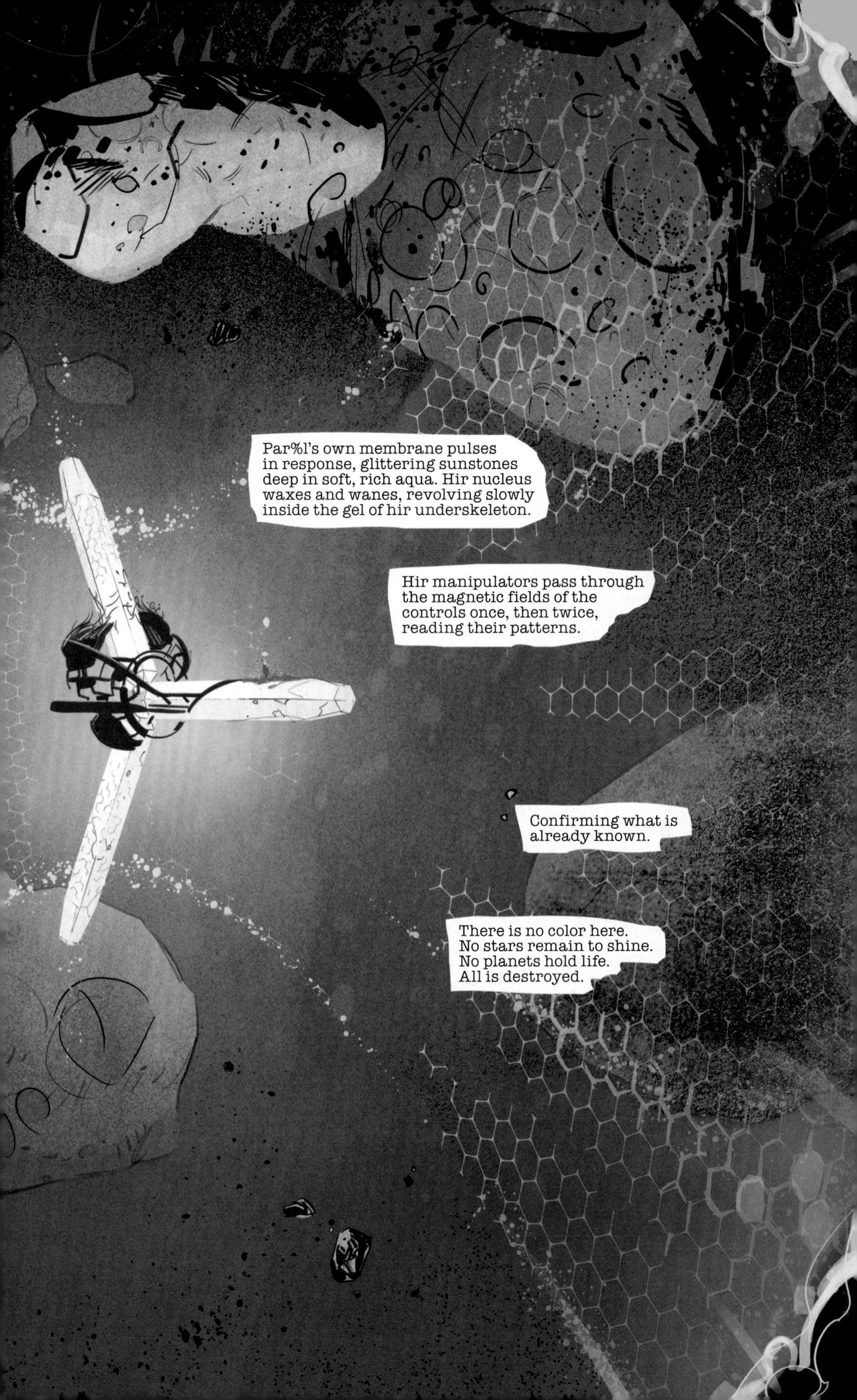
Par%l's own membrane pulses in response, glittering sunstones deep in soft, rich aqua. Hir nucleus waxes and wanes, revolving slowly inside the gel of hir underskeleton.
Hir manipulators pass through the magnetic fields of the controls once, then twice, reading their patterns.
Confirming what is already known.
There is no color here. No stars remain to shine. No planets hold life. All is destroyed.

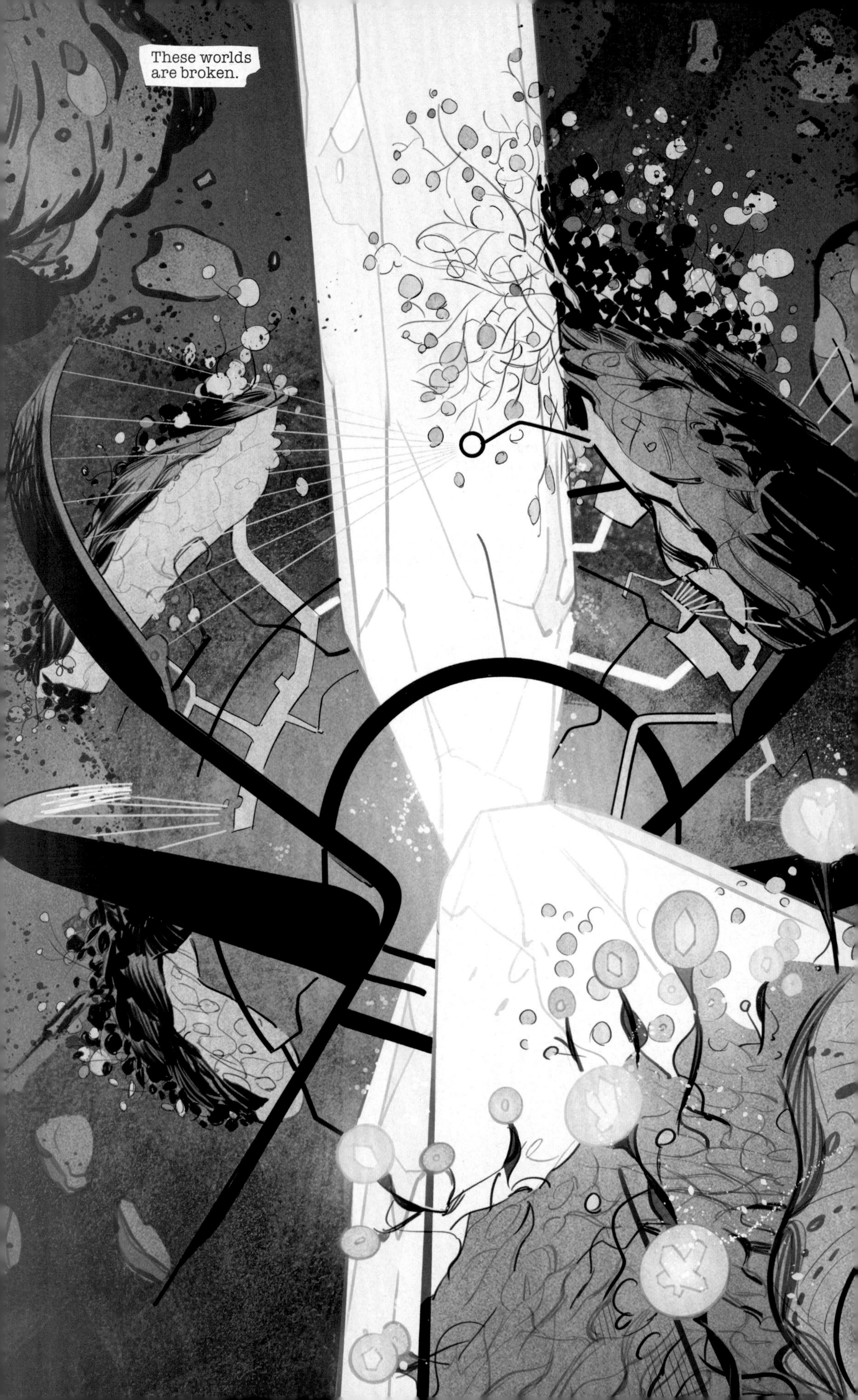
These worlds are broken.

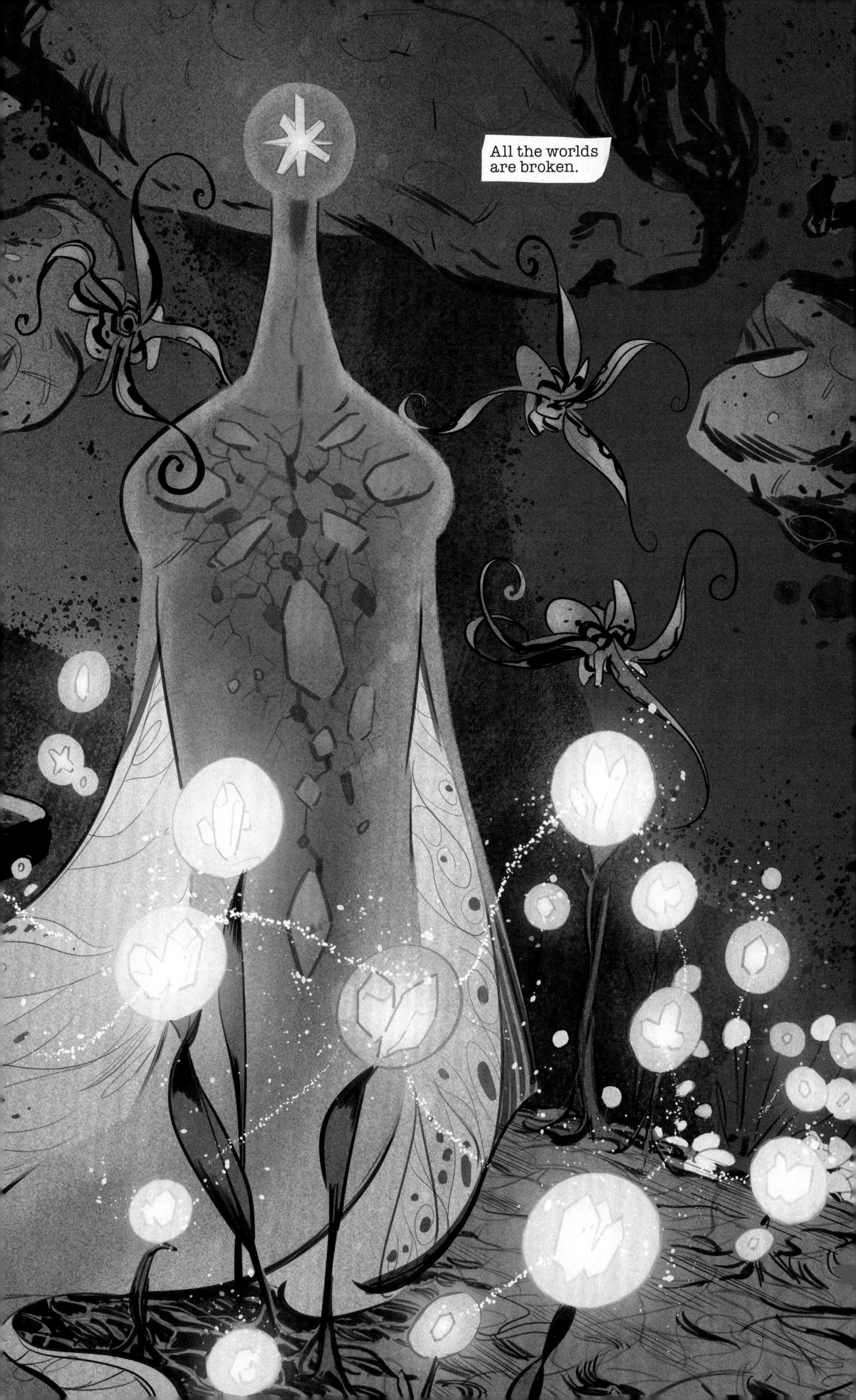
All the worlds are broken.

"It is a fearful thing to fall into the hands of the living god."

– HEBREWS 10:31

Once, the Observer's Berth tacked to the starlight, intricate pseudo-minds choreographing its motions as it danced through the orbits of planets.

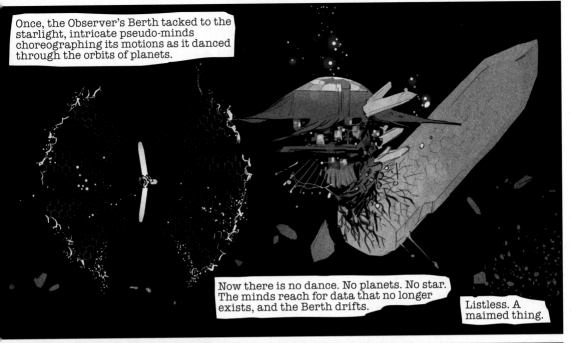

Now there is no dance. No planets. No star. The minds reach for data that no longer exists, and the Berth drifts.

Listless. A maimed thing.

It makes docking easier, but still, Par%l is careful. Should the lamina suffer damage during the linking process, there can be no repair.

Not anymore.

Par%l telepathically summons hir manipulators, carefully arranging them in the configuration for polite greeting to a superior.

The etiquette is very important.

It is all they have left.

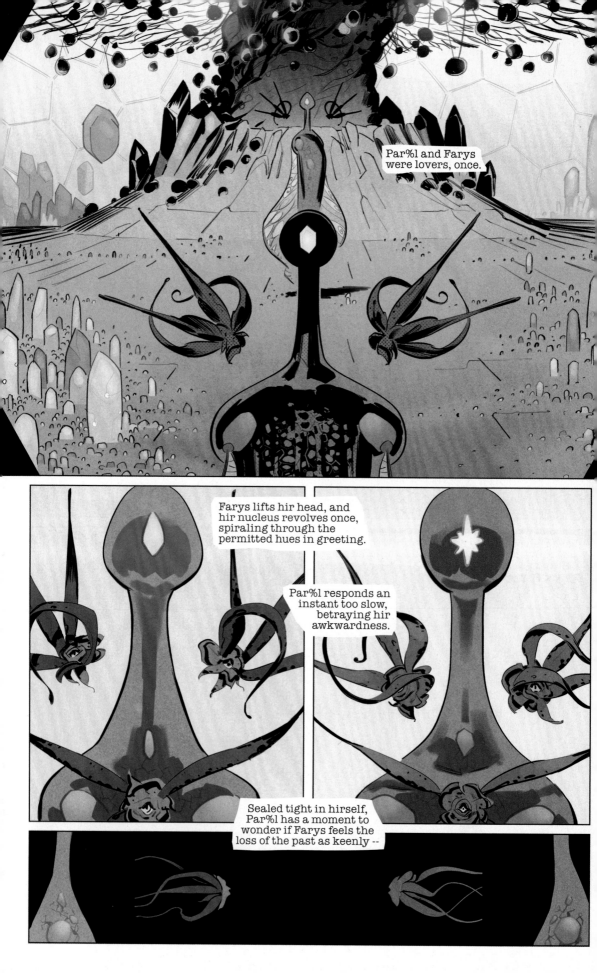

Par%l and Farys
were lovers, once.

Farys lifts hir head, and
hir nucleus revolves once,
spiraling through the
permitted hues in greeting.

Par%l responds an
instant too slow,
betraying hir
awkwardness.

Sealed tight in hirself,
Par%l has a moment to
wonder if Farys feels the
loss of the past as keenly --

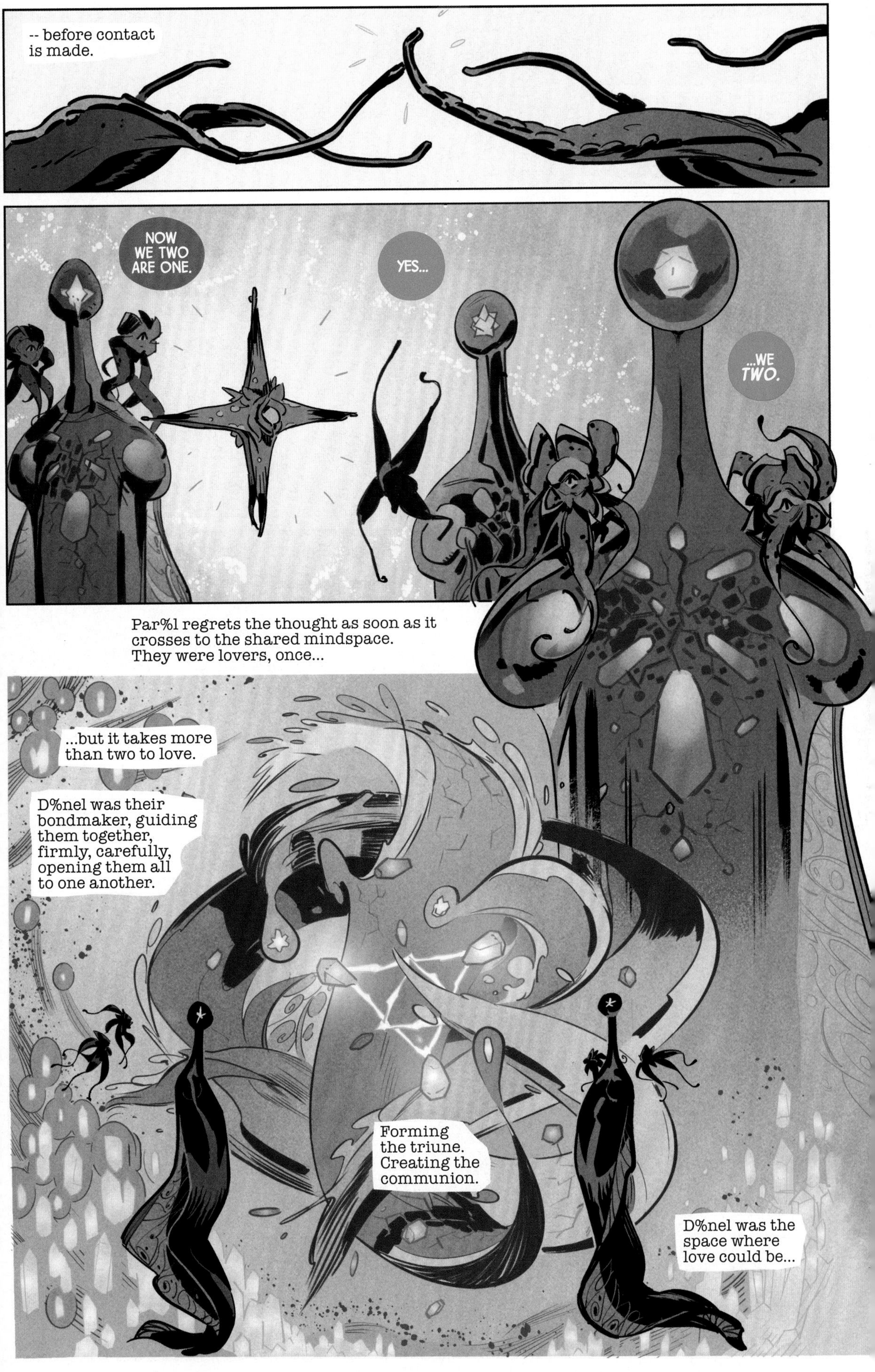
-- before contact
is made.
NOW WE TWO ARE ONE.
YES...
...WE TWO.
Par%l regrets the thought as soon as it
crosses to the shared mindspace.
They were lovers, once...
...but it takes more
than two to love.
D%nel was their
bondmaker, guiding
them together,
firmly, carefully,
opening them all
to one another.
Forming
the triune.
Creating the
communion.
D%nel was the
space where
love could be...

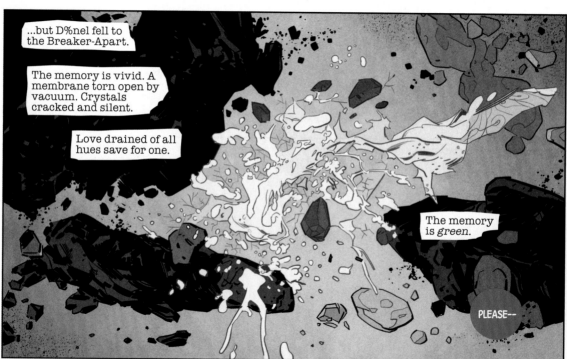

...but D%nel fell to the Breaker-Apart.

The memory is vivid. A membrane torn open by vacuum. Crystals cracked and silent.

Love drained of all hues save for one.

The memory is *green*.

PLEASE--

PLEASE. MY *OWN* PAIN IS TOO MUCH AS IT IS.

WE MUST THINK OF OUR *DUTIES*...

Par%l shrinks from the reflected sorrow. Regret becomes shame.

YES... OUR DUTIES.

WHAT HAVE YOU OBSERVED OUT HERE? I KNOW WE CAN'T GET CLOSE TO IT, BUT...DID YOU *SEE* IT?

IS THERE... CAN THE CREATURE BE *STOPPED?*

NO, PAR%L. NO, IT CANNOT BE STOPPED.

IT WILL NEVER STOP MAKING US *PAY.*

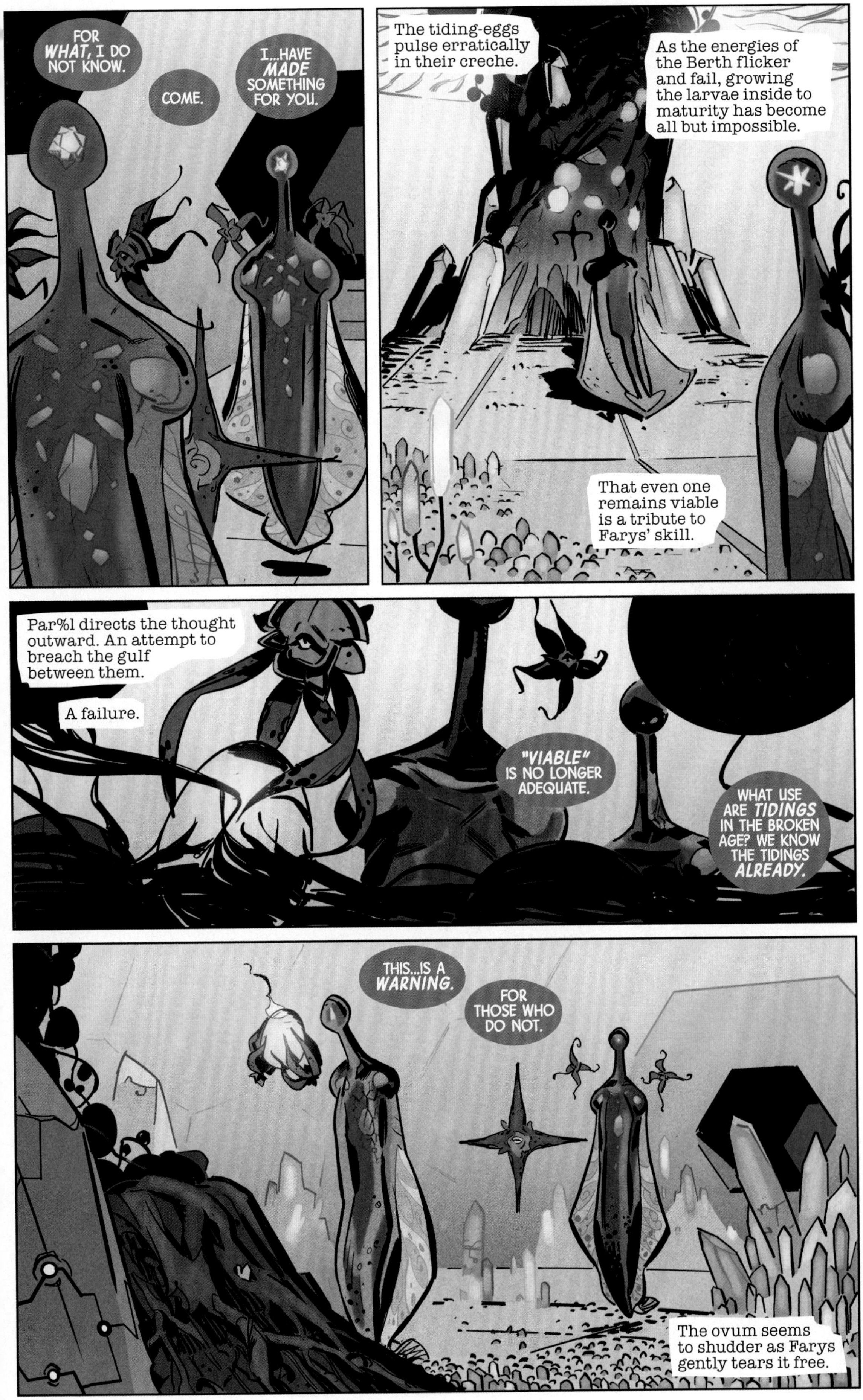
FOR WHAT, I DO NOT KNOW.
COME.
I...HAVE MADE SOMETHING FOR YOU.
The tiding-eggs pulse erratically in their creche.
As the energies of the Berth flicker and fail, growing the larvae inside to maturity has become all but impossible.
That even one remains viable is a tribute to Farys' skill.
Par%l directs the thought outward. An attempt to breach the gulf between them.
A failure.
"VIABLE" IS NO LONGER ADEQUATE.
WHAT USE ARE TIDINGS IN THE BROKEN AGE? WE KNOW THE TIDINGS ALREADY.
THIS...IS A WARNING.
FOR THOSE WHO DO NOT.
The ovum seems to shudder as Farys gently tears it free.

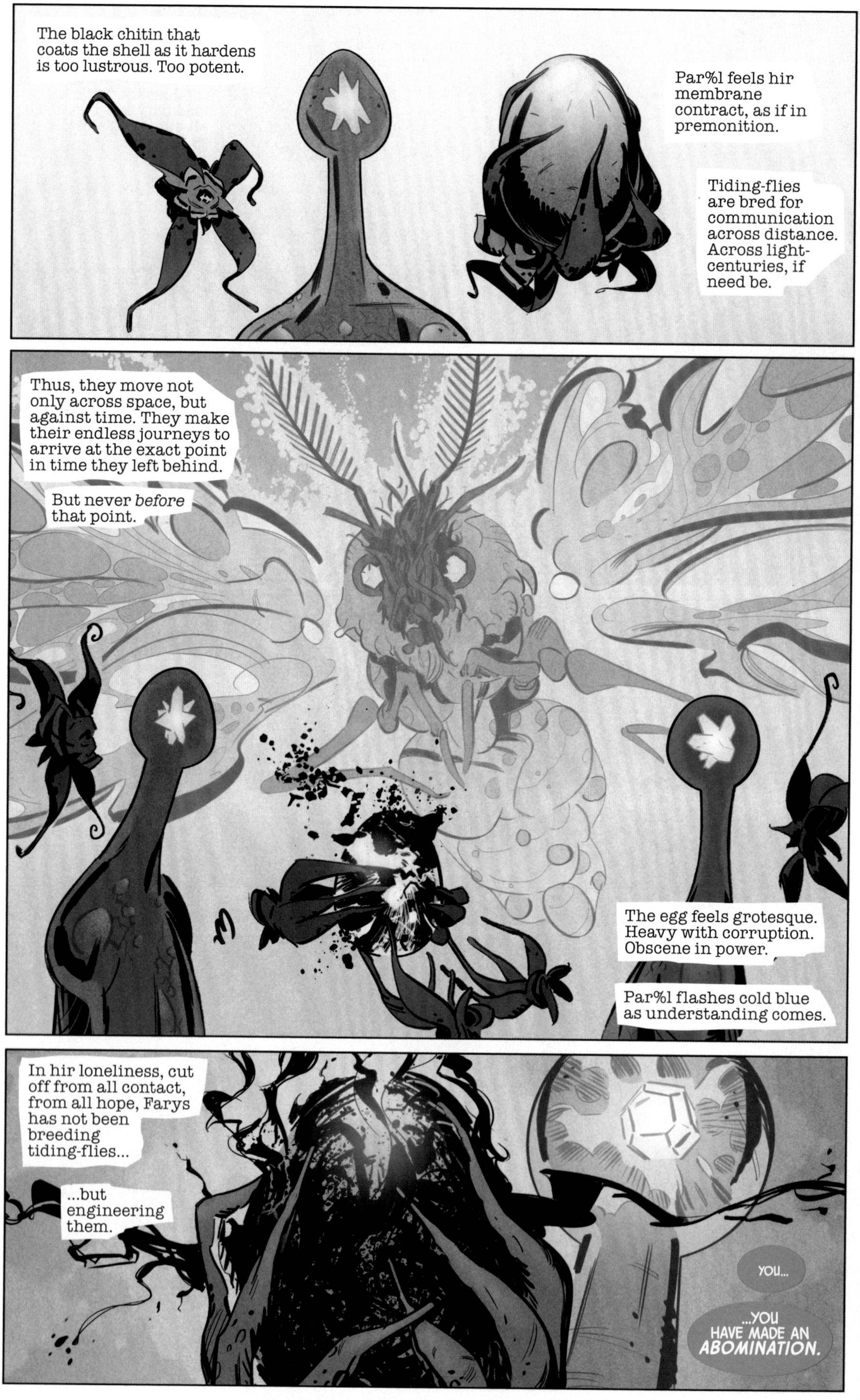
The black chitin that coats the shell as it hardens is too lustrous. Too potent.
Par%l feels hir membrane contract, as if in premonition.
Tiding-flies are bred for communication across distance. Across light-centuries, if need be.
Thus, they move not only across space, but against time. They make their endless journeys to arrive at the exact point in time they left behind.
But never *before* that point.
The egg feels grotesque. Heavy with corruption. Obscene in power.
Par%l flashes cold blue as understanding comes.
In hir loneliness, cut off from all contact, from all hope, Farys has not been breeding tiding-flies...
...but engineering them.
YOU...
...YOU HAVE MADE AN *ABOMINATION.*

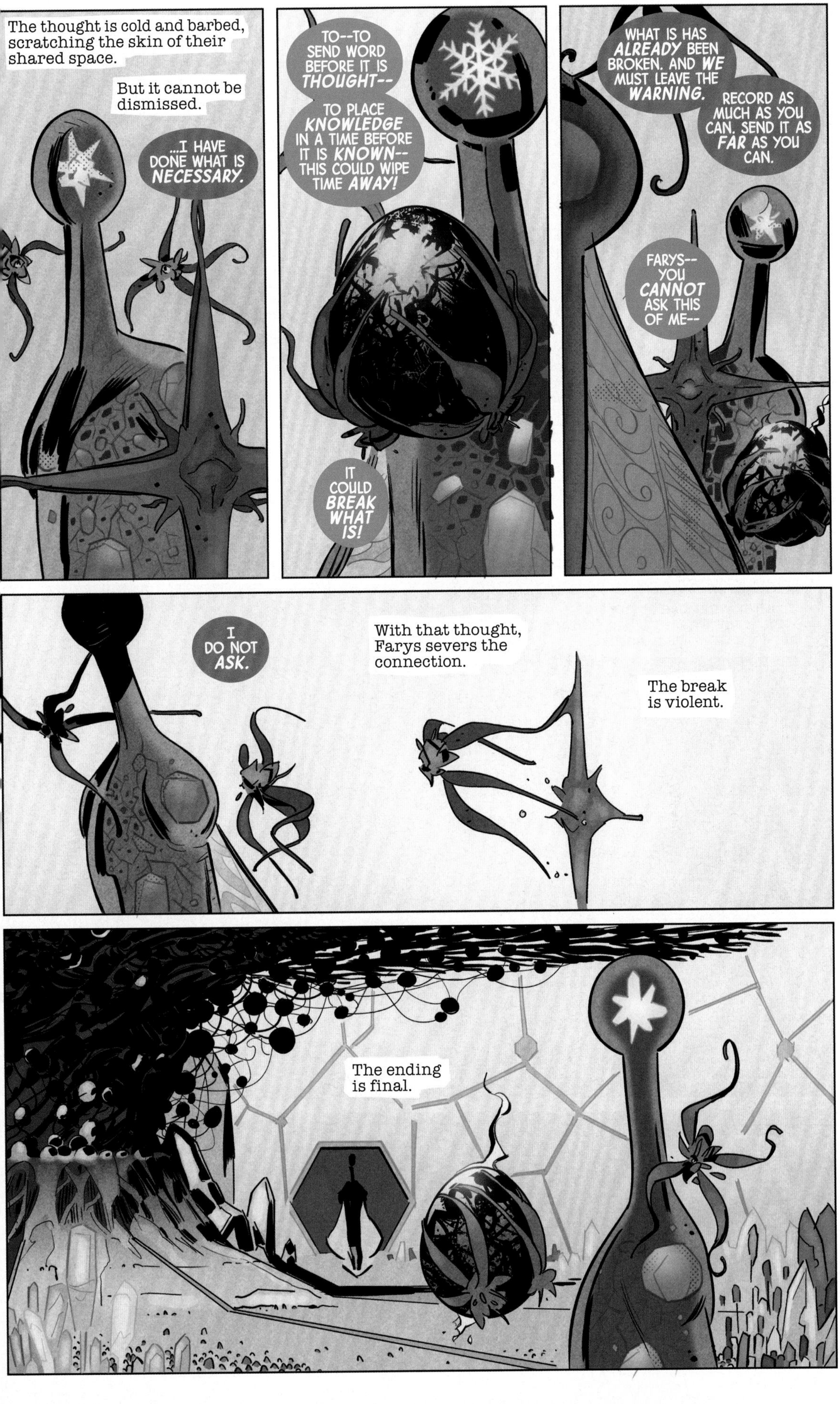
The thought is cold and barbed, scratching the skin of their shared space.
But it cannot be dismissed.
...I HAVE DONE WHAT IS NECESSARY.
TO--TO SEND WORD BEFORE IT IS THOUGHT--
TO PLACE KNOWLEDGE IN A TIME BEFORE IT IS KNOWN-- THIS COULD WIPE TIME AWAY!
IT COULD BREAK WHAT IS!
WHAT IS HAS ALREADY BEEN BROKEN. AND WE MUST LEAVE THE WARNING.
RECORD AS MUCH AS YOU CAN. SEND IT AS FAR AS YOU CAN.
FARYS-- YOU CANNOT ASK THIS OF ME--
I DO NOT ASK.
With that thought, Farys severs the connection.
The break is violent.
The ending is final.

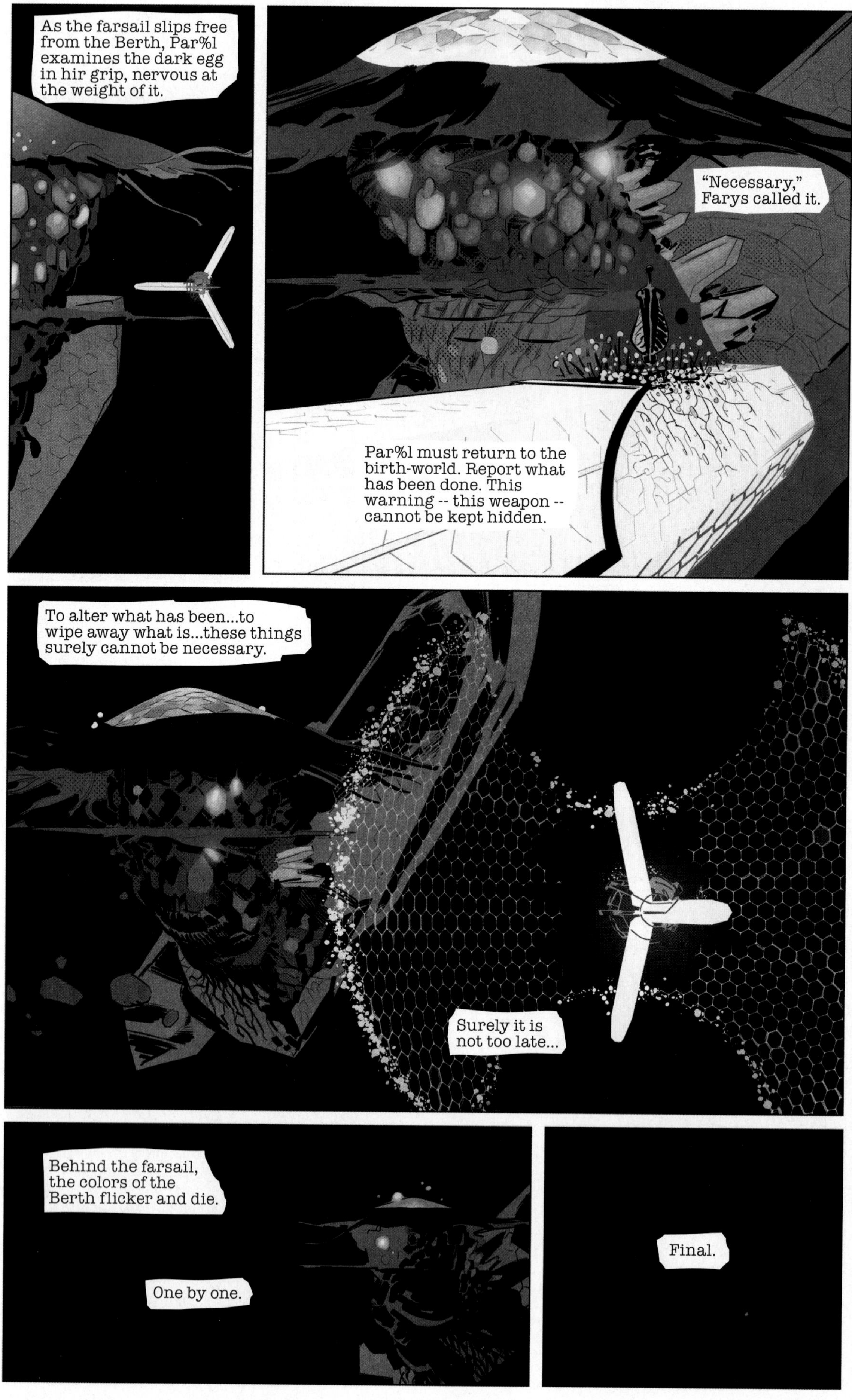
As the farsail slips free from the Berth, Par%l examines the dark egg in hir grip, nervous at the weight of it.
"Necessary," Farys called it.
Par%l must return to the birth-world. Report what has been done. This warning -- this weapon -- cannot be kept hidden.
To alter what has been...to wipe away what is...these things surely cannot be necessary.
Surely it is not too late...
Behind the farsail, the colors of the Berth flicker and die.
One by one.
Final.

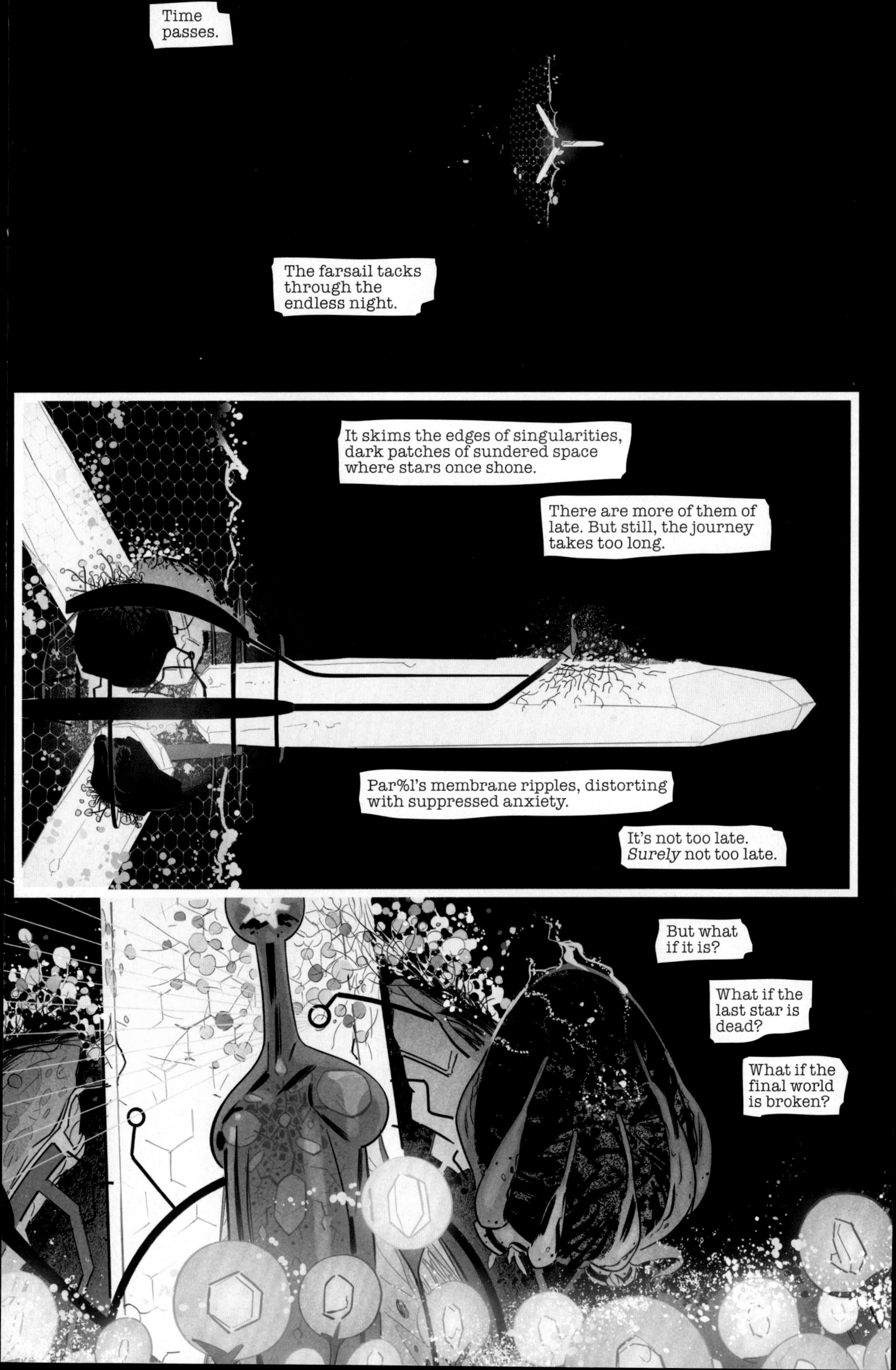
Time passes.
The farsail tacks through the endless night.
It skims the edges of singularities, dark patches of sundered space where stars once shone.
There are more of them of late. But still, the journey takes too long.
Par%l's membrane ripples, distorting with suppressed anxiety.
It's not too late. *Surely* not too late.
But what if it is?
What if the last star is dead?
What if the final world is broken?

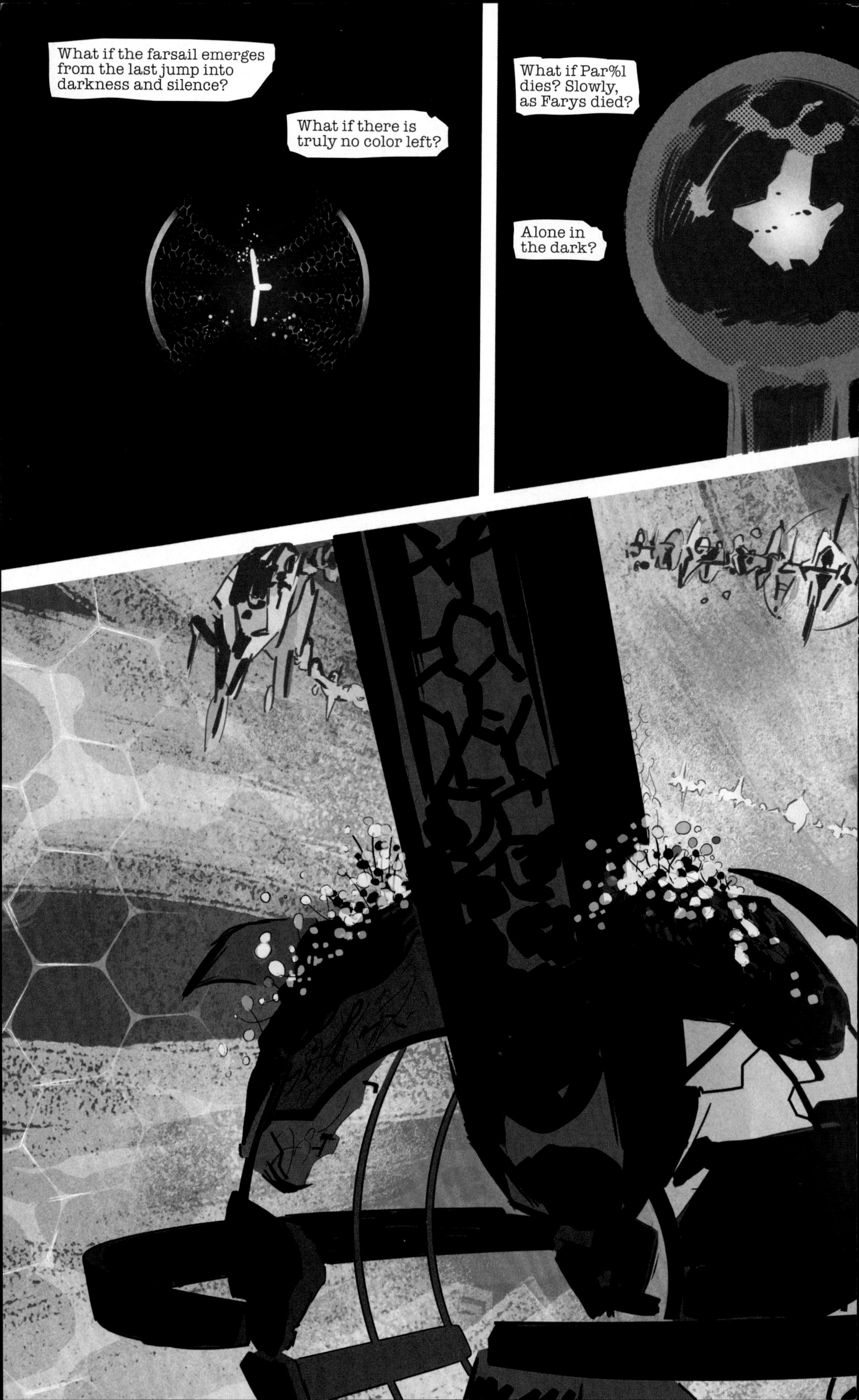
What if the farsail emerges from the last jump into darkness and silence?
What if there is truly no color left?
What if Par%l dies? Slowly, as Farys died?
Alone in the dark?

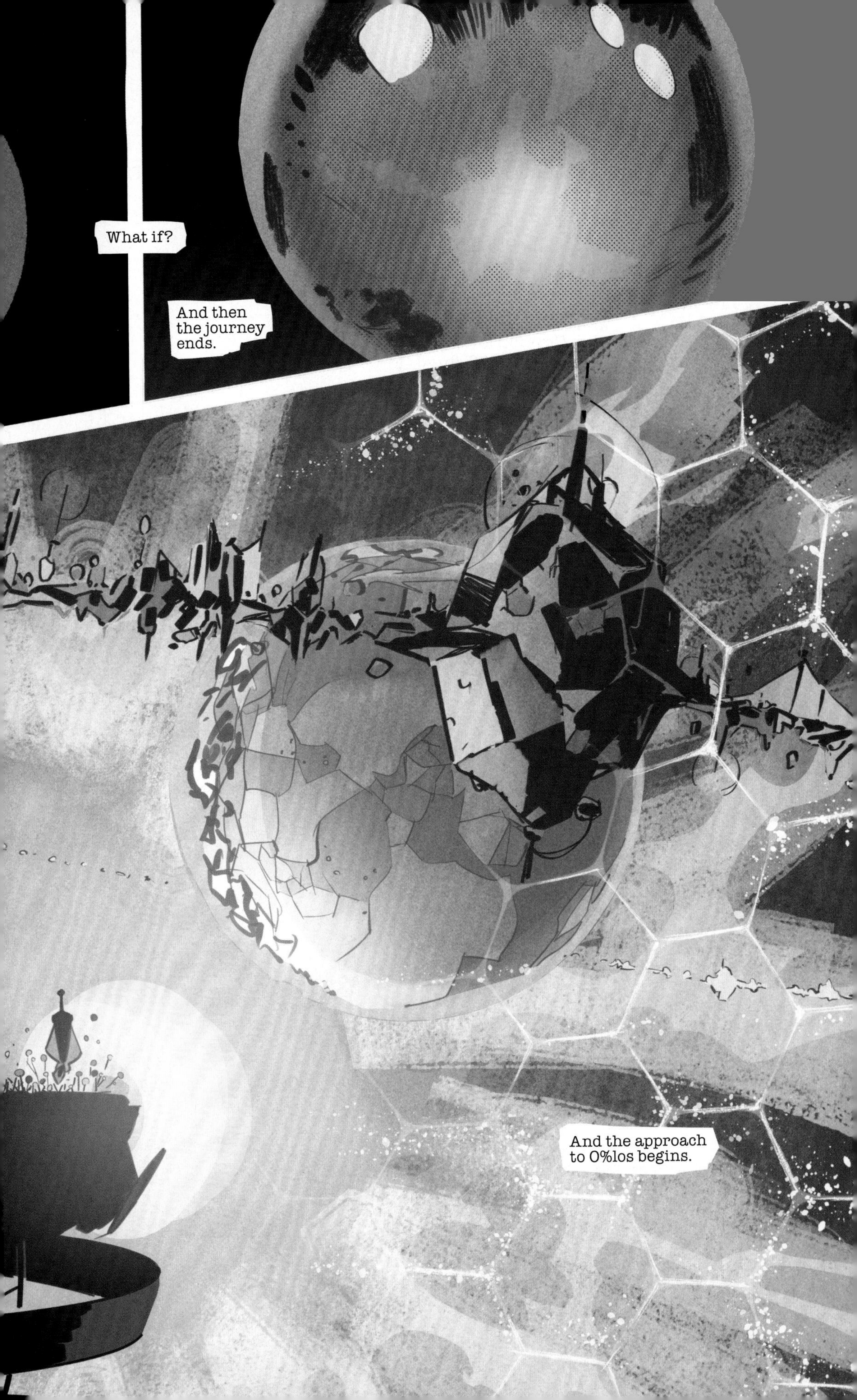
What if?
And then the journey ends.
And the approach to O%los begins.

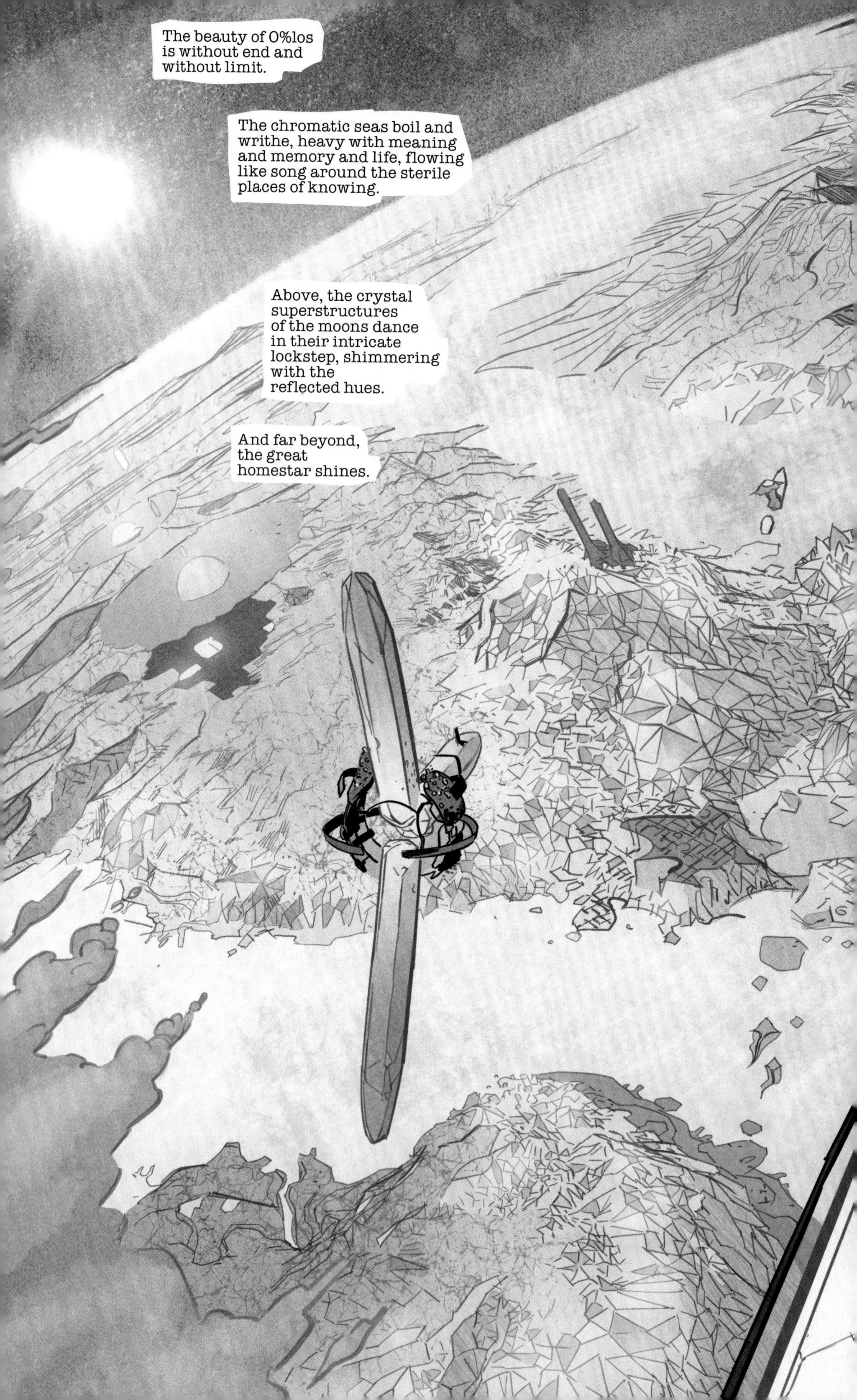
The beauty of O%los is without end and without limit.
The chromatic seas boil and writhe, heavy with meaning and memory and life, flowing like song around the sterile places of knowing.
Above, the crystal superstructures of the moons dance in their intricate lockstep, shimmering with the reflected hues.
And far beyond, the great homestar shines.

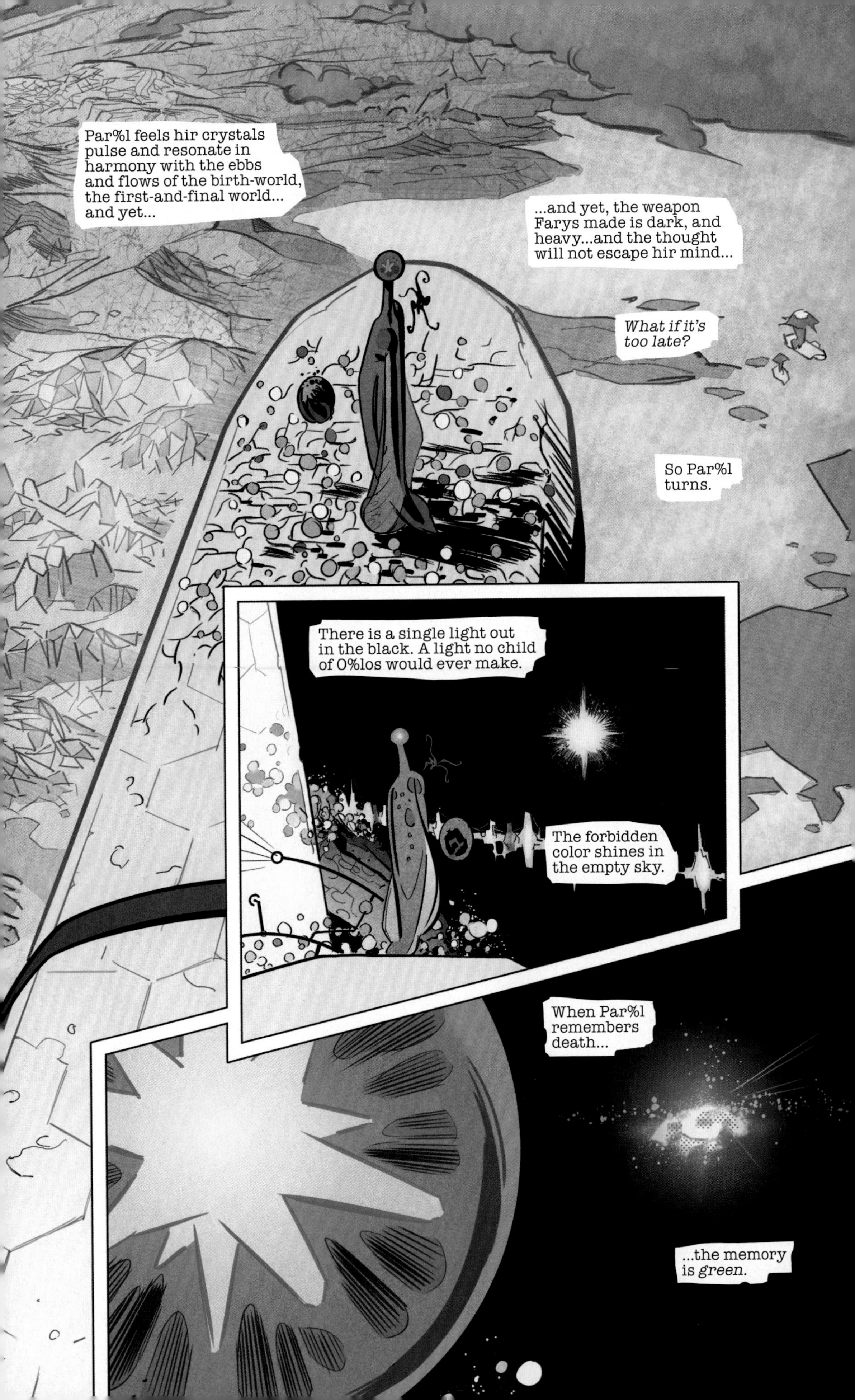
Par%l feels hir crystals pulse and resonate in harmony with the ebbs and flows of the birth-world, the first-and-final world... and yet...
...and yet, the weapon Farys made is dark, and heavy...and the thought will not escape hir mind...
What if it's too late?
So Par%l turns.
There is a single light out in the black. A light no child of O%los would ever make.
The forbidden color shines in the empty sky.
When Par%l remembers death...
...the memory is *green*.

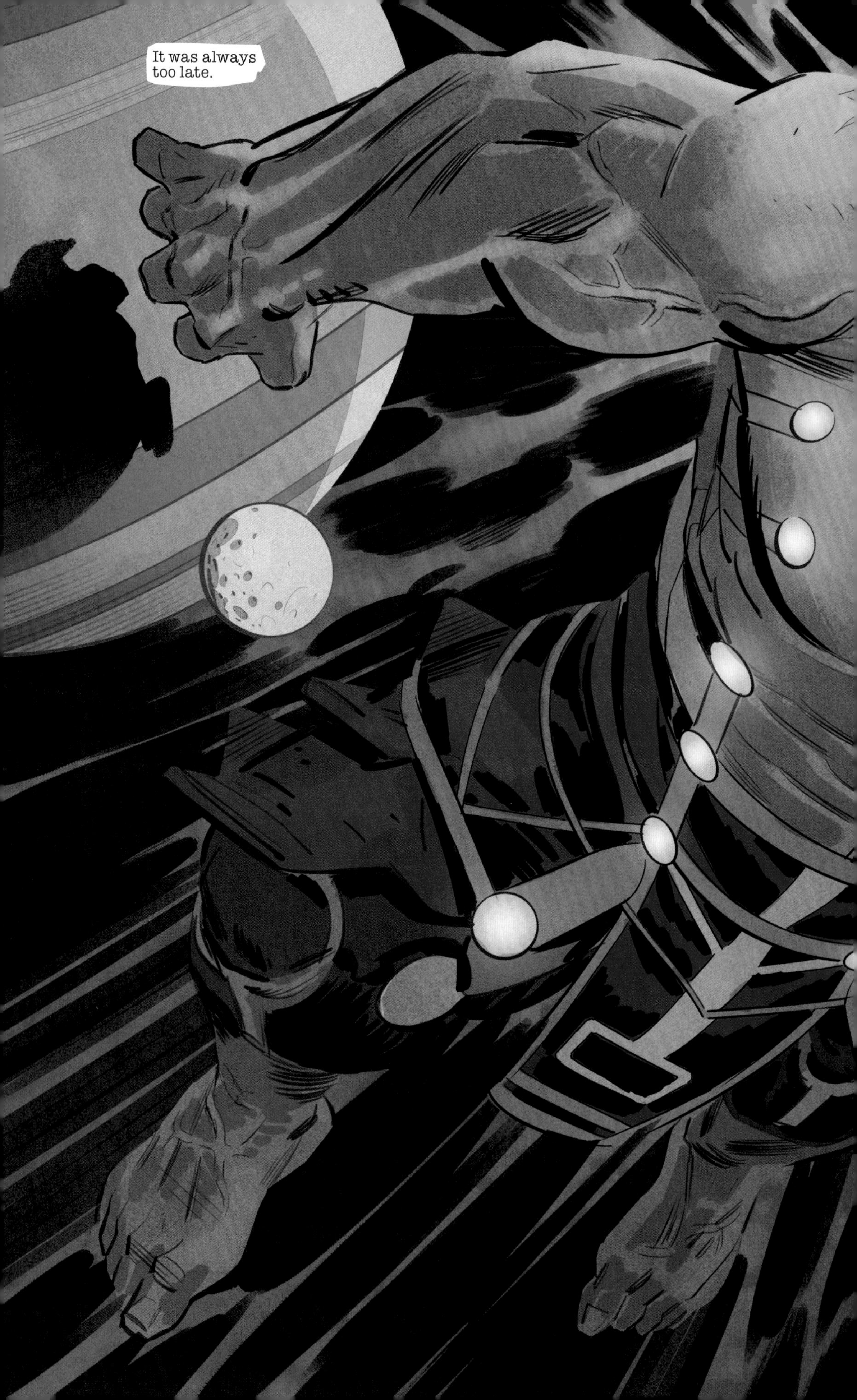
It was always too late.

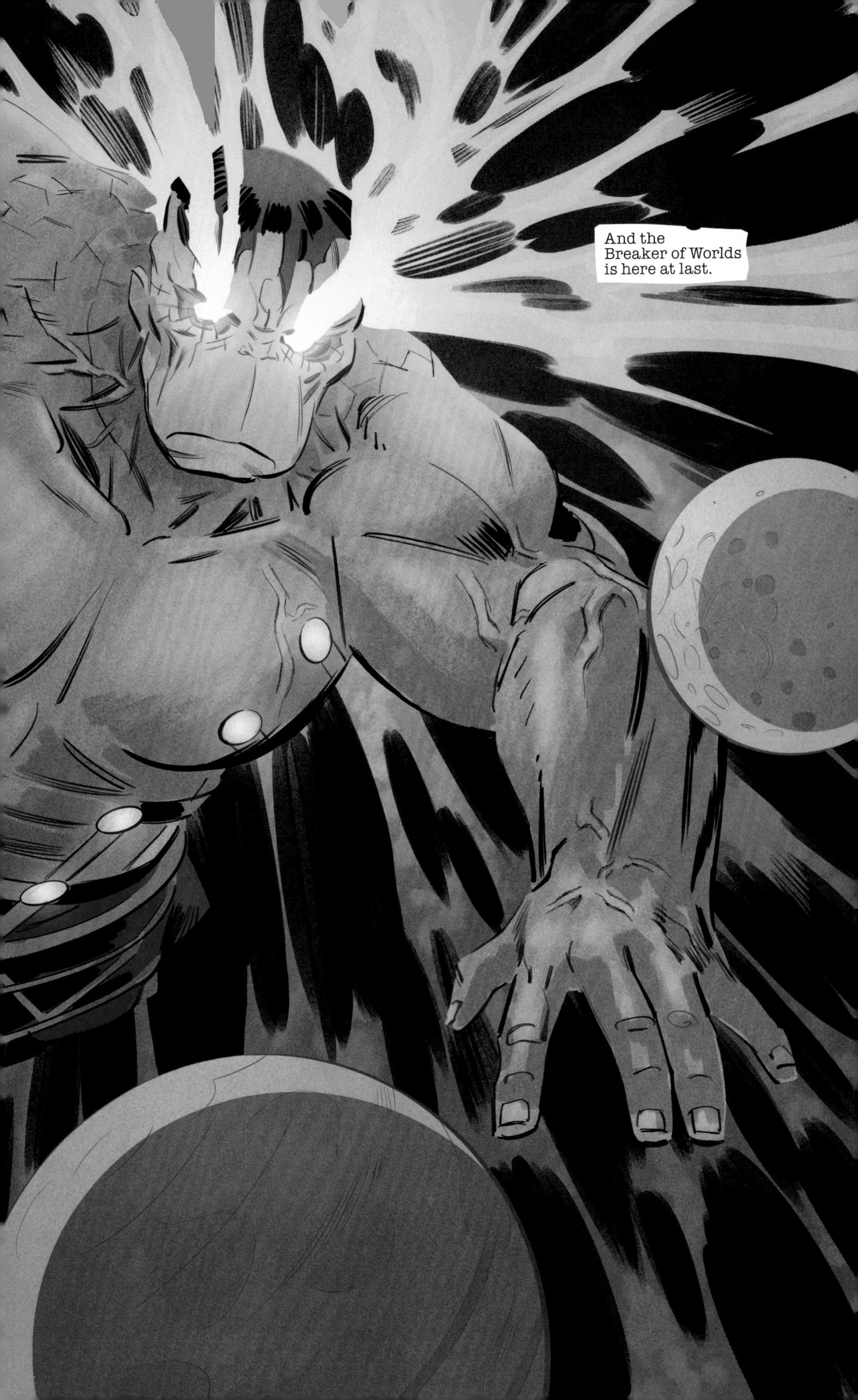
And the Breaker of Worlds is here at last.

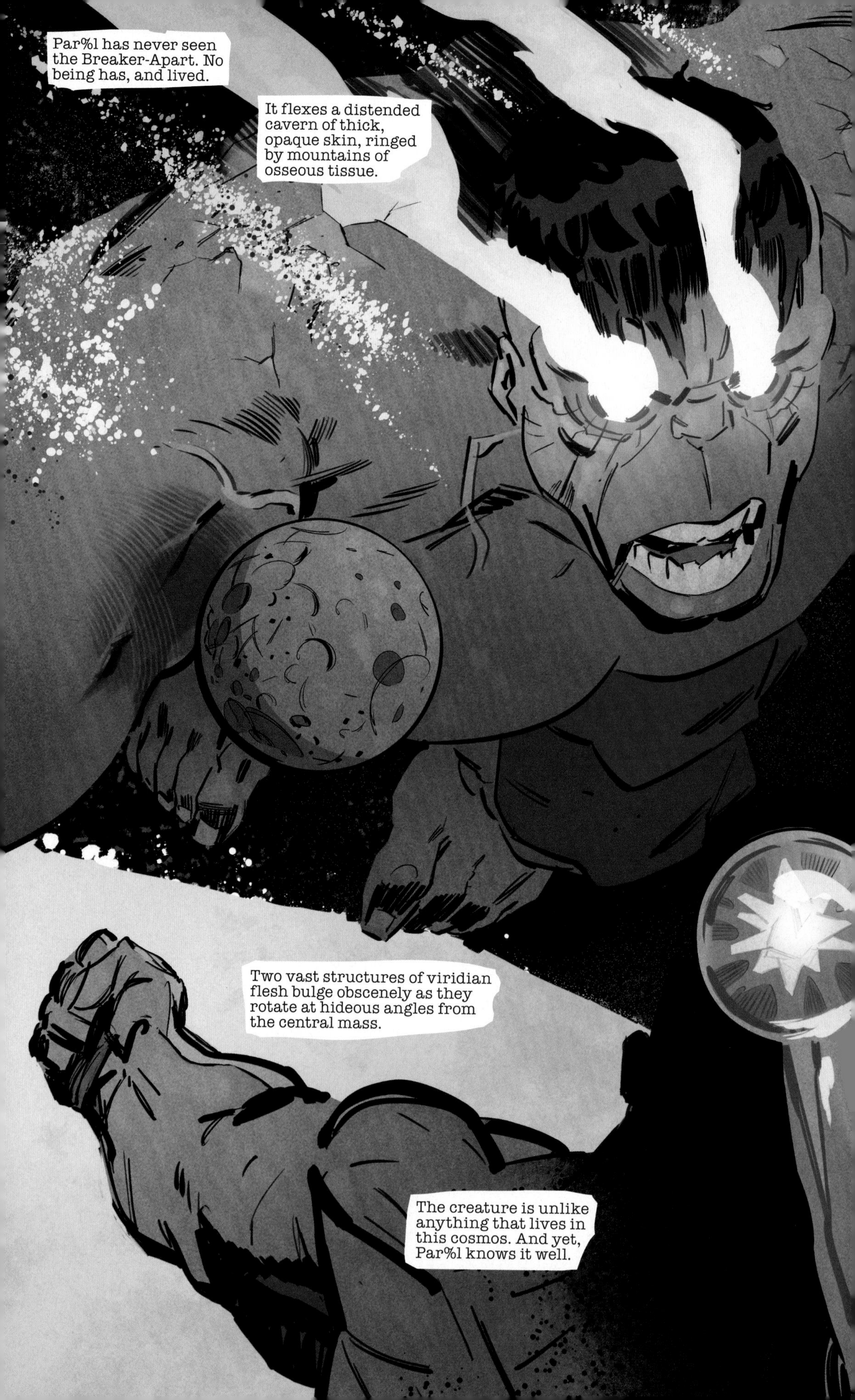
Par%l has never seen the Breaker-Apart. No being has, and lived.
It flexes a distended cavern of thick, opaque skin, ringed by mountains of osseous tissue.
Two vast structures of viridian flesh bulge obscenely as they rotate at hideous angles from the central mass.
The creature is unlike anything that lives in this cosmos. And yet, Par%l knows it well.

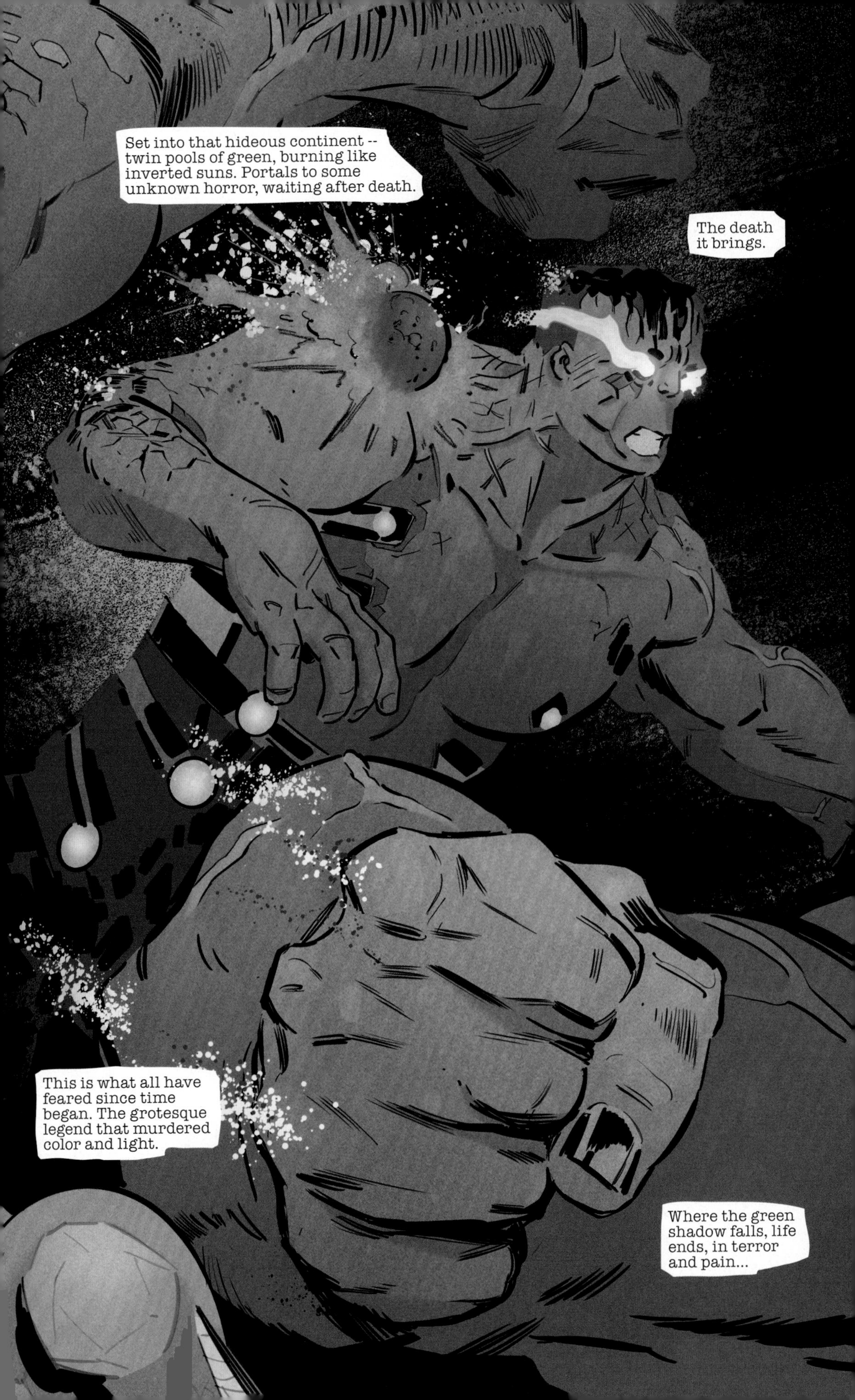
Set into that hideous continent -- twin pools of green, burning like inverted suns. Portals to some unknown horror, waiting after death.
The death it brings.
This is what all have feared since time began. The grotesque legend that murdered color and light.
Where the green shadow falls, life ends, in terror and pain...

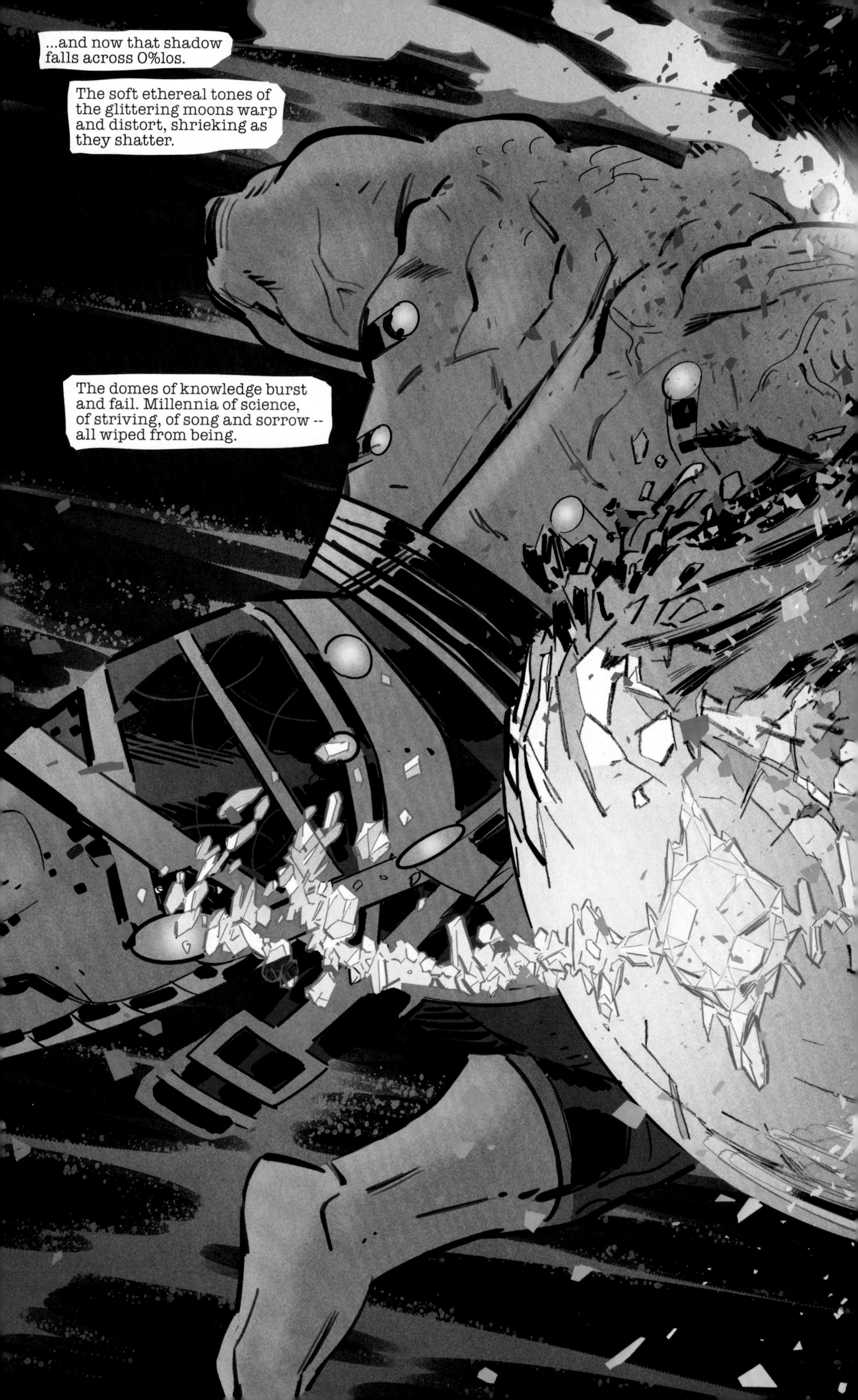
...and now that shadow falls across O%los.
The soft ethereal tones of the glittering moons warp and distort, shrieking as they shatter.
The domes of knowledge burst and fail. Millennia of science, of striving, of song and sorrow -- all wiped from being.

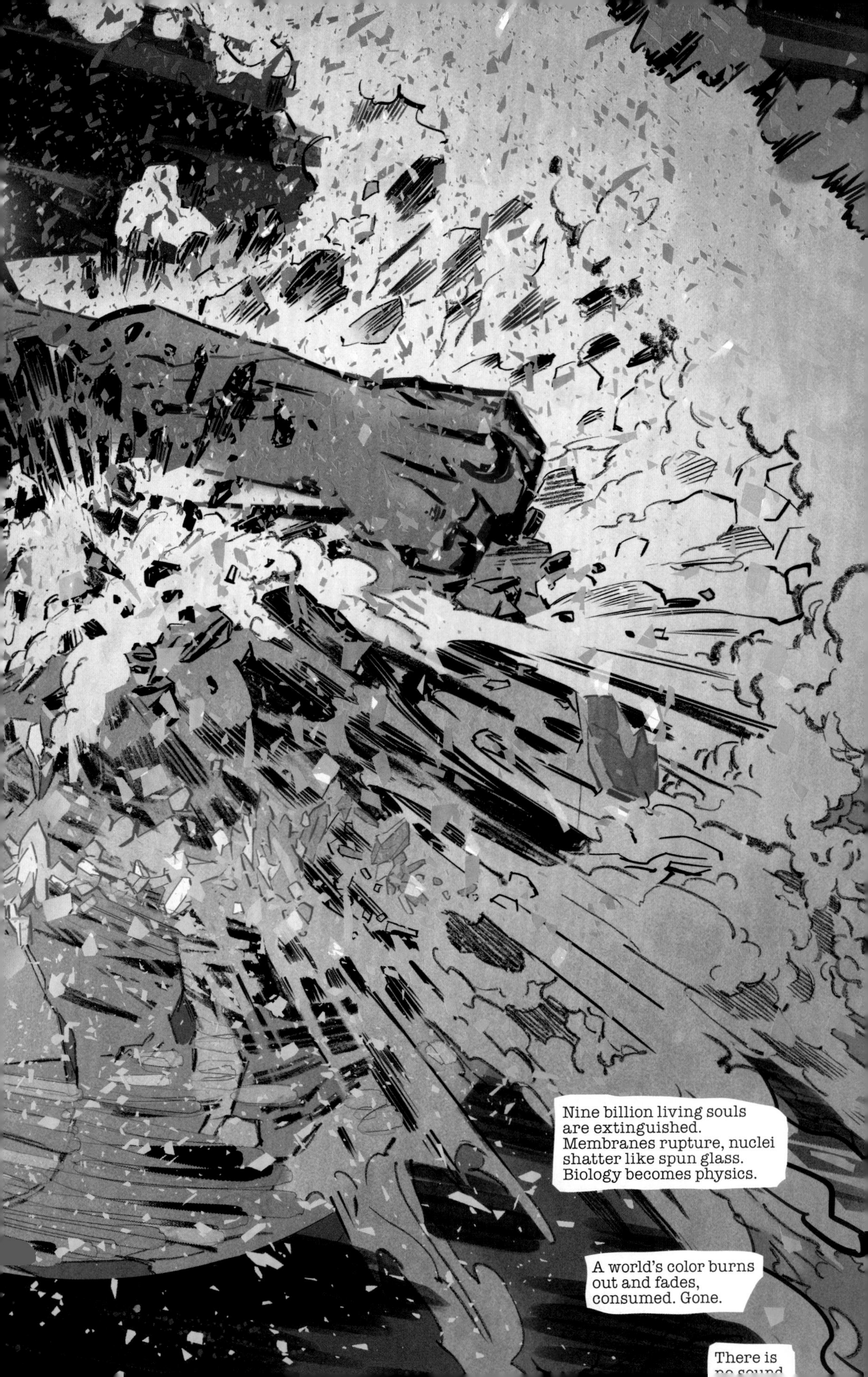
Nine billion living souls are extinguished. Membranes rupture, nuclei shatter like spun glass. Biology becomes physics.
A world's color burns out and fades, consumed. Gone.
There is

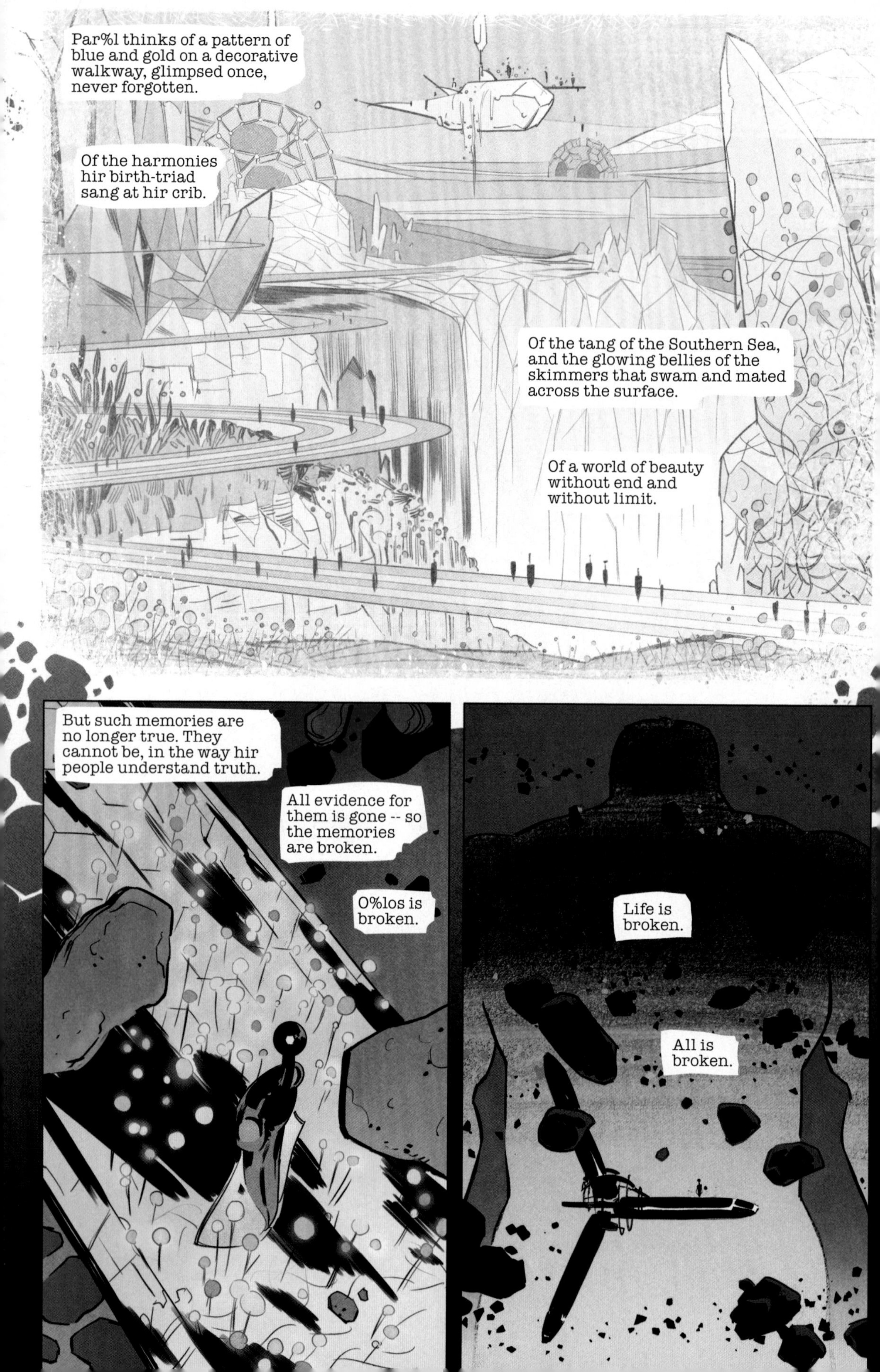

Par%l thinks of a pattern of blue and gold on a decorative walkway, glimpsed once, never forgotten.
Of the harmonies hir birth-triad sang at hir crib.
Of the tang of the Southern Sea, and the glowing bellies of the skimmers that swam and mated across the surface.
Of a world of beauty without end and without limit.
But such memories are no longer true. They cannot be, in the way hir people understand truth.
All evidence for them is gone -- so the memories are broken.
O%los is broken.
Life is broken.
All is broken.

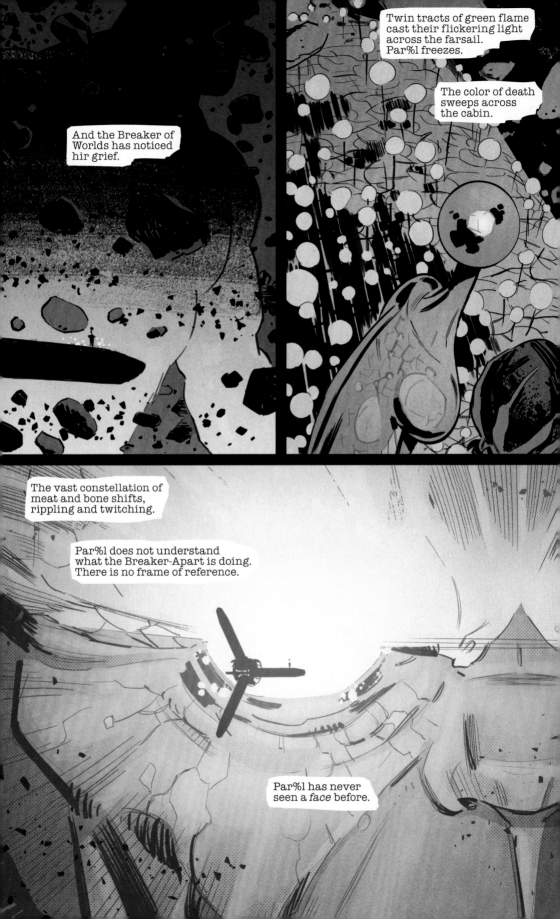

Twin tracts of green flame
cast their flickering light
across the farsail.
Par%l freezes.

The color of death
sweeps across
the cabin.

And the Breaker of
Worlds has noticed
hir grief.

The vast constellation of
meat and bone shifts,
rippling and twitching.

Par%l does not understand
what the Breaker-Apart is doing.
There is no frame of reference.

Par%l has never
seen a *face* before.

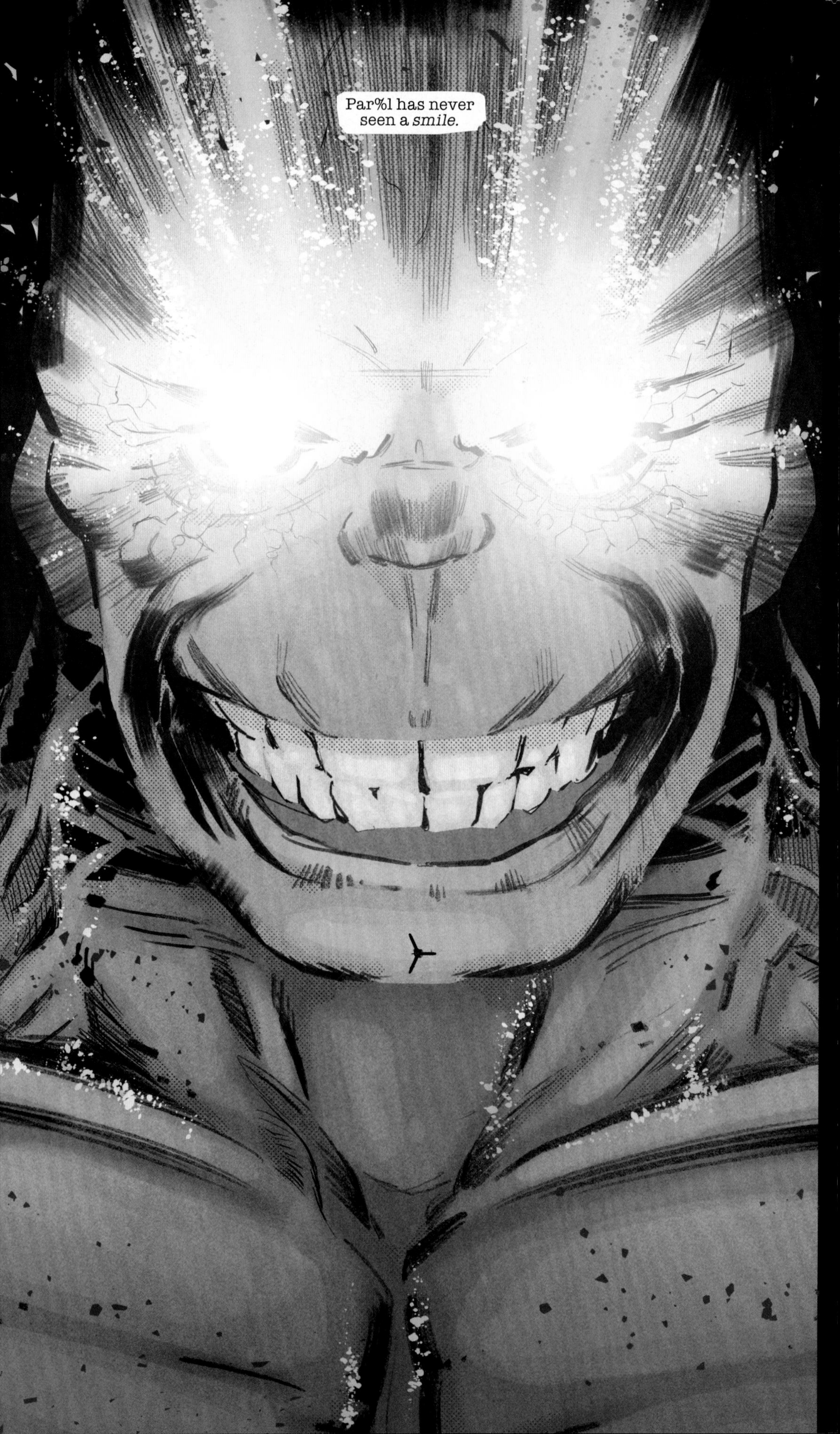
Par%l has never seen a *smile.*

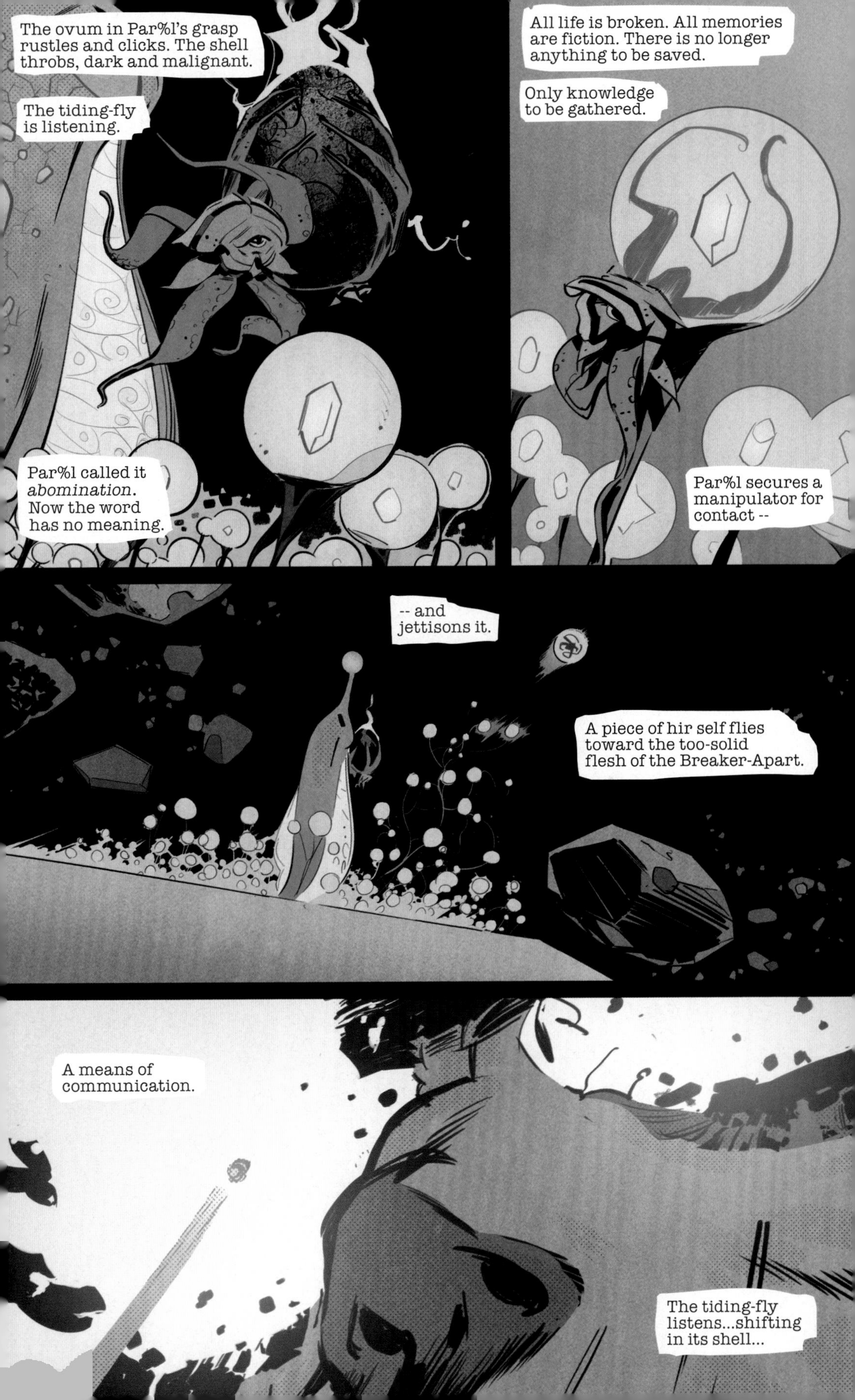
The ovum in Par%l's grasp rustles and clicks. The shell throbs, dark and malignant.
The tiding-fly is listening.
Par%l called it *abomination*. Now the word has no meaning.
All life is broken. All memories are fiction. There is no longer anything to be saved.
Only knowledge to be gathered.
Par%l secures a manipulator for contact --
-- and jettisons it.
A piece of hir self flies toward the too-solid flesh of the Breaker-Apart.
A means of communication.
The tiding-fly listens...shifting in its shell...

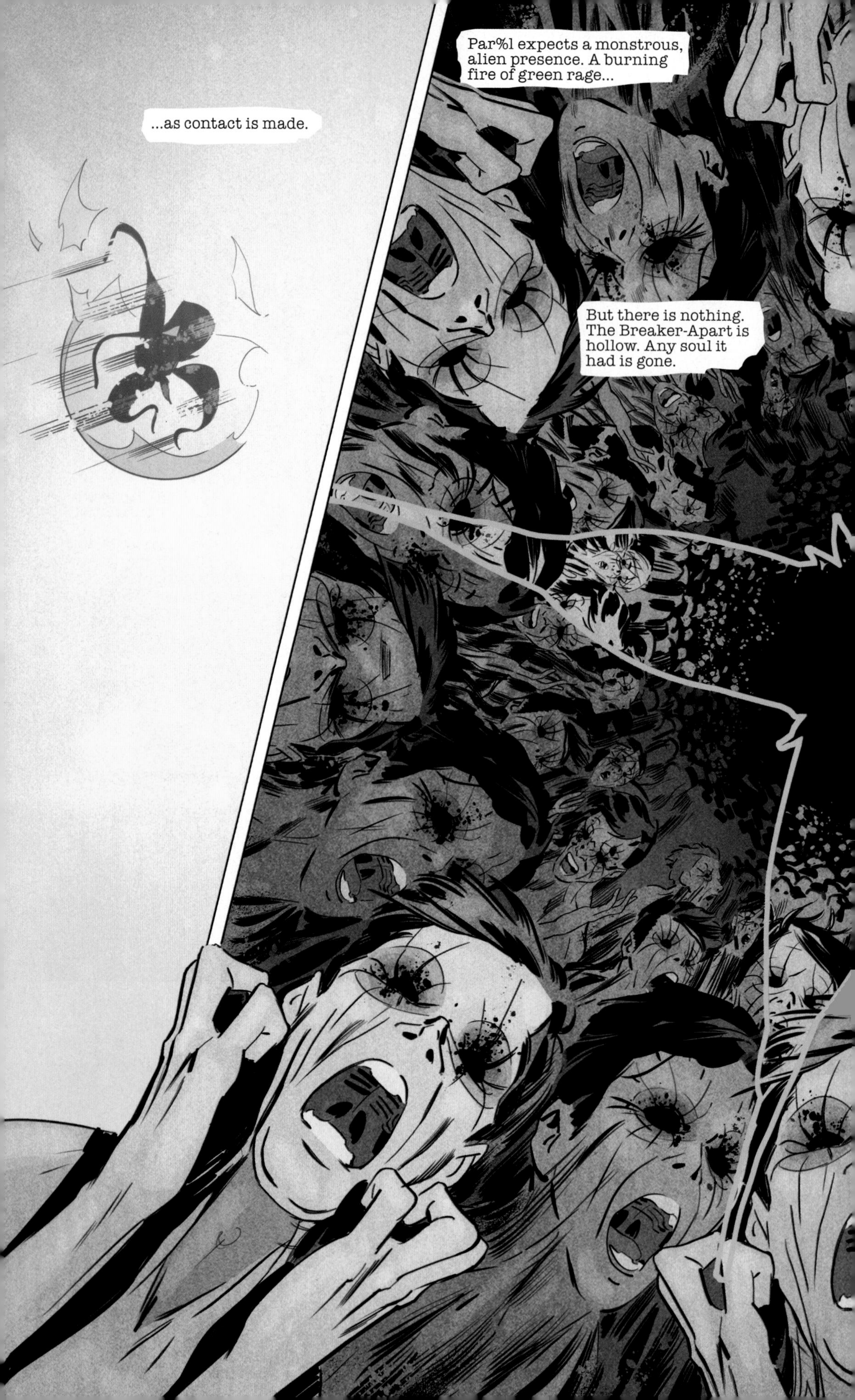
...as contact is made.
Par%l expects a monstrous, alien presence. A burning fire of green rage...
But there is nothing. The Breaker-Apart is hollow. Any soul it had is gone.

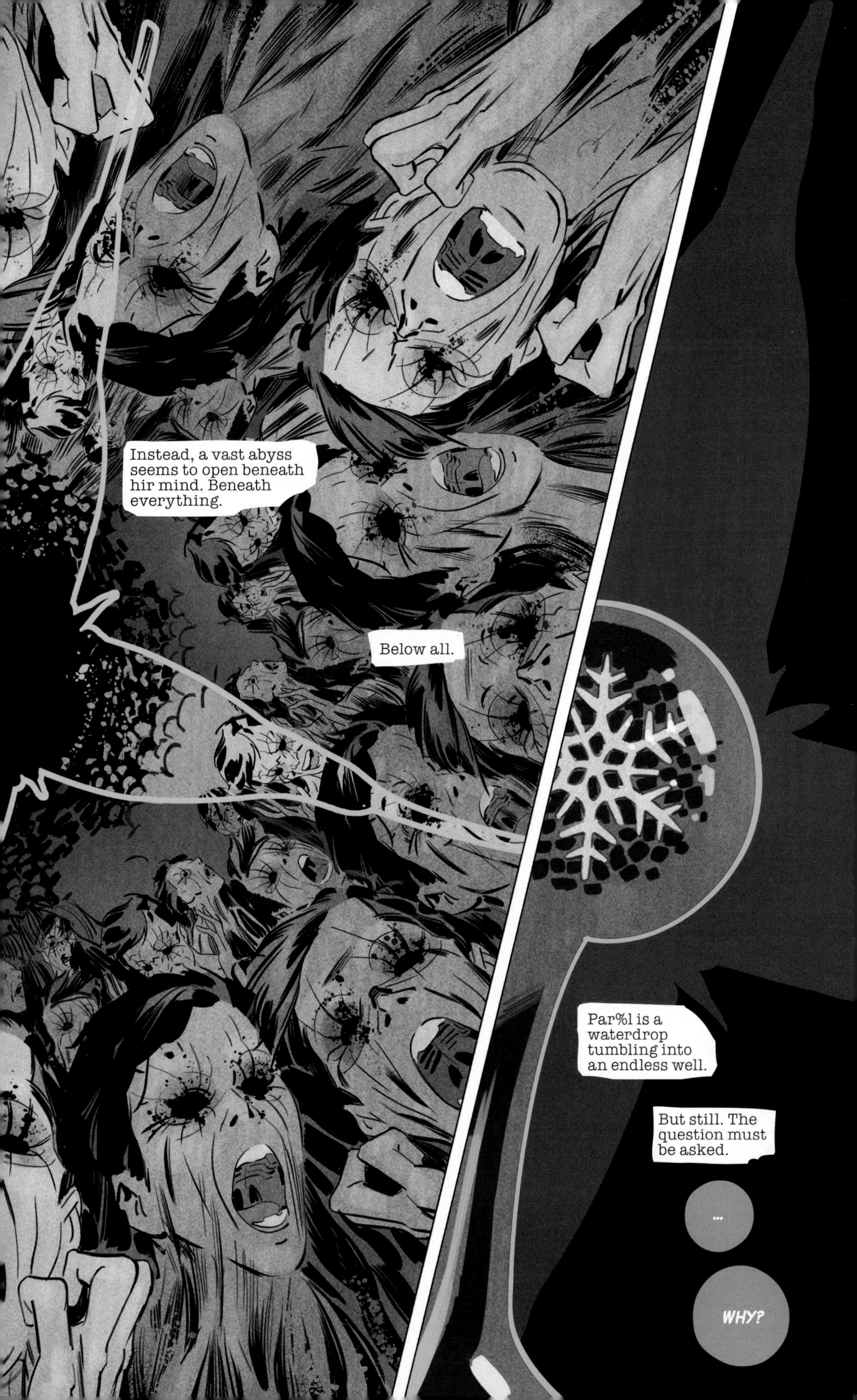
Instead, a vast abyss seems to open beneath hir mind. Beneath everything.
Below all.
Par%l is a waterdrop tumbling into an endless well.
But still. The question must be asked.
...
WHY?

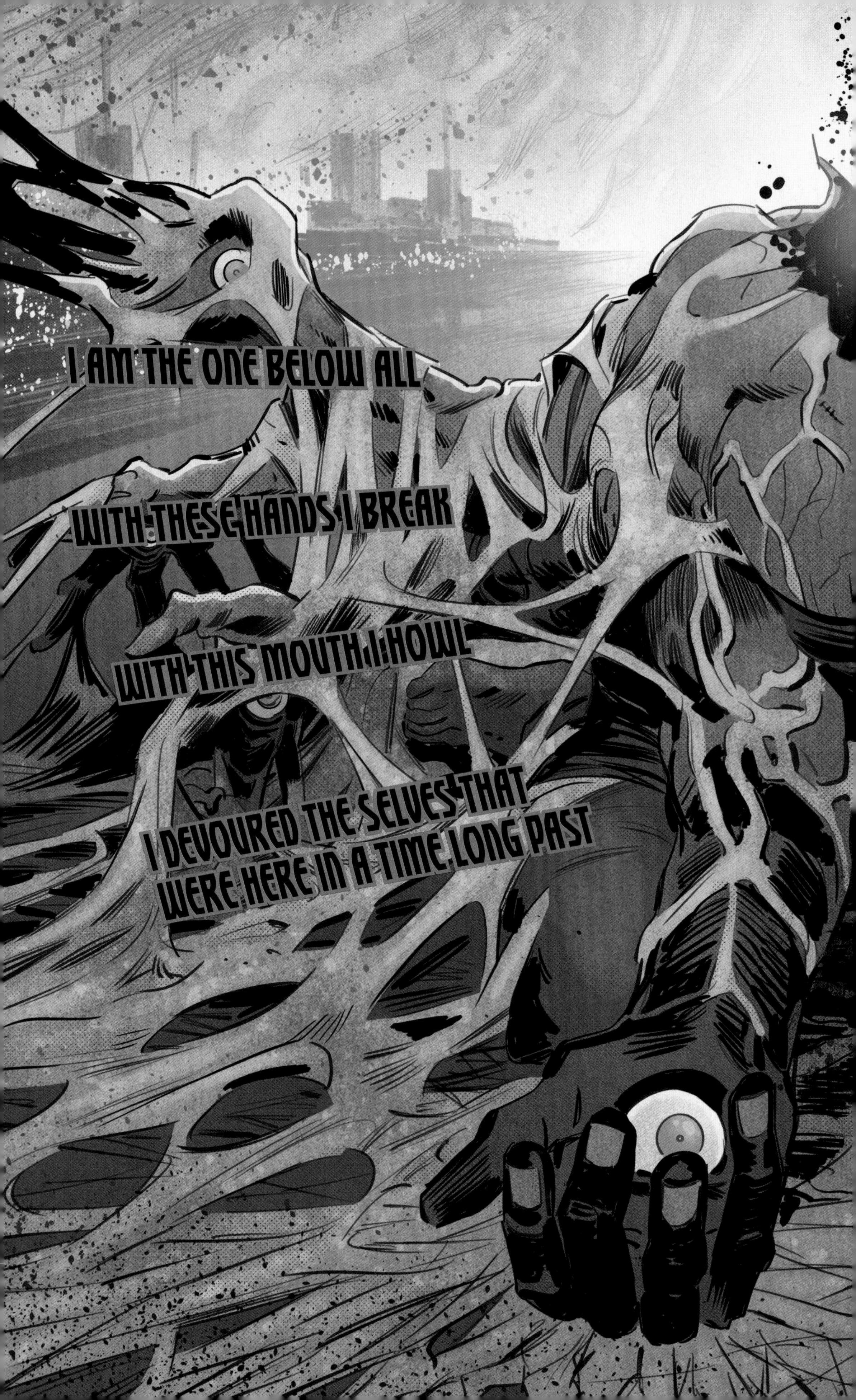
I AM THE ONE BELOW ALL
WITH THESE HANDS I BREAK
WITH THIS MOUTH I HOWL
I DEVOURED THE SELVES THAT WERE HERE IN A TIME LONG PAST

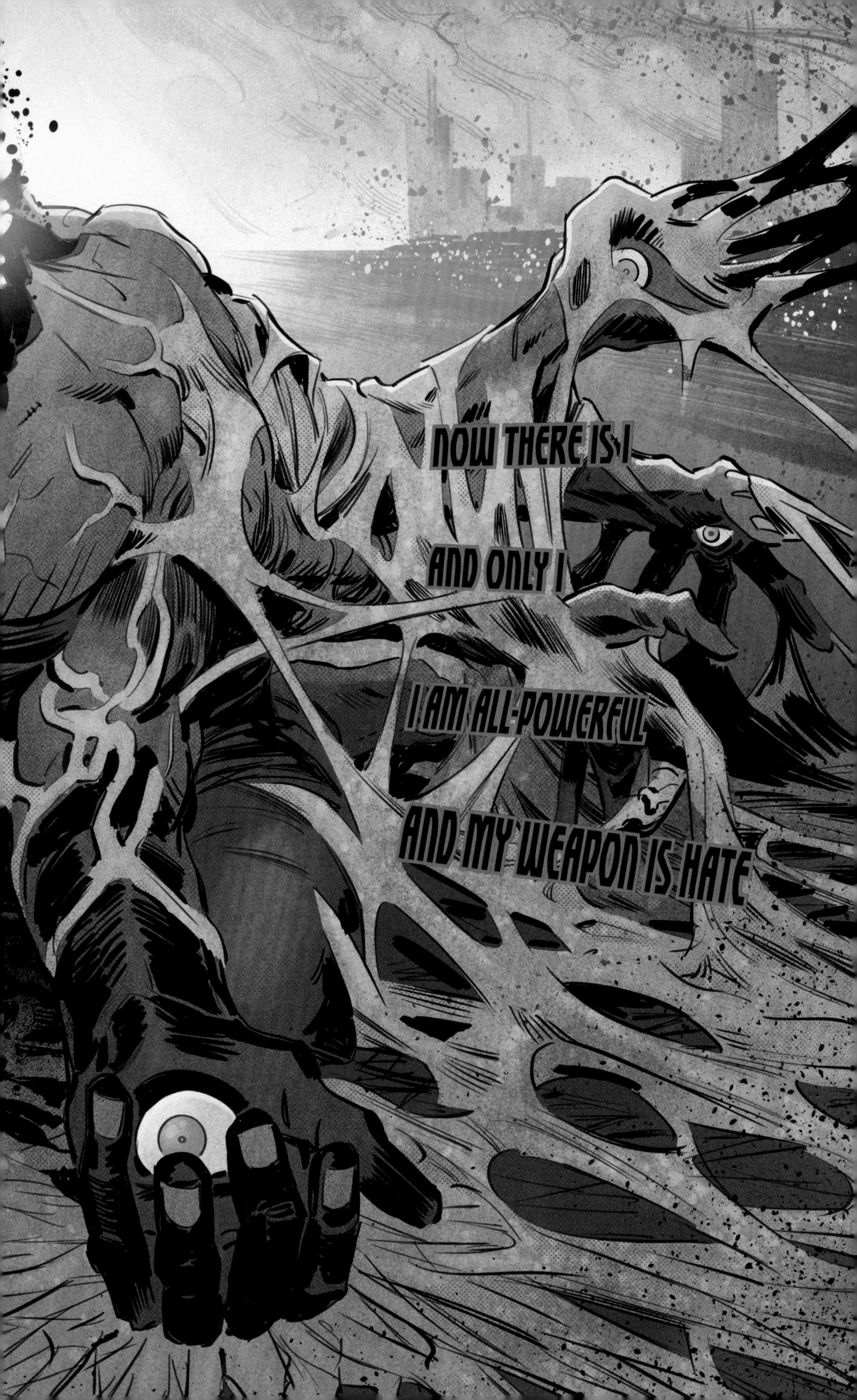
NOW THERE IS I
AND ONLY I
I AM ALL-POWERFUL
AND MY WEAPON IS HATE

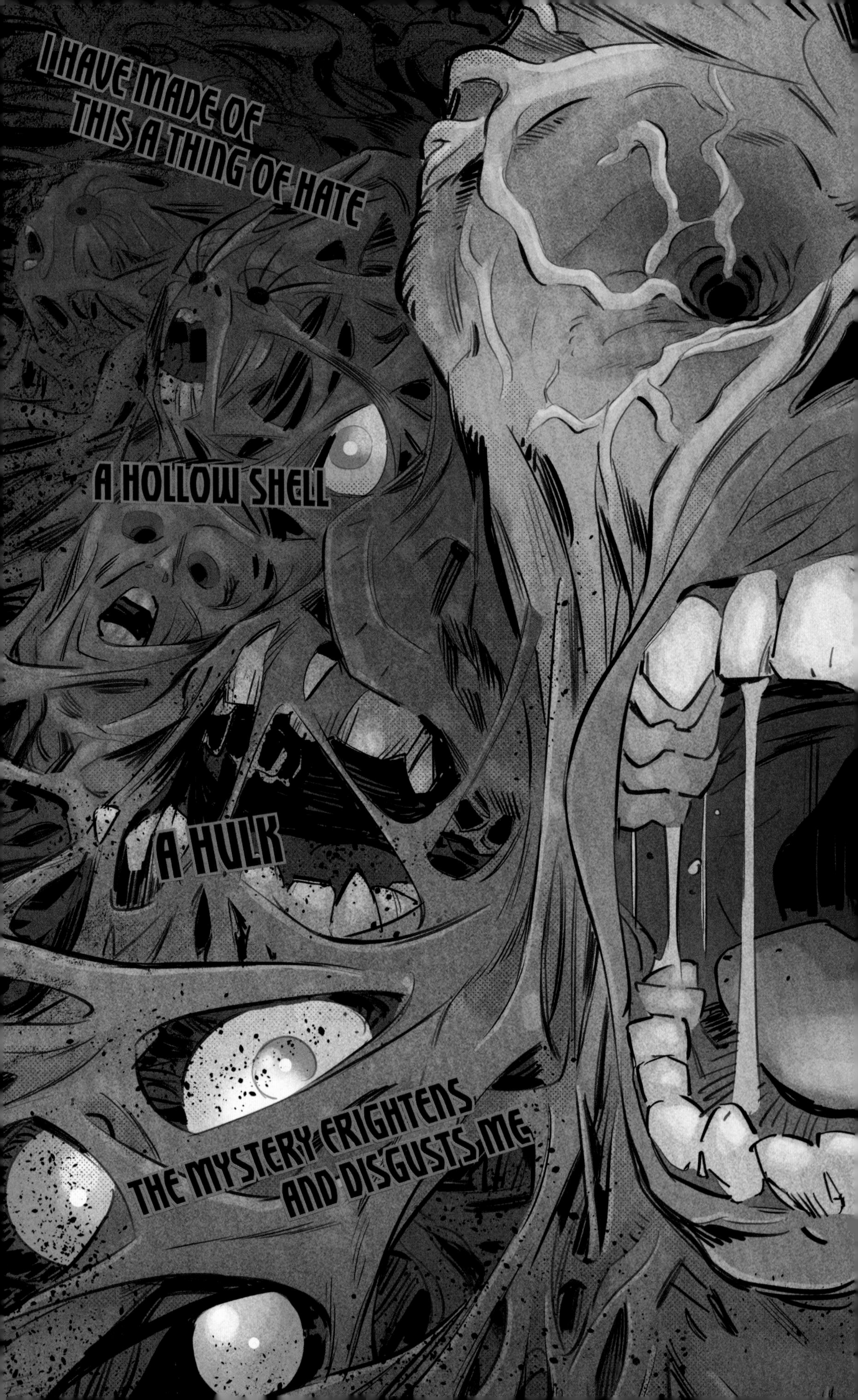
I HAVE MADE OF THIS A THING OF HATE
A HOLLOW SHELL
A HULK
THE MYSTERY FRIGHTENS AND DISGUSTS ME

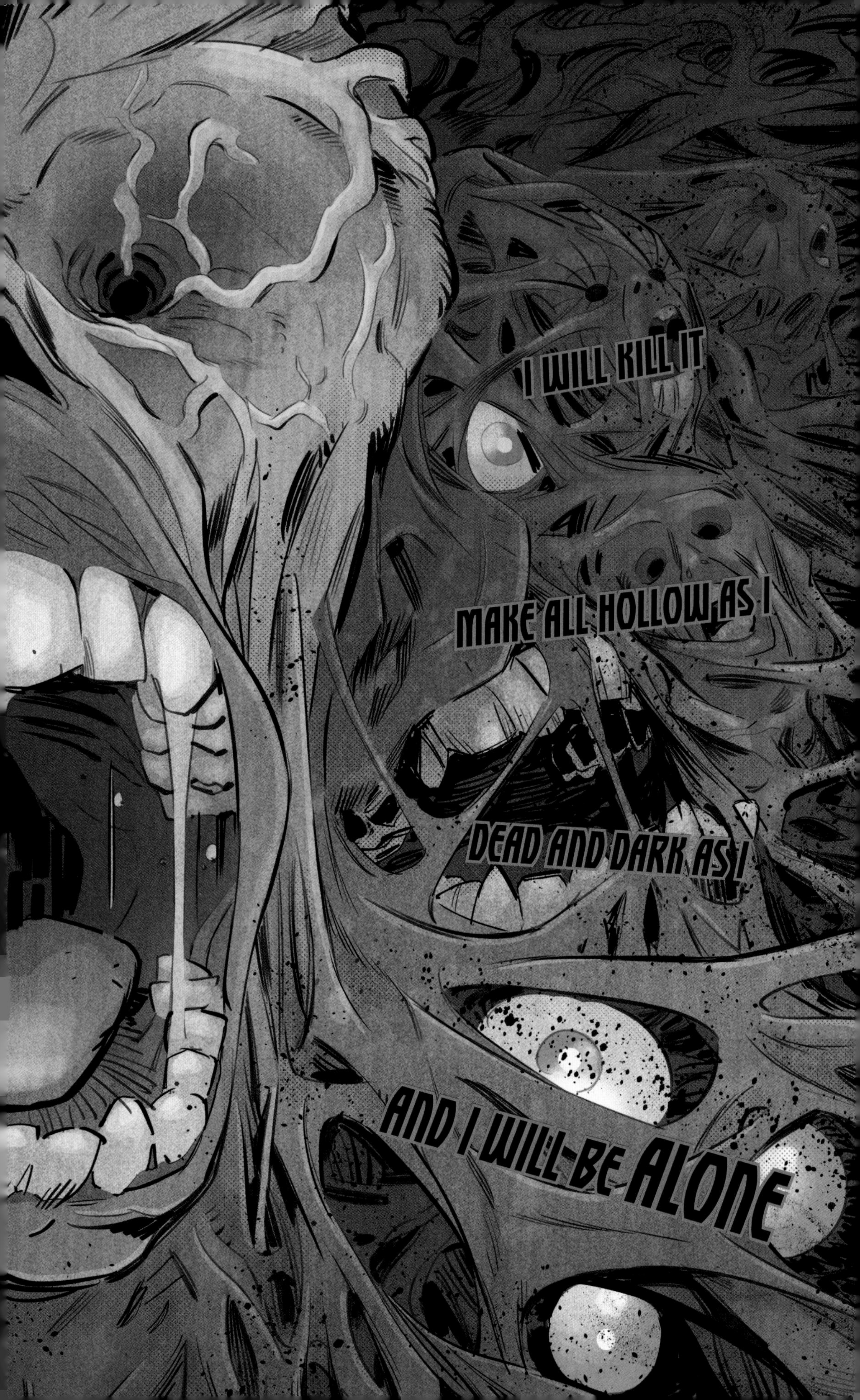
I WILL KILL IT
MAKE ALL HOLLOW AS I
DEAD AND DARK AS I
AND I WILL BE ALONE

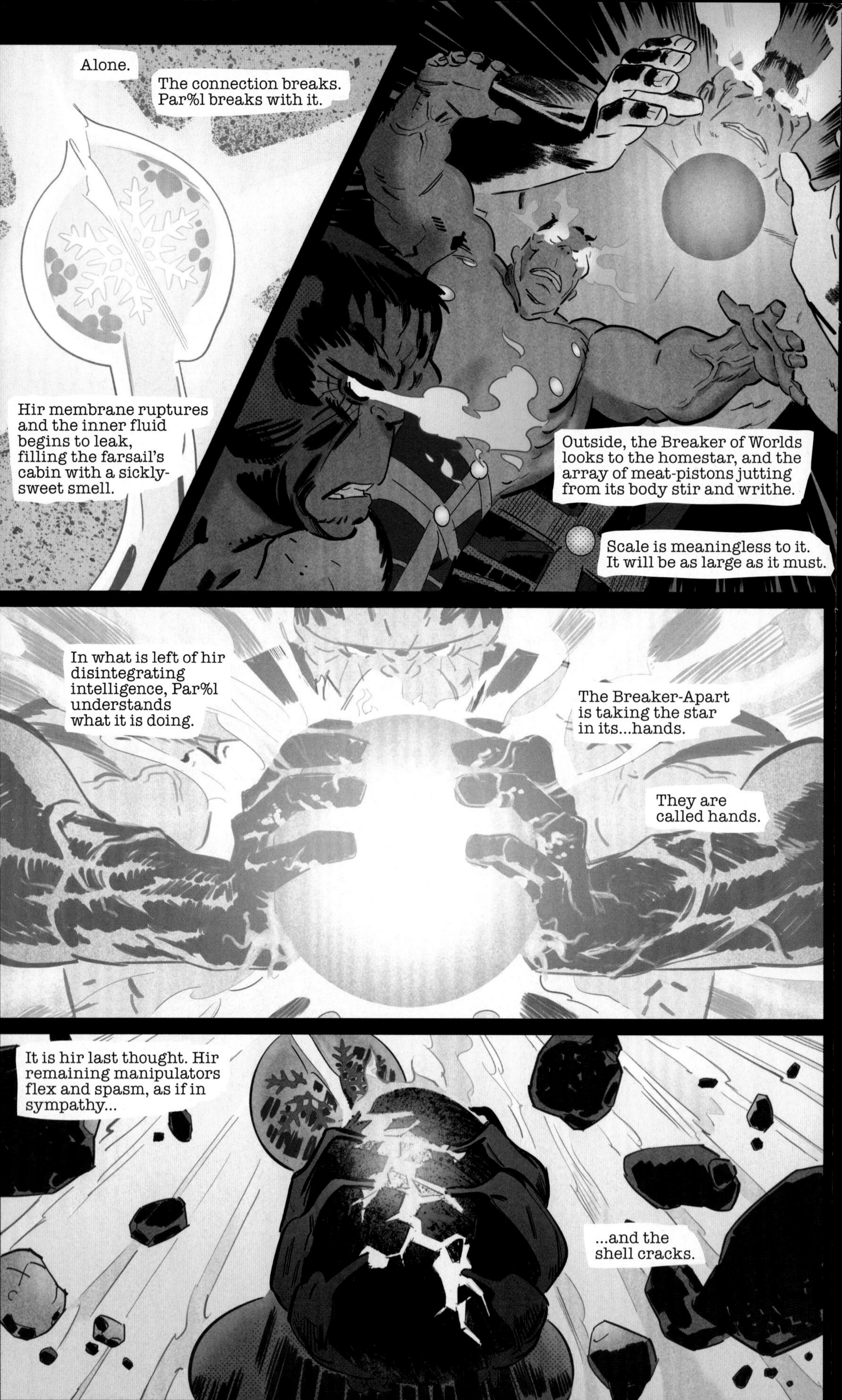

Alone.
The connection breaks. Par%l breaks with it.
Hir membrane ruptures and the inner fluid begins to leak, filling the farsail's cabin with a sickly-sweet smell.
Outside, the Breaker of Worlds looks to the homestar, and the array of meat-pistons jutting from its body stir and writhe.
Scale is meaningless to it. It will be as large as it must.
In what is left of hir disintegrating intelligence, Par%l understands what it is doing.
The Breaker-Apart is taking the star in its...hands.
They are called hands.
It is hir last thought. Hir remaining manipulators flex and spasm, as if in sympathy...
...and the shell cracks.

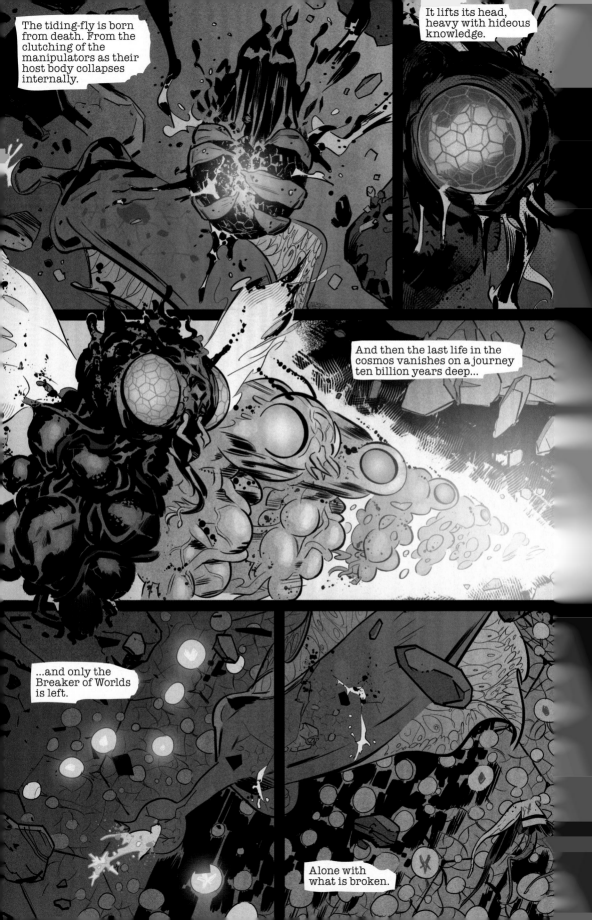

The tiding-fly is born from death. From the clutching of the manipulators as their host body collapses internally.

It lifts its head, heavy with hideous knowledge.

And then the last life in the cosmos vanishes on a journey ten billion years deep...

...and only the Breaker of Worlds is left.

Alone with what is broken.

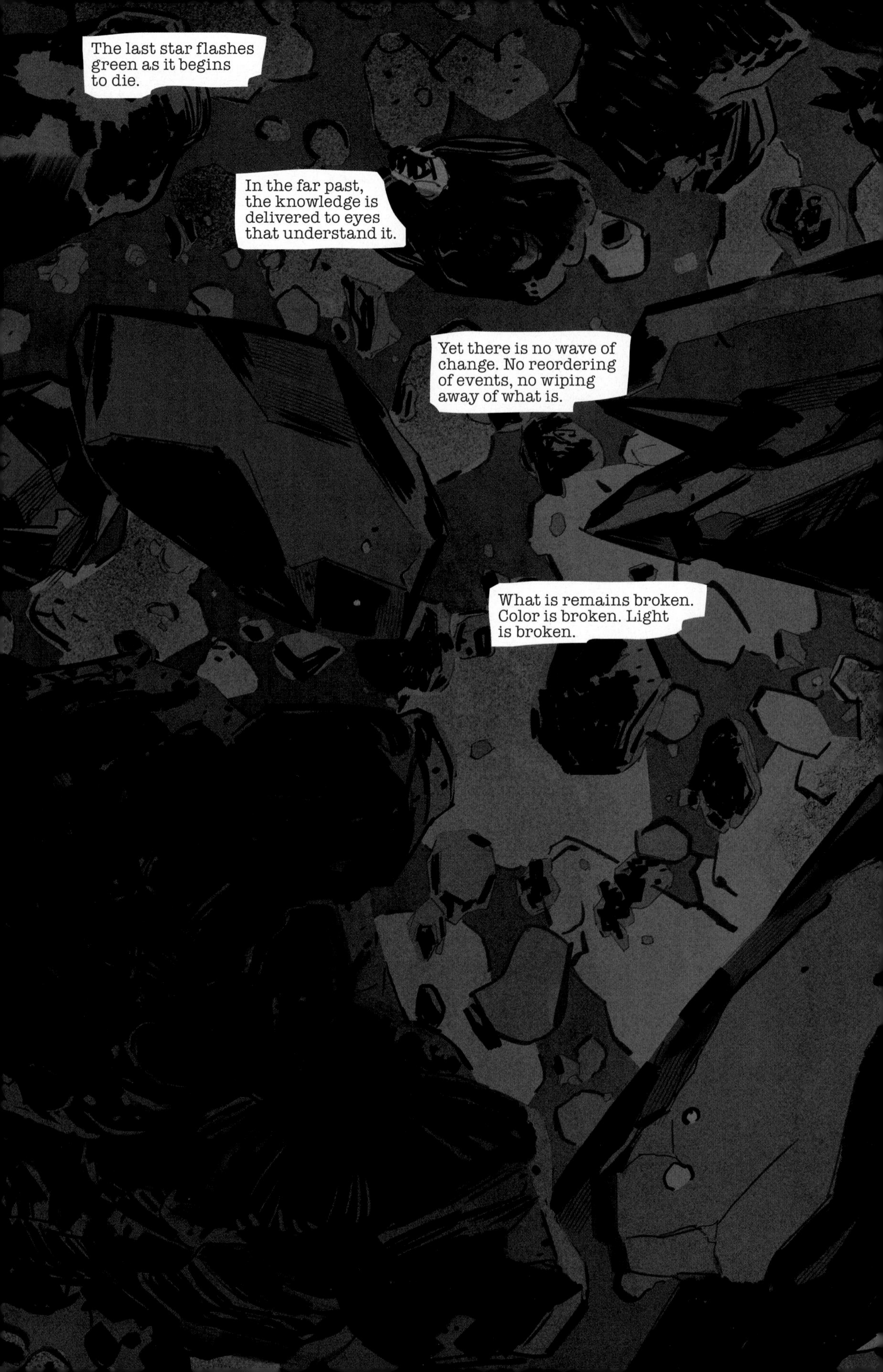
The last star flashes green as it begins to die.
In the far past, the knowledge is delivered to eyes that understand it.
Yet there is no wave of change. No reordering of events, no wiping away of what is.
What is remains broken. Color is broken. Light is broken.

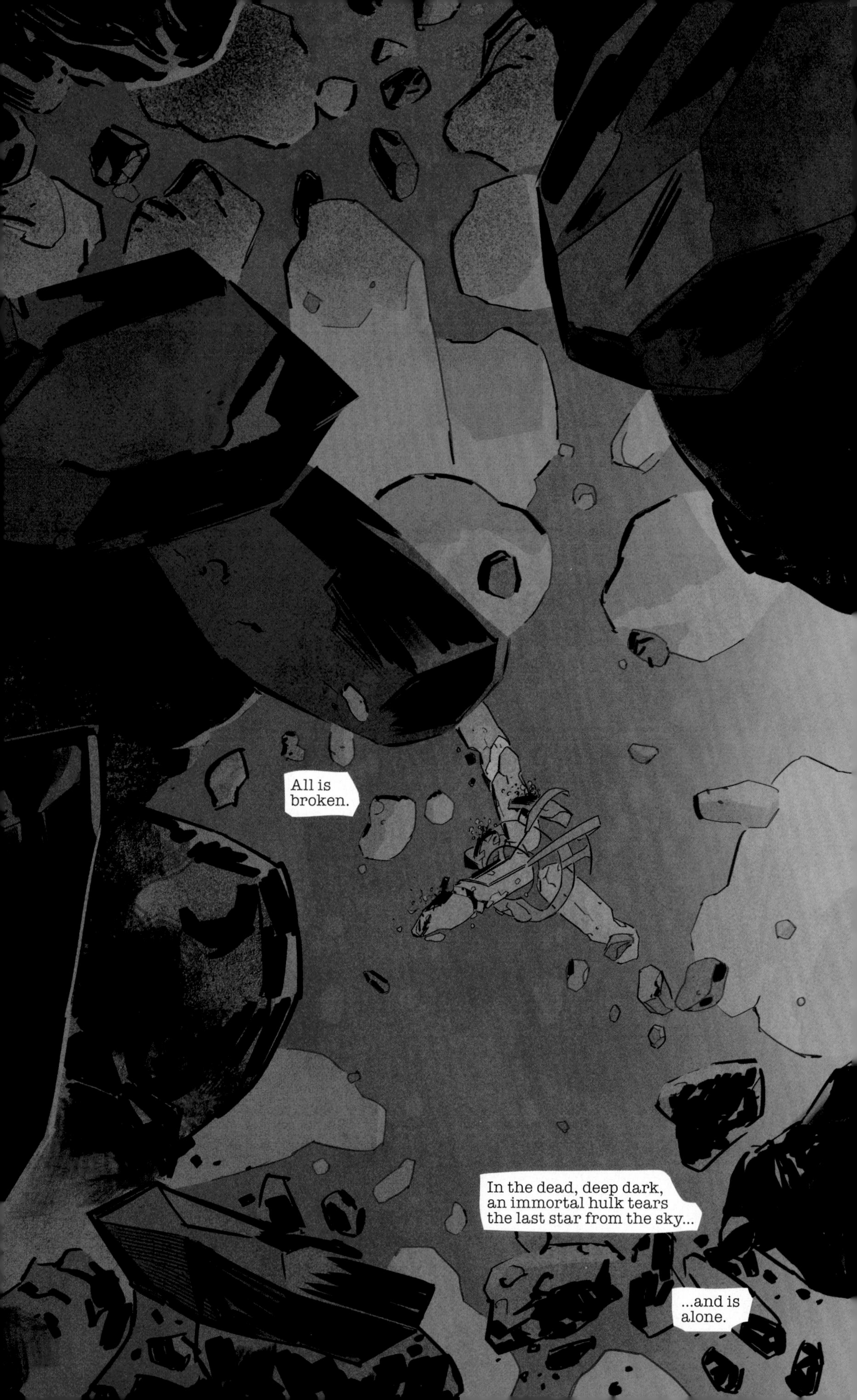
All is broken.
In the dead, deep dark, an immortal hulk tears the last star from the sky...
...and is alone.

"Joe?

IS THAT YOU? ARE YOU THERE?

I NEED HELP, JOE. I CAN'T SEE.

SOMETHING'S EATING ME.

I THINK...

I THINK IT KILLED THE HULK."

– BRUCE BANNER

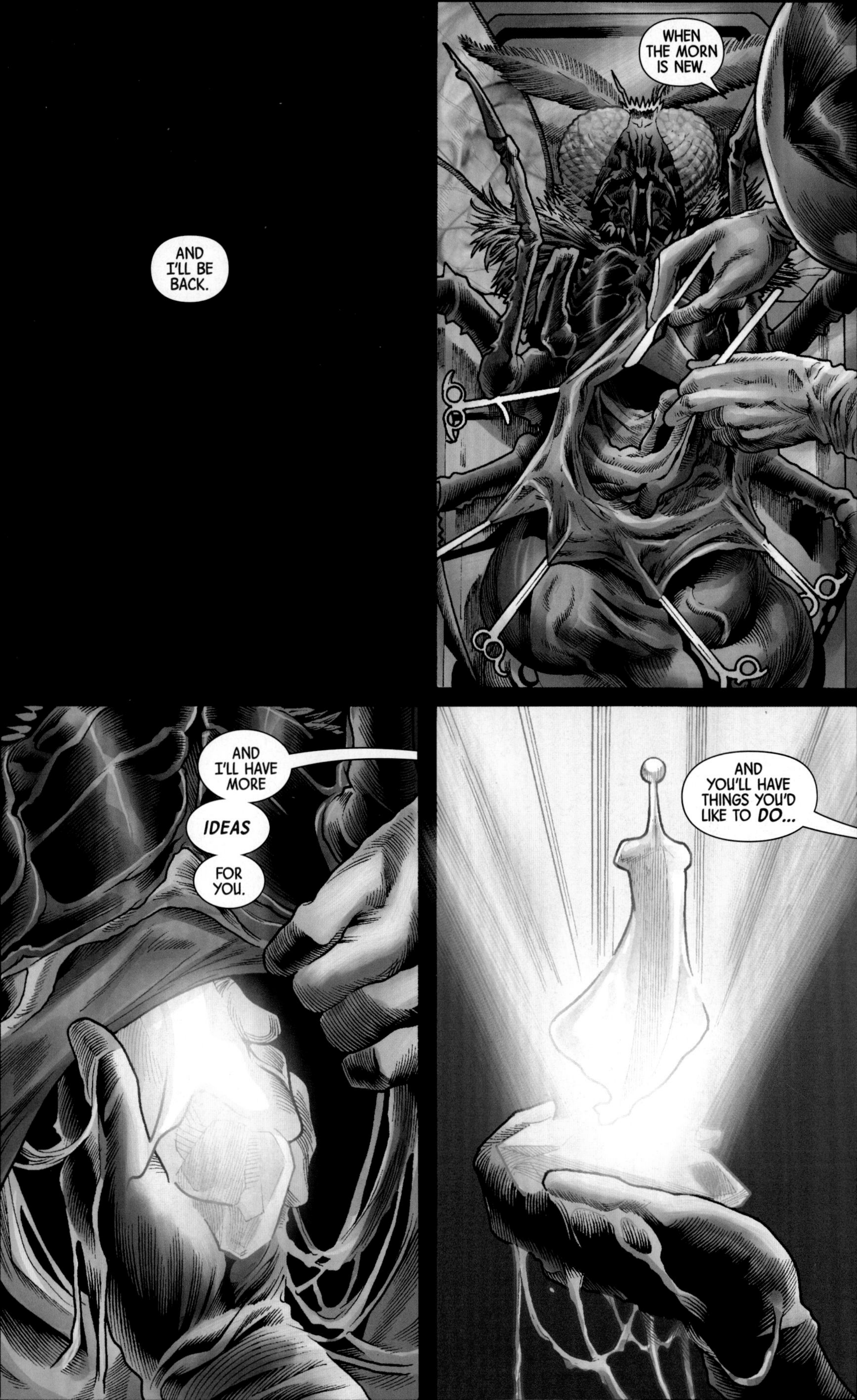
AND I'LL BE BACK.
WHEN THE MORN IS NEW.
AND I'LL HAVE MORE
IDEAS
FOR YOU.
AND YOU'LL HAVE THINGS YOU'D LIKE TO DO...

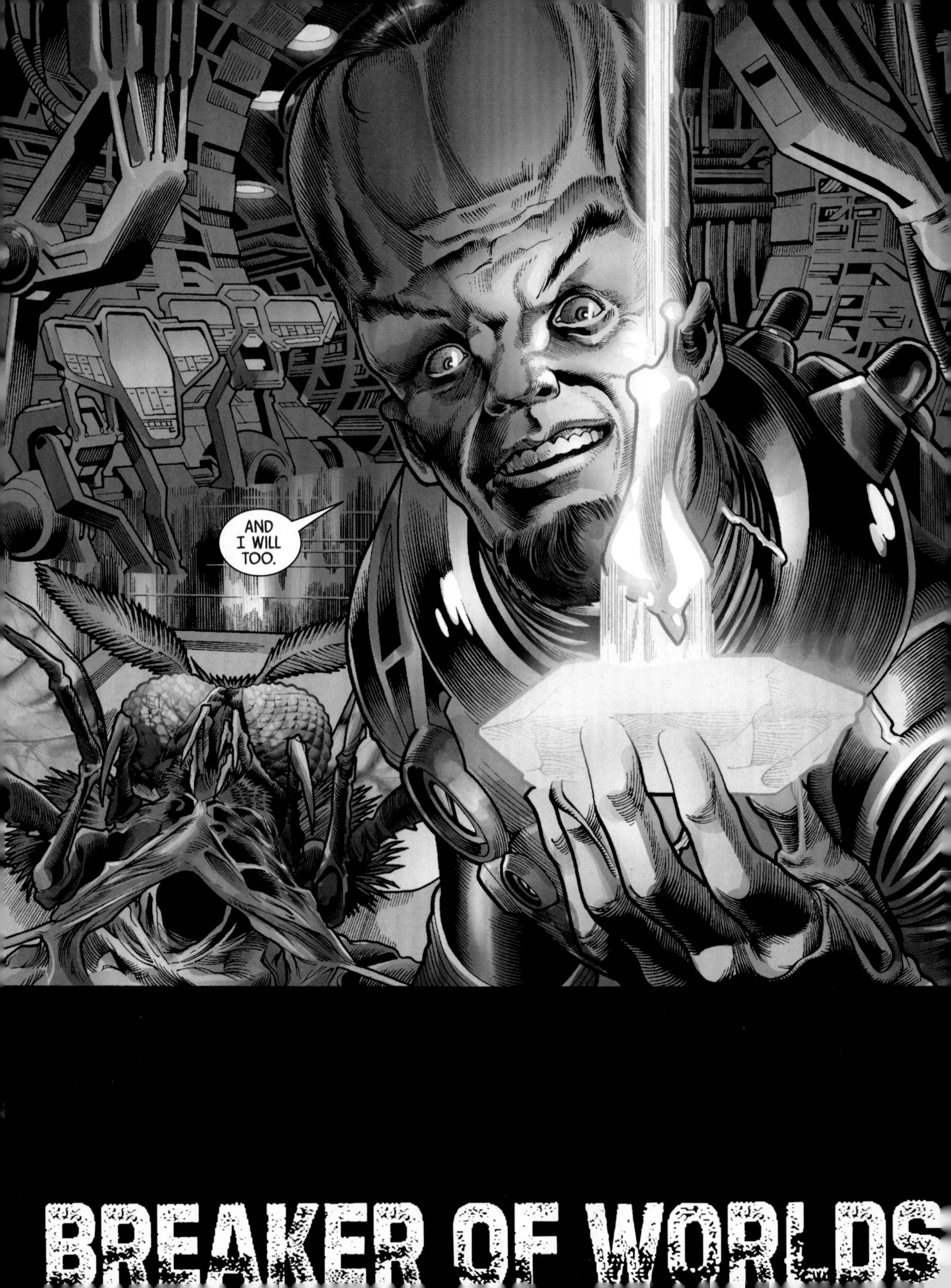
AND I WILL TOO.

BREAKER OF WORLDS

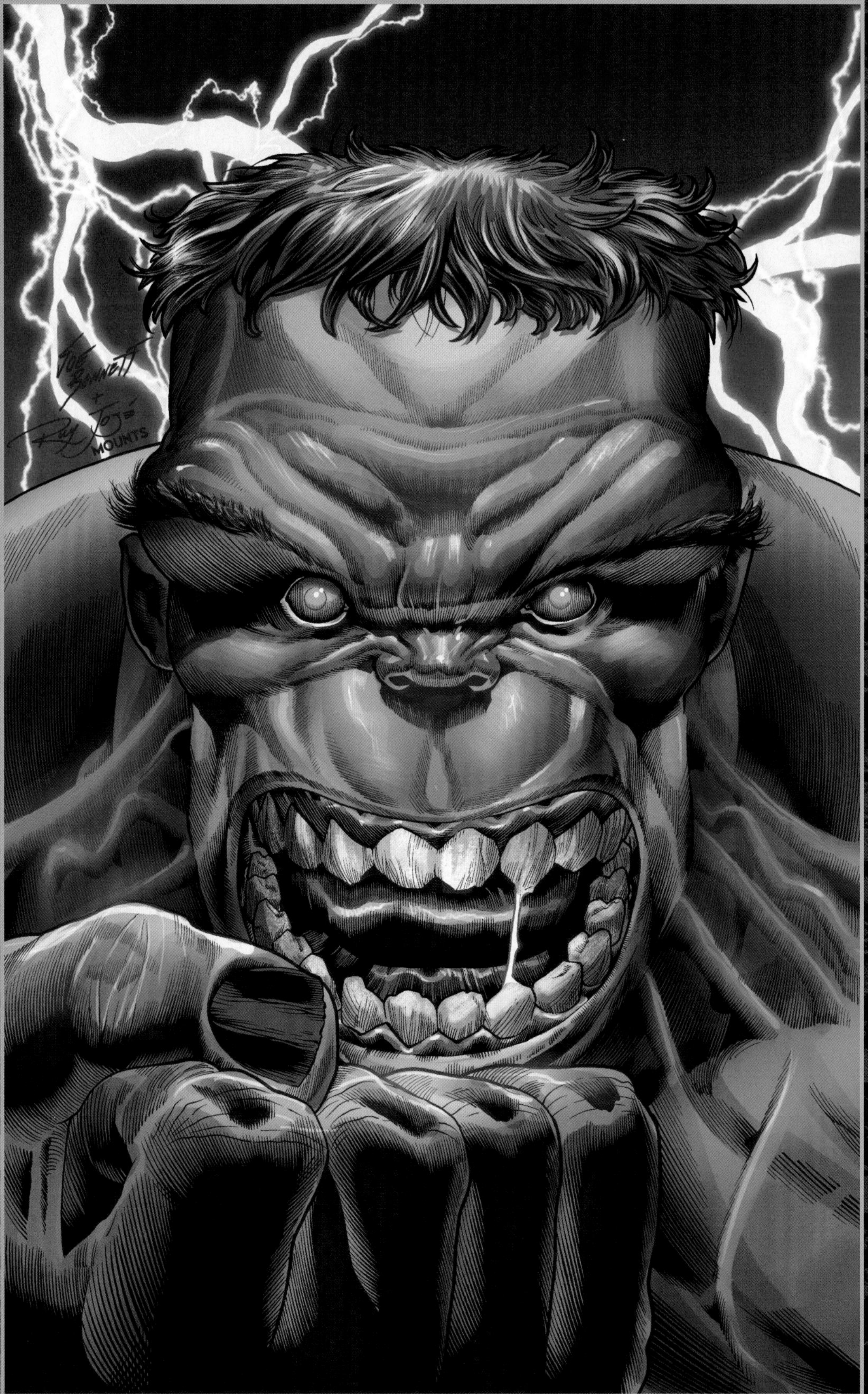
MOUNTS

JOE BENNETT, RUY JOSÉ & PAUL MOUNTS
#25 VARIANT

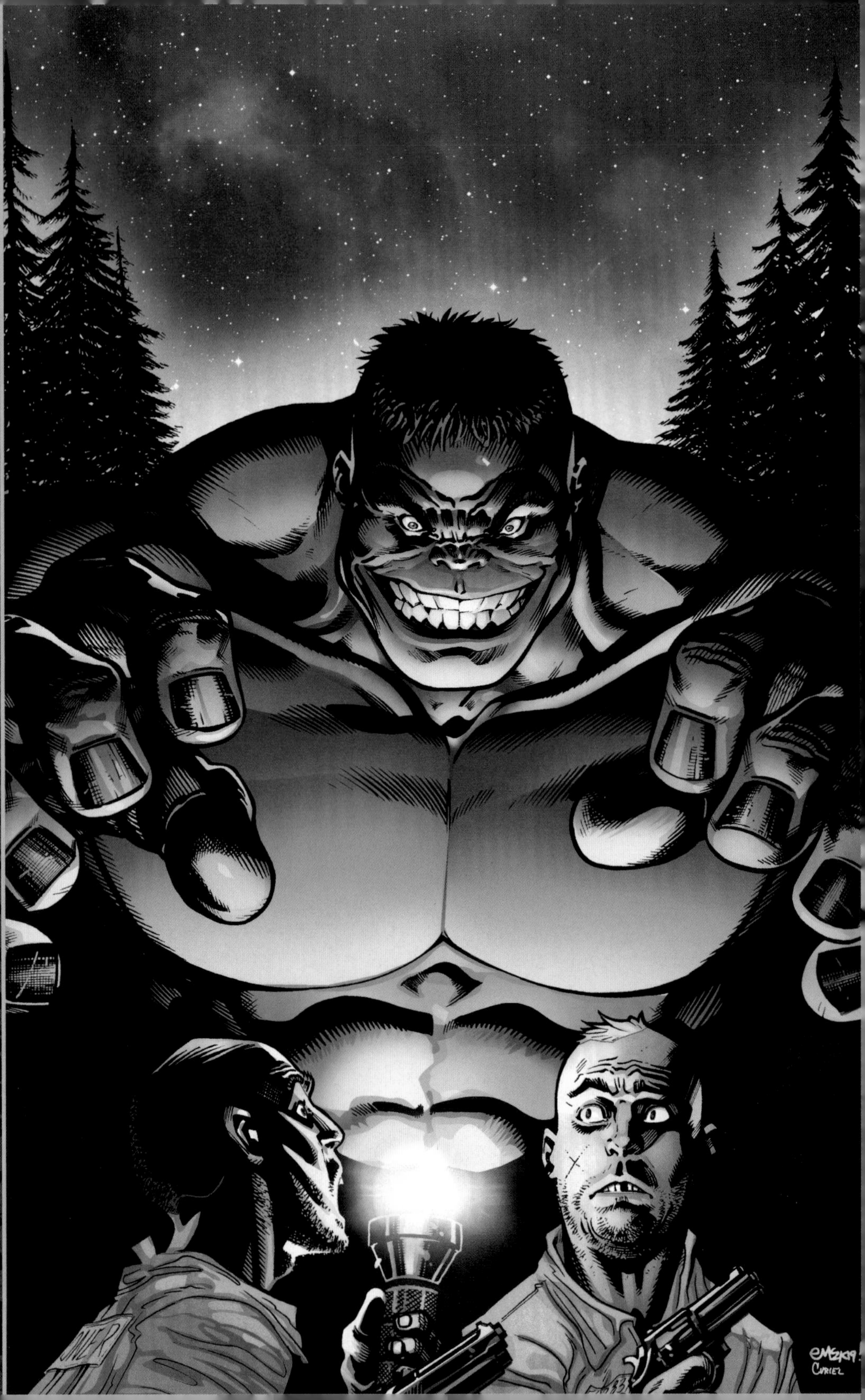